lonely planet

Dutch

PHRASEBOOK & DICTIONARY

D0774821

Acknowledgments
Associate Publisher Mina Patria
Managing Editor Angela Tinson
Editor Branislava Vladisavljevic
Series Designer Mark Adams
Managing Layout Designer Jane Hart
Layout Designer Clara Monitto
Language Writer Annelies Mertens
Cover Image Researcher Naomi Parker

Thanks
Ruth Cosgrove, Briohny Hooper, Carol Jackson, Wayne Murphy

Published by Lonely Planet Publications Pty Ltd
ABN 36 005 607 983

2nd Edition – Sep 2013
ISBN 978 1 74179 274 4
Text © Lonely Planet 2013
Cover Image Tulip fields, Bergen, Frans Lemmens/Alamy©

Printed in China   10 9 8 7 6 5 4 3

Contact lonelyplanet.com/contact

Although the authors and Lonely Planet try to make the information as accurate as possible, we accept no responsibility for any loss, injury or inconvenience sustained by anyone using this book.

Paper in this book is certified against the Forest Stewardship Council™ standards. FSC™ promotes environmentally responsible, socially beneficial and economically viable management of the world's forests.

MIX
Paper from
responsible sources
FSC™ C021741

acknowledgments

Editor Branislava Vladisavljevic would like to acknowledge the following people for their contributions to this phrasebook:

Annelies Mertens for the comprehensive translations and the cultural information.

Annelies is a native Dutch speaker hailing from the Kempen region in Belgium. At the age of 18 she moved to the Flemish 'student city' of Leuven to study Arts and Linguistics. After obtaining her Honours in Romance studies and graduating as a French and Spanish teacher, she moved to the baroque port city of Antwerp to sample more of the good things life (and Belgium) have on offer. Having travelled the length and breadth of Europe as a kid with mum and dad, Annelies has continued to travel as often as she can to all corners of the world, and now lives in Melbourne, Australia with husband Tony, and works at Lonely Planet as a Managing Editor. During her visits to Belgium she indulges in the cuisine, the vibrant cultural life, the most *gezellige* pubs imaginable, the beers, the chocolates, and can be seen wandering seemingly aimlessly through its historic cities.

Annelies would like to thank colleague and fellow native Dutch speaker Barbara Delissen, originally from Gouda, the Netherlands, for providing extra Dutch language and cultural expertise, as well as support during the production of this book. Thanks also to editor Brana Vladisavljevic with whom the manuscript was in super-safe and capable hands. Last but not least, a big thank you to Moeke, Katleen, Tony, Els, Dirk and Jules – you all know why!

Thanks also to Wendy Wright for the inside illustrations.

make the most of this phrasebook ...

Anyone can speak another language! It's all about confidence. Don't worry if you can't remember your school language lessons or if you've never learnt a language before. Even if you learn the very basics (on the inside covers of this book), your travel experience will be the better for it. You have nothing to lose and everything to gain when the locals hear you making an effort.

finding things in this book

For easy navigation, this book is in sections. The Basics chapters are the ones you'll thumb through time and again. The Practical section covers basic travel situations like catching transport and finding a bed. The Social section gives you conversational phrases, pick-up lines, the ability to express opinions – so you can get to know people. Food has a section all of its own: gourmets and vegetarians are covered and local dishes feature. Safe Travel equips you with health and police phrases, just in case. Remember the colours of each section and you'll find everything easily; or use the comprehensive Index. Otherwise, check the two-way traveller's Dictionary for the word you need.

being understood

Throughout this book you'll see coloured phrases on each page. They're phonetic guides to help you pronounce the language. Start with them to get a feel for how the language sounds. The pronunciation chapter in Basics will explain more, but you can be confident that if you read the coloured phrase, you'll be understood. As you become familiar with the spoken language, move on to using the actual text in the language which will help you perfect your pronunciation.

communication tips

Body language, ways of doing things, sense of humour – all have a role to play in every culture. 'Local talk' boxes show you common ways of saying things, or everyday language to drop into conversation. 'Listen for ...' boxes supply the phrases you may hear. They start with the language (so a local can find the phrase they want and point it out to you) and then lead in to the phonetic guide and the English translation.

MAKE THE MOST OF THIS PHRASEBOOK

dutch

NORTH SEA

Schiermonnikoog
Ameland
Terschelling
Vlieland
Leeuwarden
Groningen
Texel
Drachten
Waddenzee
Den Helder
Assen
Sneek
Emmen
Alkmaar
Hoorn
Purmerend
Lelystad
Zwolle
Haarlem
Amsterdam
Leiden
Amersfoort
Apeldoorn
Enschede
Den Haag
Utrecht
NETHERLANDS
Arnhem
Rotterdam
Nijmegen
Schouw...
Dordrecht
Den Bosch
Germany
Noord-Beveland
Breda
Vlissingen
Tilburg
Zeebrugge
Eindhoven
Helmond
Oostende
Brugge
Antwerpen
Herentals
Gent
Aalst
Heerlen
Ieper
Kortrijk
Leuven
Hasselt
Maastricht
Brussel/
Bruxelles
BELGIUM
Tournai
Liège
France
Mons
Namur
Charleroi
Bastogne
Luxembourg
Arlon

EUROPE

NORTH SEA

0 — 50 km
0 — 30 mi

BELGIUM
Brussel/
Bruxelles

■ Dutch-speaking areas   ■ French-speaking areas   ■ German-speaking areas

For more details, see the **introduction**.

ABOUT DUTCH

8

When it comes to Dutch, you can safely put aside those negative stereotypes about 'double Dutch'. The reality is that Dutch and English are closely related, both being members of the Germanic family of languages. Such are the similarities that Bill Bryson was moved to remark in *Neither Here Nor There* that 'when one hears Dutch, one feels one ought to be able to understand it.'

The connection between English and Dutch has been reinforced by numerous word borrowings – some 2000 English words are said to be of Dutch origin. The impetus behind this phenomenon was the Dutch Golden Age (1584–1702), when the Dutch sailed across the seven seas founding colonies and establishing a trading empire. As you might expect, many of the adopted words are of maritime origin: buoy, dock, skipper, whiting and yacht are only a few.

at a glance ...

language name:
Dutch

name in language:
Nederlands
ney·duhr·lants

language family:
Germanic

approximate number of speakers: 20 million

close relatives:
Afrikaans, English, Frisian, German

donations to English:
buoy, cookie, cruise, dock, landscape (among many others)

Dutch is more than just the language spoken in the Netherlands. Flemish (*Vlaams* vlaams), spoken in the northern part of Belgium (known as Flanders), is really the same language as Dutch, but for historical and cultural reasons the name 'Flemish' is often used. Officially, eg in the school curriculum, it's always referred to as *Nederlands* ney·duhr·lants (Dutch). There are slight differences in pronunciation and vocabulary between Flemish and the Dutch spoken in the Netherlands. In this phrasebook, the differences are indicated with Ⓝ and Ⓑ

introduction

(signifying the Netherlands and Belgium). Both countries are members of the *Nederlandse Taalunie* (Dutch Language Union), the supreme authority on modern language standards. The same rules for spelling and grammar are followed throughout both countries and the same dictionaries are used as reference. There are also some dialect divisions within the language as a result of historical circumstances, but they are limited to the spoken language and informal surroundings only. Everyone is taught standard Dutch at school. The standard language is based on the northern dialects, mainly as spoken around Amsterdam. Due to historical events, Dutch is also spoken by a few thousand mainly older people in the very northeastern corner of France, around the city of Dunkirk.

With over 20 million speakers, Dutch has a strong presence on the world linguistic stage. The explorers and traders of the Dutch Golden Age, who brought their language to many corners of the globe, helped establish it as an official language in Aruba, the Dutch Antilles and Suriname. The greatest achievement of the Dutch linguistic expansion is its famous offspring, Afrikaans, now considered a separate language and spoken by around six million people in South Africa.

Some travellers might wonder about the necessity of using Dutch when so many Dutch and Flemish people seem to speak excellent English. While it's true that the Dutch and Flemish are avid linguists, a little effort on your part to speak the local language will be warmly received as a sign of goodwill. And remember that a country's language is also a key to its culture. Taking this book with you will open the door to a truly *gezellige* khuh·ze·li·khuh travel experience. If you want to discover firsthand the true meaning of this quintessentially Dutch word ('convivial' just doesn't do it justice), then don't leave home without this little book!

abbreviations used in this book

a	adjective	m	masculine
adv	adverb	n	neuter (after Dutch)
Ⓑ	Belgium	n	noun (after English)
f	feminine	Ⓝ	the Netherlands
Ind	Indonesian (food)	pl	plural
inf	informal	pol	polite
lit	literal	sg	singular

To most foreigners, Dutch has a delightfully distinctive sound – with its guttural r and kh sounds and its array of vowels.

If you put aside your inhibitions and read our coloured pronunciation guides as if you're speaking English, you'll have no trouble getting your message across. It's such a rarity for foreigners to make the effort to speak Dutch that when you do, you'll win friends quicker than you can say *Nederlands ney·duhr·lants* (Dutch).

vowel sounds

Dutch has a rich reservoir of vowel sounds. Most vowels have a long and a short version, which simply means that you hold vowels for a greater or lesser length of time. It's important to make the distinction between long and short versions, as they can distinguish meaning – eg *maan* maan means 'moon' but *man* man means 'man'.

There are also a few vowel sounds that are a bit trickier for English speakers to pronounce as they have no equivalent in English, such as the öy and eu sounds. The many-hued Dutch vowels often merge together into swooping diphthongs (vowel sound combinations). While the vowels might take a little practice, they're a key part of the unique flavour of spoken Dutch. If you listen carefully to native speakers and follow our coloured pronunciation guides, you shouldn't have any problems being understood.

pronunciation

symbol	english equivalent	dutch example	transliteration
a	run (but more clearly pronounced, as in 'pasta')	*vak*	vak
aa	father	*vaak, maken*	vaak, *maa*·kuhn
aw	saw	*lauw, koud*	law, kawt
e	bet	*bed*	bet
ee	see	*niet*	neet
eu	nurse	*leuk*	leuk
ew	ee pronounced with rounded lips	*u, uur*	ew, ewr
ey	as in 'bet', but longer	*beet, reis, mijn*	beyt, reys, meyn
i	hit	*ik*	ik
o	pot	*bot*	bot
oh	note	*boot*	boht
oo	zoo	*boer*	boor
öy	her year (without the 'r')	*buik*	böyk
u	put	*geluk*	khuh·*luk*
uh	ago	*het, een*	huht, uhn

consonant sounds

Dutch consonants are pretty straightforward to pronounce as they're also found in English. You might need a little practice with the kh sound, which is guttural and harsher than the English 'h' (although in Flanders it's a lot 'softer' than in Holland). The distinctive trilled r sound is traditionally made with the tongue forward, although these days a lot of people pronounce it more like a French 'r' – held back and restricting the flow of air in the throat.

symbol	english equivalent	dutch example	transliteration
b	**b**ed	*bed*	bet
ch	**ch**eat	*kindje*	kin·**ch**uh
d	**d**og	*dag*	dakh
f	**f**at	*fiets*	feets
g	**g**o	*gate*	geyt
h	**h**at	*hoed*	hoot
k	**k**it	*klok*	klok
kh	as the 'ch' in the Scottish *loch*	*goed, schat*	khoot, skhat
l	**l**ot	*lied*	leet
m	**m**an	*man*	man
n	**n**ot	*niet*	neet
ng	ri**ng**	*haring*	*haa*·ring
p	**p**et	*pot*	pot
r	**r**ed (trilled)	*rechts*	rekhs
s	**s**un	*slapen*	**S***laa*·puhn
sh	**sh**ot	*alsjeblieft*	a·**shuh**·*bleeft*
t	**t**op	*tafel*	*taa*·fuhl
v	**v**ery	*vlucht*	vlukht
w	**w**in	*water*	*waa*·tuhr
y	**y**es	*je*	yuh
z	**z**ero	*zomer*	*zoh*·muhr
zh	plea**s**ure	*garage*	kha·*raa*·zhuh

word stress

There are no universal rules on stress in Dutch. Just follow our pronunciation guides, in which the stressed syllables are always indicated with italics.

reading & writing

Dutch is written with the Latin alphabet, which is exactly the same as in English. For spelling purposes (eg if you need to spell your name out to book into a hotel) the pronunciation of each letter is given in the box below.

alphabet					
A a	aa	*J j*	yey	*S s*	es
B b	bey	*K k*	kaa	*T t*	tey
C c	sey	*L l*	el	*U u*	ew
D d	dey	*M m*	em	*V v*	vey
E e	ey	*N n*	en	*W w*	wey
F f	ef	*O o*	oh	*X x*	iks
G g	khey	*P p*	pey	*Y y*	ey/*eep*·see·lon
H h	haa	*Q q*	kew	*Z z*	zet
I i	ee	*R r*	er		

a–z phrasebuilder
grammatica – bouwblokken

contents

The list below shows which grammatical structures you can use to say what you want. Look under each function – listed in alphabetical order – for information on how to build your own sentences. For example, to tell the taxi driver where your hotel is, look for **giving instructions** and you'll be directed to information on **demonstratives**, etc. A **glossary** of grammatical terms is included at the end of this chapter to help you.

a–z phrasebuilder

diminutives

Dutch speakers love a diminutive or two, so much so that it has become a feature of the language. They don't only use them to indicate the smallness of something, like in *autootje* aw·toh·chuh (little car), but also to express endearment when talking with or about children (*kindjes kin*·chus 'small/ cute children'), lovers (*schatje skhat*·yuh, *liefje leef*·yuh, both meaning 'darling') or pets (*hondje hon*·chuh 'doggy') – or anything else kind or cute. They'll even add it to your first name! Similarly, anything that's considered cosy will have a diminutive ending whacked onto it – a seven-course dinner with friends is an *etentje ey*·tuhn·chuh (cosy meal) with a *glaasje wijn khlaas*·yuh weyn (a cosy glass of wine) rather than just a *glas wijn* khlas weyn. Diminutives can also indicate relativity – you'd rather wait an *uurtje ewr*·chuh (60 minutes passing quickly and pleasantly) than an *uur* ewr. And strange but true, a diminutive can be a euphemism for something big – if someone says you have a *buikje böyk*·yuh (little belly), it's not really meant as a compliment. Dutch speakers are masters at using diminutives to say 'A' when they mean 'B' or to make understatements, eg *een mondje Frans spreken* uhn *mon*·chuh frans *sprey*·kuhn (lit: to speak a little-mouthfull of French) actually means 'to speak French quite well'. Ultimately, it's often the context determining what's the real effect of the diminutive – a *nummer nu*·muhr is a 'number', but a *nummertje nu*·muhr·chuh is a 'short, lighthearted song or performance' or … 'sexual intercourse'. There's a set of rules governing the spelling of diminutive endings depending on the final sound of the base word, which you shouldn't worry about too much – if you see or hear the ending -*je* ·yuh (also often pronounced ·chuh) tucked onto the end of a word, you're looking at a *verkleinwoordje* vuhr·*kleyn*·wohr·chuh (ie little diminutive).

adjectives & adverbs

Dutch adjectives mostly come before the noun they describe and after the article, if one is present (see also **articles**). When they are placed before the noun, the ending -e is added to adjectives.

(the) good friend *(de) goede vriend* (duh) khoo·duh vreent
(lit: (the) good friend)
(the) good hotel *(het) goede hotel* (huht) khoo·duh hoh·tel
(lit: (the) good-neuter hotel-neuter)

The exception to this rule is when adjectives come before a neuter singular noun which has the indefinite article *een* uhn (a) in front of it. No -e ending is added in this case.

a good hotel *een goed hotel* uhn khoot hoh·tel
(lit: a good-neuter hotel-neuter)

Adjectives can also come after the noun (eg when they're connected to the noun with 'is' or 'are'). When this is the case, no -e ending is added either.

The train is full.
De trein is vol. duh treyn is vol
(lit: the train is full)

Adverbs are basically the same as adjectives in Dutch – the only difference is that you don't need to add an -e ending to adverbs. There's no equivalent to the English '-ly' ending. In Dutch, adverbs are generally placed after the verb they refer to. See also **verbs**.

The music's loud.
De muziek is luid. duh mew·zeek is löyt
(lit: the music is loud)

He's talking loudly.
Hij spreekt luid. hey spreykt löyt
(lit: he speaks loud)

articles

When you're referring to someone or something in particular, the definite article (the equivalent of 'the' in English) is used in Dutch. The definite article is *de* duh for common gender nouns and *het* huht for neuter nouns. When you're referring to plural definite nouns, the article *de* duh is used for both the common and neuter genders (see **gender** and **plurals**).

the train	*de trein*	duh treyn
the house	*het huis* n	huht höys
the trains	*de treinen*	duh trey·nuhn
the houses	*de huizen* n pl	duh höy·zuhn

The indefinite article (the same as English 'a') is *een* uhn for both genders. As in English, there's no plural form of the indefinite article – you just use the plural noun on its own.

a train	*een trein*	uhn treyn
a house	*een huis* n	uhn höys

be

As in many languages, the verb 'be' is quite irregular in Dutch. Here are the present and past tense forms of *zijn* zeyn (be):

zijn – present tense					
I	am	*ik*	*ben*	ik	ben
you sg inf	are	*jij*	*bent*	yey	bent
you sg pol	are	*u*	*bent*	ew	bent
he/she/it	is	*hij/zij/ het*	*is*	hey/zey/ huht	is
we	are	*wij*	*zijn*	wey	zeyn
you pl inf	are	*jullie*	*zijn*	yew·lee	zeyn
you pl pol	are	*u*	*bent*	ew	bent
they	are	*zij*	*zijn*	zey	zeyn

BASICS

18

zijn – past tense					
I	was	*ik*	*was*	ik	was
you sg inf	were	*jij*	*was*	yey	was
you sg pol	were	*u*	*was*	ew	was
he/she/it	was	*hij/ zij/ het*	*was*	hey/ zey/ huht	was
we	were	*wij*	*waren*	wey	*waa*·ruhn
you pl inf	were	*jullie*	*waren*	yew·lee	*waa*·ruhn
you pl pol	were	*u*	*was*	ew	was
they	were	*zij*	*waren*	zey	*waa*·ruhn

demonstratives

giving instructions · indicating location · pointing things out

The Dutch words for 'this' and 'that' vary according to the gender of the noun that they precede – just like the definite articles. The plural demonstratives ('these' and 'those') are the same for both genders. See also **articles**, **gender** and **plurals**.

demonstratives			
m&f	this man/woman	*deze man/vrouw*	*dey*·zuh man/vraw
n	this house	*dit huis*	dit höys
pl	these houses	*deze huizen*	*dey*·zuh *höy*·zuhn
m&f	that man/woman	*die man/vrouw*	dee man/vraw
n	that house	*dat huis*	dat höys
pl	those houses	*die huizen*	dee *höy*·zuhn

gender

Dutch nouns have either masculine, feminine or neuter gender. The distinction is purely grammatical and not related to a noun's meaning. You need to learn the gender for each noun as you go, but you can recognise it by the definite article that's used with it: *de* duh for masculine and feminine gender and *het* huht for neuter gender.

The grammatical distinction between masculine and feminine is only relevant in archaic forms, so we've only indicated the neuter nouns with n in this phrasebook. Masculine and feminine nouns are known as 'common gender' and have been left unmarked in this phrasebook. There are some exceptions that have distinct masculine and feminine forms, for example for professions. Where this happens, we've marked them with m and f respectively. See also **adjectives & adverbs**, **articles** and **demonstratives**.

have

The present and past tense forms of *hebben he·buhn* (have) are given in the next two tables. The verb is used the same way as in English. For negative statements with 'have', see **negatives**.

hebben – present tense					
I	have	*ik*	*heb*	ik	hep
you sg inf	have	*jij*	*hebt*	yey	hept
you sg pol	have	*u*	*heeft*	ew	heyft
he/she/it	has	*hij/zij/ het*	*heeft*	hey/zey/ huht	heyft
we	have	*wij*	*hebben*	wey	*he·buhn*
you pl inf	have	*jullie*	*hebben*	*yew·lee*	*he·buhn*
you pl pol	have	*u*	*heeft*	ew	heyft
they	have	*zij*	*hebben*	zey	*he·buhn*

hebben – past tense					
I	had	*ik*	had	ik	hat
you sg inf	had	*jij*	had	yey	hat
you sg pol	had	*u*	had	ew	hat
he/she	had	*hij/zij*	had	hey/zey	hat
we	had	*wij*	hadden	wey	*ha*·duhn
you pl inf	had	*jullie*	hadden	yew·lee	*ha*·duhn
you pl pol	had	*u*	had	ew	hat
they	had	*zij*	hadden	zey	*ha*·duhn

negatives

In Dutch, negative statements are made by adding the word *niet* neet (not) to a sentence – note that it goes after the verb.

I understand.
  Ik begrijp het.   ik buh·*khreyp* huht
  (lit: I understand it)

I don't understand.
  Ik begrijp het niet.   ik buh·*khreyp* huht neet
  (lit: I understand it not)

The position of *niet* varies but it's often placed at the end of the phrase or just before the part of the phrase you're negating.

I'm not coming today.
  Ik kom vandaag niet.   ik kom van·*daakh* neet
  (lit: I come today not)

I'm not coming at four o'clock.
  Ik kom niet om vier uur.   ik kom neet om veer ewr
  (lit: I come not at four hour)

To make a negative expression that equates to 'I have no …' or 'There aren't any …', use *geen* kheyn (none) instead of *niet*.

I don't have any money.
  Ik heb geen geld.   ik hep kheyn khelt
  (lit: I have none money)

personal pronouns

Personal pronouns ('I', 'you', etc) have different forms in Dutch depending on whether they're the subject or the object in a sentence. It's the same in English, which has 'I' as the subject pronoun but 'me' as the object pronoun (eg 'I see her' and 'She sees me'). These are the Dutch subject pronouns:

subject pronouns					
I	*ik*	ik	we	*wij (we)*	wey (wuh)
you sg inf	*jij (je)*	yey (yuh)	you pl inf	*jullie*	*yew·lee*
you sg pol	*u*	ew	you object	*u*	ew
he	*hij*	hey			
she	*zij (ze)*	zey (zuh)	they	*zij (ze)*	zey (zuh)
it	*het*	huht			

Often, the unemphatic forms (shown in brackets in the table above) are used. It's only when you particularly want to emphasise the subject that you use the emphatic forms.

She went to the museum.

> *Ze bezocht het*   zuh buh·*zokht* huht
> *museum.*   mew·*zey*·yum
> (lit: she-unemphatic visited the museum)

***She* went to the museum, but he didn't.**

> *Zij bezocht het*   zey buh·*zokht* huht
> *museum, maar hij niet.*   mew·*zey*·yum maar hey neet
> (lit: she-emphatic visited the museum, but he not)

The forms of the direct object pronouns are listed in the next table. The unemphatic forms are given in brackets.

direct object pronouns					
me	*mij (me)*	mey (muh)	us	*ons*	ons
you sg inf	*jou (je)*	yaw (yuh)	you pl inf	*jullie*	yew·lee
you sg pol	*u*	ew	you pl pol	*u*	ew
him	*hem**	hem			
her	*haar (ze)*	haar (zuh)	them	*hen (ze)*	hen (zuh)
it	*het**	huht			

*In spoken Dutch, you're likely to hear *hem* and *het* shortened to *'m* and *'t*.

The indirect object pronouns are the same as the emphatic direct object pronouns in Dutch, as shown with the following examples.

I saw her.
Ik zag haar.   ik zakh haar
(lit: I saw her)

I gave the guidebook to her.
Ik gaf de reisgids aan haar.   ik khaf duh *reys*·khits aan haar
(lit: I gave the guidebook to her)

I gave it to her.
Ik gaf het haar.   ik khaf huht haar
(lit: I gave it her)

As the previous tables show, Dutch has two forms for the English 'you'. The polite form *u* ew, which has the same form for singular and plural, is used when meeting people for the first time, people in a position of authority or people you don't know well. Note that *u* takes third-person singular verb forms. An informal 'you' is either *jij* yey for singular or *jullie* yew·lee for plural.

In this book, we've used the pronouns appropriate to the context – generally the informal 'you' – and we've indicated the alternative forms with inf and pol respectively where required. For more information, see the box **all about you** on page 109.

plurals

There are two main plural endings for nouns: -en (or just -n if the noun already ends in an -e) and -s. The -(e)n form is the more common one of the two. The -s ending is mainly used when nouns end in -el, -er, -em or -en.

	singular		plural	
train(s)	*trein*	treyn	*treinen*	*trey*·nuhn
hotel(s)	*hotel*	hoh·*tel*	*hotels*	hoh·*tels*

Some words of Latin origin follow the Latin pattern for plurals: eg *museum* mew·*zee*·yuhm becomes *musea* mew·*zey*·ya. Words ending in -heid ·heyt change that ending to -heden ·hey·duhn in the plural, eg *schoonheid* skhohn·heyt (beauty) becomes *schoonheden* skhohn·hey·duhn (beauties). Words ending in a long vowel written only once (with no accent on it) take the 's ·s in plural, eg *auto* aw·toh (car) becomes *auto's* aw·tohs.

possessives

In Dutch, possessive adjectives (words for 'my', 'your' etc) function just like their English equivalents, as shown below.

possessive adjectives					
my	*mijn (m'n)*	meyn (muhn)	**our**	*onze**	*on*·zuh
your sg inf	*jouw (je)*	yaw (yuh)	**your** pl inf	*jullie*	*yew*·lee
your sg pol	*uw*	ew	**your** pl pol	*uw*	ew
his	*zijn (z'n)*	zeyn (zuhn)	**their**	*hun*	hun
hers	*haar*	haar			

*onze becomes ons ons before neuter singular nouns. The unemphatic forms you might hear are given in brackets above.

That's my backpack.

> *Dat is mijn rugzak.*   dat is meyn *rukh*·zak
> (lit: that is my backpack)

To say 'mine', 'yours' etc, use the common or neuter gender forms from the following table (separated with a slash), depending on the gender of what you're referring to.

possessive pronouns					
mine	*de/het mijne*	duh/huht *mey*·nuh	ours	*de/het onze*	duh/huht *on*·zuh
yours sg inf	*de/het jouwe*	duh/huht *yaw*·wuh	yours pl inf	*die/dat van jullie*	dee/ dat van *yew*·lee
yours sg pol	*de/het uwe*	duh/huht *ew*·wuh	yours pl pol	*de/het uwe*	duh/huht *ew*·wuh
his/ hers	*de/het zijne*	duh/huht *zey*·nuh	theirs	*de/het hunne*	duh/huht *hu*·nuh
hers	*de/het hare*	duh/huht *haa*·ruh			

Alternatively, you can use a demonstrative followed by the construction 'is/are' + *van* … + emphatic direct object pronoun (see **demonstratives** and **personal pronouns**).

This/That is mine.

> *Dit/Dat is van mij.*   dit/dat is van mey
> (lit: this/that is from me)

That backpack is mine.

> *Die rugzak is van mij.*   dee *rukh*·zak is van mey
> (lit: that backpack is from me)

prepositions

giving instructions • indicating location • pointing things out

Like English, Dutch uses prepositions to explain where things are in time or space. Common Dutch prepositions are listed on the next page with their approximate English equivalents.

prepositions					
after	*na*	naa	in (time)	*over*	in
before	*voor*	vohr	since	*sinds*	sins
in (place)	*in*	in	until	*tot*	tot

questions

Forming yes/no questions is quite simple in Dutch – just swap the order of the verb and the pronoun in the statement.

She took a photo.
   Zij nam een foto.   zey nam uhn *foh*·toh
   (lit: she took a photo)

Did she take a photo?
   Nam zij een foto?   nam zey uhn *foh*·toh
   (lit: took she a photo)

Note also that when the word order is reversed, the ending 't' is dropped from the singular informal 'you' form (*jij* yey). As in English, there are also question words for more specific questions. These words go at the start of the sentence.

question words					
How?	*Hoe?*	hoo	Where?	*Waar?*	waar
What?	*Wat?*	wat	Who?	*Wie?*	wee
When?	*Wanneer?*	wa·*neyr*	Why?	*Waarom?*	waa·*rom*

verbs

Dutch verbs mostly follow regular patterns. The infinitive (ie the dictionary form of a verb) usually ends in -*en* or -*n*. To form different tenses, you remove these infinitive endings to get the verb stem and then add a regular series of endings.

BASICS

present tense

The present tense is formed by adding either -t or -en to the verb stem, as shown in the table below. There might be some changes in the verb stem due to Dutch spelling rules related to vowel length, but you'll still be understood even if you don't get it exactly right. Here are the present tense forms of the verb *danken* dang·kuhn (thank).

danken – present tense					
I	thank	*ik*	*dank*	ik	dangk
you sg inf	thank	*jij*	*dankt* *	yey	dangkt
you sg pol	thank	*u*	*dankt*	ew	dangkt
he/ she	thanks	*hij/ zij*	*dankt*	hey/ zey	dangkt
we	thank	*wij*	*danken*	wey	*dang*·kuhn
you pl inf	thank	*jullie*	*danken*	yew·lee	*dang*·kuhn
you pl pol	thank	*u*	*dankt*	ew	dangkt
they	thank	*zij*	*danken*	zey	*dang*·kuhn

* When word order is reversed (eg in questions), the ending 't' is dropped from the singular informal 'you' form (*jij* yey).

past tense

Dutch verbs can be 'strong' or 'weak' and form their past tense according to which group they belong to. Unlike weak verbs, strong verbs have a vowel change in the verb stem in the past tense (like 'begin' becomes 'began/begun' in English). The past tense endings are then added to the strong verb stem, as shown in the table on the following page for the verb *vragen* vraa·khuhn (ask).

For space reasons we can't include the past tense stems of strong verbs in this chapter, but you could try getting hold of a book on Dutch verbs such as *201 Dutch verbs* by Henry Stern (Barron's Educational Series 1980) as a useful reference.

a–z phrasebuilder

27

vragen – past tense					
I	asked	*ik*	*vroeg*	ik	vrookh
you sg inf	asked	*jij*	*vroeg*	yey	vrookh
you sg pol	asked	*u*	*vroeg*	ew	vrookh
he/she	asked	*hij/zij*	*vroeg*	hey/zey	vrookh
we	asked	*wij*	*vroegen*	wey	vroo·khuhn
you pl inf	asked	*jullie*	*vroegen*	yew·lee	vroo·khuhn
you pl pol	asked	*u*	*vroeg*	ew	vrookh
they	asked	*zij*	*vroegen*	zey	vroo·khuhn

As shown in the next table with the verb *reizen* rey·zuhn (travel), weak verbs simply add an ending to form the past tense, with no change in the verb stem (like 'jump' becomes 'jumped' in English). The ending for most verbs is -de(n), but if a verb stem ends in *ch*, *f*, *k*, *p*, *s* or *t*, the endings are -te and -ten instead.

reizen – past tense					
I	travelled	*ik*	*reisde*	ik	reys·duh
you sg inf	travelled	*jij*	*reisde*	yey	reys·duh
you sg pol	travelled	*u*	*reisde*	ew	reys·duh
he/she	travelled	*hij/zij*	*reisde*	hey/zey	reys·duh
we	travelled	*wij*	*reisden*	wey	reys·duhn
you pl inf	travelled	*jullie*	*reisden*	yew·lee	reys·duhn
you pl pol	travelled	*u*	*reisde*	ew	reys·duh
they	travelled	*zij*	*reisden*	zey	reys·duhn

future tense

The future tense in Dutch is easy – it works the same as in English. To form the future tense, you simply combine the auxiliary verb *zullen* zu·luhn (will) with the infinitive of the main verb, just like you use 'will + infinitive' in English (eg 'I will go'). The forms of *zullen* are given in the table below. If it's clear you're speaking about the future or if you use an expression of time, you can just use the present tense.

I'll visit Maastricht.
  Ik zal Maastricht bezoeken.   ik zal maas·*trikht* buh·*zoo*·kuhn
  (lit: I will Maastricht to-visit)

I'll return soon.
  Ik kom gauw terug.   ik kom khaw tuh·*rukh*
  (lit: I come soon back)

zullen (will)

I will	*ik zal*	ik zal	**we will**	*wij zullen*	wey zu·luhn
you will sg inf	*jij zult/ zal **	yey zult/ zal	**you will** pl inf	*jullie zullen*	yew·lee zu·luhn
you will sg pol	*u zult*	u zult	**you will** pl pol	*u zult*	ew zult
he will	*hij zal*	hey zal	**they will**	*zij zullen*	zey zu·luhn
she will	*zij zal*	zey zal			

* both forms are correct

word order

The word order in Dutch in simple sentences is the same as in English: subject–verb–object.

She sent an email.
  Zij stuurde een email.   zey *stewr*·duh uhn *ee*·meyl
  (lit: she sent an email)

See also **negatives** and **questions**.

glossary

adjective	a word that describes something – 'his bike had **faulty** brakes'
adverb	a word that explains how an action is done – 'the mechanic changed the wheel **quickly**'
article	the words 'a', 'an' and 'the'
auxiliary verb	a *verb* used with another verb to indicate tense – 'he **will** win'
demonstrative	a word that means 'this' or 'that'
direct object	the thing or person in the sentence that has the action directed to it – 'he won **the race**'
gender	classification of *nouns* into classes (like masculine, feminine and neuter), requiring other words (eg *adjectives*) to belong to the same class
indirect object	the person or thing in the sentence that is the recipient of the action – 'they gave **him** a drug test'
infinitive	dictionary form of a *verb* – '**to fix** a flat tyre'
noun	a thing, person or idea – 'the big **chainring**'
number	whether a word is singular or plural – 'the **peloton** caught the **breakaways**'
personal pronoun	a word that means 'I', 'you' etc
possessive adjective	a word that means 'my', 'your' etc
possessive pronoun	a word that means 'mine', 'yours' etc
preposition	a word like 'for' or 'before' in English
subject	the thing or person in the sentence that does the action – 'his **chain** snapped'
tense	form of a *verb* that tells you whether the action is in the present, past or future – eg 'ride' (present), 'rode' (past), 'will ride' (future)
verb	a word that tells you what action happened – 'he **attacked** the peloton'
verb stem	part of a *verb* that doesn't change – eg '**cycle**' in '**cycle**ing' and '**cycle**d'

language difficulties
taalproblemen

Do you speak (English)?
Spreekt u (Engels)? pol — spreykt ew (*eng*·uhls)

Does anyone speak (English)?
Is er hier iemand die — is uhr heer *ee*·mant dee
(Engels) spreekt? — (*eng*·uhls) spreykt

Do you understand (me)?
Begrijpt u (mij)? pol — buh·*khreypt* ew (mey)

I (don't) understand.
Ik begrijp het (niet). — ik buh·*khreyp* huht (neet)

I speak (English).
Ik spreek (Engels). — ik spreyk (*eng*·uhls)

I don't speak (Dutch).
Ik spreek geen (Nederlands). — ik spreyk kheyn (*ney*·duhr·lants)

I speak a little.
Ik spreek het een beetje. — ik spreyk huht uhn *bey*·chuh

What does (dag) mean?
Wat betekent (dag)? — wat buh·*tey*·kuhnt (dakh)

I'd like to practise (Dutch).
Ik wil graag mijn — ik wil khraakh meyn
(Nederlands) wat — (*ney*·duhr·lants) wat
oefenen. — *oo*·fuh·nuhn

Let's speak (Dutch).
Laat ons (Nederlands) — laat ons (*ney*·duhr·lants)
spreken. — *sprey*·kuhn

Could you please speak more slowly?
Kunt u alstublieft wat — kunt ew al·stew·*bleeft* wat
langzamer spreken? pol — *lang*·zaa·muhr *sprey*·kuhn

Could you — *Kunt u dat* — kunt ew dat
please ...? — *alstublieft ...?* pol — al·stew·*bleeft* ...
  repeat that — *herhalen* — her·*haa*·luhn
  write it down — *opschrijven* — *op*·skhrey·vuhn

language difficulties

How do you …?	Hoe …?	hoo …
pronounce this	spreek je dit uit	spreyk yuh dit öyt
write	schrijf je	skhreyf yuh
(*dank u wel*)	(*dank u wel*)	(dangk ew wel)

tongue twisters

*De knappe kapper knipt en kapt knap, maar de knappe
knecht van de knappe kapper knipt en kapt nog knapper
dan de knappe kapper knipt en kapt.*

duh *kna*·puh *ka*·puhr knipt en kapt knap, maar duh
kna·puh knekht van duh *kna*·puh *ka*·puhr knipt en kapt
nokh *kna*·puhr dan duh *kna*·puh *ka*·puhr knipt en kapt

(The handsome hairdresser cuts and chops beautifully, but the handsome helper of the handsome hairdresser cuts and chops even more beautifully than the handsome hairdresser cuts and chops.)

*Frans zei in het Frans tegen Frans dat Frans in het Frans
Frans wordt geschreven, nee zei Frans in het Frans tegen
Frans, Frans wordt in het Frans niet Frans geschreven,
Frans wordt in het Frans François geschreven.*

frans zey in huht frans *tey*·khuhn frans dat frans in huht
frans frans wort khuh·*skhrey*·vuhn ney zey frans in huht
frans *tey*·khun frans frans wort in huht frans neet frans
khuh·*skhrey*·vuhn frans wort in huht frans fran·*swa*
khuh·*skhrey*·vuhn

(Frans said to Frans in French that Frans in French is written as Frans, no said Frans in French to Frans, Frans is not written as Frans in French, Frans is written as François in French.)

*Zeven Zwevegemse zotten zwommen zeven zondagen
zonder zwembroek, ze zeiden, ze zijn zeker zot zonder
zwembroek zwemmen.*

zey·vuhn *zwey*·vuh·khem·suh *zo*·tuhn *zwo*·muhn *zey*·vuhn
zon·daa·khuhn *zon*·duhr *zwem*·brook zuh *zey*·duhn zuh
zeyn *zey*·kuhr zot *zon*·duhr *zwem*·brook *zwe*·muhn

(Seven fools from Zwevegem went swimming seven Sundays without bathers, they said, they must be crazy to go swimming without bathers.)

numbers & amounts
getallen & hoeveelheden

cardinal numbers

		hoofdtelwoorden
0	*nul*	nul
1	*één*	eyn
2	*twee*	twey
3	*drie*	dree
4	*vier*	veer
5	*vijf*	veyſ
6	*zes*	zes
7	*zeven*	*zey*·vuhn
8	*acht*	akht
9	*negen*	*ney*·khuhn
10	*tien*	teen
11	*elf*	elf
12	*twaalf*	twaalf
13	*dertien*	*der*·teen
14	*veertien*	*veyr*·teen
15	*vijftien*	*veyf*·teen
16	*zestien*	*zes*·teen
17	*zeventien*	*zey*·vuhn·teen
18	*achttien*	*akh*·teen
19	*negentien*	*ney*·khuhn·teen
20	*twintig*	*twin*·tikh
21	*eenentwintig*	*eyn*·en·*twin*·tikh
22	*tweeëntwintig*	*twey*·en·*twin*·tikh
30	*dertig*	*der*·tikh
40	*veertig*	*feyr*·tikh
50	*vijftig*	*feyf*·tikh
60	*zestig*	*ses*·tikh
70	*zeventig*	*sey*·vuhn·tikh
80	*tachtig*	*takh*·tikh
90	*negentig*	*ney*·khuhn·tikh

numbers & amounts

33

100	*honderd*	*hon·duhrt*
200	*tweehonderd*	*twey·hon·duhrt*
1000	*duizend*	*döy·zuhnt*
1,000,000	*een miljoen*	uhn mil·*yoon*

ordinal numbers

To form the ordinal number, add *-de* ·duh to the cardinal number, except for *eerste/1ste* (first) and *derde/3de* (third), which are irregular. Also, *achtste/8ste* (eight) and multiples of 10 use the ending *-ste* ·stuh instead of *-de*, eg *twintigste/20ste* (twentieth) and *honderdste/100ste* (hundredth). Note that ordinal numbers can be used in dates – eg *7de/zevende april* (7 April).

1st	*eerste/1ste*	eyr·stuh
2nd	*tweede/2de*	twey·duh
3rd	*derde/3de*	der·duh
4th	*vierde/4de*	veer·duh
5th	*vijfde/5de*	veyf·duh

fractions & decimals

a quarter	*een kwart*	uhn kwart
a third	*een derde*	uhn *der*·duh
a half (of a number)	*een half*	uhn half
three and a half	*drie en half*	dree en half
a half (of something)	*een helft*	uhn helft
a half of the cake	*een helft van de cake*	uhn helft van duh keek
three-quarters	*drie vierde*	dree *veer*·duh
all	*alle*	*a*·luh
none	*geen*	kheyn

Decimals are written – and pronounced – with a comma, not a dot as in English.

three point fourteen (3.14)	*drie comma veertien (3,14)*	dree ko·ma veyr·teen
four point two (4.2)	*vier comma twee (4,2)*	veer ko·ma twey
five point one (5.1)	*vijf comma één (5,1)*	veyf ko·ma eyn

useful amounts

How much/many?	*Hoeveel?*	hoo·veyl
Please give me ...	*Ik wil graag ...*	ik wil khraakh ...
(100) grams	*(honderd) gram*	(hon·duhrt) khram
half a dozen	*een half dozijn*	uhn half do·zeyn
half a kilo	*een halve kilo*	uhn hal·vuh kee·loh
a kilo	*een kilo*	uhn kee·loh
a bottle	*een fles*	uhn fles
a jar	*een pot* ⓝ	uhn pot
	een bokaal ⓑ	uhn boh·kaal
a packet	*een pak*	uhn pak
a piece	*een stuk*	uhn stuk
(three) pieces	*(drie) stuks*	(dree) stuks
a slice	*een plak/snee* ⓝ/ⓑ	uhn plak/sney
(six) slices	*(zes) plakken* ⓝ	(zes) pla·kuhn
	(zes) sneetjes ⓑ	(zes) sney·chuhs
a tin	*een blik*	uhn blik
a few	*enkele*	eng·kuh·luh
less	*minder*	min·duhr
(just) a little	*een (klein) beetje*	uhn (kleyn) bey·chuh
a lot	*veel*	veyl
many	*vele*	vey·luh
more	*meer*	meyr
some	*enkele*	eng·kuh·luh

For more amounts, see **self-catering**, page 177.

frisian

If you thought it was only Belgium that had a complex linguistic situation – with Dutch, French and German as its three official languages – you're mistaken. The Netherlands, too, has a second language in addition to Dutch – Frisian (called *Fries* frees in Dutch and *Frysk* freesk in Frisian itself) has official status in the northern Dutch province of Friesland. In 1997 the spelling of the province's name was officially altered from the Dutch *Friesland* frees·lant to *Fryslân* frees·lan, the local version of the name. There are about 700,000 speakers of Frisian – around 400,000 live in Friesland, while the rest live mostly in Germany. The language spoken in Friesland is, more precisely, West Frisian, with closely related East Frisian and North Frisian spoken in Germany – but it's simply referred to as 'Frisian' in the Netherlands.

Frisian is a member of the West Germanic family of languages and is historically the closest relative of English (there's even an old saying that goes 'as milk is to cheese, are English and Freese'). It developed from Old Frisian, spoken in the Middle Ages along the North Sea coast from Belgium to Germany. Over the centuries, however, Old Frisian and Old English drifted apart considerably, so that a modern-day English speaker won't be able to make much sense of Frisian – just like the Dutch have difficulty understanding it. The majority of Frisians, on the other hand, are perfectly conversant in standard Dutch. You're actually more likely to hear Frisian coming from older people than the younger generation, but most of the locals know some as a sign of cultural pride. In Friesland, Frisian is used alongside Dutch in the media, public administration, in the courts and in education (either taught as a compulsory subject or used as the medium of instruction in schools). Most native speakers of Frisian live in the rural areas.

You'll usually see written examples of Frisian, such as place names and street signs. Here are the most important place names in Friesland, given in both languages:

Frisian	Dutch
Frjentsjer	*Franeker*
Harns	*Harlingen*
Hylpen	*Hindeloopen*
Ljouwert	*Leeuwarden*
Snits	*Sneek*

telling the time

In everyday language, the 12-hour clock is used. You'll only see the 24-hour clock on train and bus timetables. The terms 'am' and 'pm' are not used as such in Dutch – the time of day is specified using one of the expressions below, such as *'s avonds* saa·vonts (in the evening).

What time is it?	*Hoe laat is het?*	hoo laat is huht
It's (10) o'clock.	*Het is (tien) uur.*	huht is (teen) ewr
Five past (10).	*Vijf over (tien).*	veyf (oh·vuhr) teen
Quarter past (10).	*Kwart over (tien).*	kwart (oh·vuhr) teen
Half past (10).	*Half (elf).*	half (elf)
	(lit: half eleven)	
Quarter to (11).	*Kwart voor (elf).*	kwart vohr (elf)
Twenty to (11).	*Tien over half (elf).*	teen oh·ver half (elf)
	(lit: ten past half eleven)	
Ten to (11).	*Tien voor (elf).*	teen vohr (elf)
am (night)	*'s nachts*	snakhts
am (morning)	*'s ochtends*	sokh·tuhns
pm (afternoon)	*'s middags*	smi·dakhs
pm (evening)	*'s avonds*	saa·vonts
At what time ...?	*Hoe laat ...?*	hoo laat ...
At (five).	*Om (vijf uur).*	om (veyf ewr)

At (7.57pm). (in everyday speech)
Om (drie voor acht   om (dree vohr akht
's avonds)./Om (7.57).   saa·vonts)
(lit: at three to eight in-the-evening)

At (7.57pm). (in timetables)
Om (negentien uur   om (ney·khuhn·teen ewr
zevenenvijftig)./Om (19.57).   zey·vuhn·en·feyf·tikh)
(lit: at nineteen hour fifty-seven)

the calendar

days of the week

Monday	*maandag*	*maan*·dakh
Tuesday	*dinsdag*	*dins*·dakh
Wednesday	*woensdag*	*woons*·dakh
Thursday	*donderdag*	*don*·duhr·dakh
Friday	*vrijdag*	*vrey*·dakh
Saturday	*zaterdag*	*zaa*·tuhr·dakh
Sunday	*zondag*	*zon*·dakh

months

January	*januari*	*ya*·new·waa·ree
February	*februari*	*fey*·brew·waa·ree
March	*maart*	maart
April	*april*	a·*pril*
May	*mei*	mey
June	*juni*	*yew*·nee
July	*juli*	*yew*·lee
August	*augustus*	aw·*khus*·tus
September	*september*	sep·*tem*·buhr
October	*oktober*	ok·*toh*·buhr
November	*november*	noh·*vem*·buhr
December	*december*	dey·*sem*·buhr

dates

What date is it today?
    De hoeveelste is het   duh hoo·*veyl*·stuh is huht
    vandaag?   van·*daakh*

It's (7 April).
    Het is de (zevende april).   huht is duh (*zey*·vuhn·duh a·*pril*)

seasons

spring	*lente*	*len*·tuh
summer	*zomer*	*zoh*·muhr
autumn/fall	*herfst*	herfst
winter	*winter*	*win*·tuhr

and the fifth season is ...

When hell freezes over. (ie never)
Als Pasen en Pinksteren   als *paa*·suhn en *pink*·stuh·ruhn
op één dag vallen.   op eyn dakh *va*·luhn
(lit: when Easter and Pentecost fall on the same day)

present

het heden

now	*nu*	new
today	*vandaag*	van·*daakh*
this morning	*vanochtend*	van·*okh*·tuhnt
this afternoon	*vanmiddag*	van·*mi*·dakh
tonight	*vanavond*	va·*naa*·vont
this week	*deze week*	*dey*·zuh weyk
this month	*deze maand*	*dey*·zuh maant
this year	*dit jaar*	dit yaar

past

het verleden

yesterday	*gisteren*	*khis*·tuh·ruhn
day before yesterday	*eergisteren*	*eyr*·khis·tuh·ruhn
(three days) ago	*(drie dagen) geleden*	(dree *daa*·khuhn) khuh·*ley*·duhn
since (May)	*sinds (mei)*	sins (mey)

last ...		
night	*gisteravond*	khis·tuhr·*aa*·vont
week	*vorige week*	*voh*·ri·khuh weyk
month	*vorige maand*	*voh*·ri·khuh maant
year	*vorig jaar*	*voh*·rikh yaar

yesterday ...		
morning	*gisterochtend*	khis·tuhr·*okh*·tuhnt
afternoon	*gistermiddag*	khis·tuhr·*mi*·dakh
evening	*gisteravond*	khis·tuhr·*aa*·vont

future

tomorrow	*morgen*	*mor*·khuhn
day after tomorrow	*overmorgen*	*oh*·vuhr·mor·khuhn
in (six days)	*over (zes dagen)*	*oh*·vuhr (zes *daa*·khuhn)
until (June)	*tot (juni)*	tot (*yew*·nee)
next year	*volgend jaar*	*vol*·khuhnt yaar

next ...	*volgende ...*	*vol*·khuhn·duh ...
week	*week*	weyk
month	*maand*	maant

tomorrow ...		
morning	*morgenochtend*	mor·khuhn·*okh*·tuhnt
afternoon	*morgenmiddag*	mor·khuhn·*mi*·dakh
evening	*morgenavond*	mor·khuhn·*aa*·vont

during the day

Note that in Flanders you may also hear *namiddag* used for 'afternoon', to distinguish it from *middag* (noon), and *morgen* as an alternative for *ochtend* (morning).

afternoon	*middag* Ⓝ	*mi*·dakh
	namiddag Ⓑ	*naa*·mi·dakh
dawn	*dageraad*	*daa*·khuh·raat
day	*dag*	dakh
evening	*avond*	*aa*·vont
midday/noon	*middag*	*mi*·dakh
midnight	*middernacht*	mi·duhr·*nakht*
morning	*ochtend* Ⓝ	*okh*·tuhnt
	morgen Ⓑ	*mor*·khuhn
night	*nacht*	nakht
sunrise	*zonsopgang*	zons·*op*·gang
sunset	*zonsondergang*	zons·*on*·duhr·gang

party on in belgium

Festival of the Flemish Community

Feest van de Vlaamse   feyst van duh *vlaam*·suh
Gemeenschap Ⓑ   khuh·*meyn*·skhap

On 11 July, the Flemish commemorate the *Guldensporenslag* *khul*·duhn·*spoh*·ruhn·slakh (Battle of the Gilded Spurs) of 1302, when they beat their French rulers and asserted their cultural and political independence – at least for a while. They've picked that day as their 'Flemish National Day'. The Francophone Walloons celebrate on 27 September, while the small German-speaking community lets their hair down on 15 November.

National Day

Nationale Feestdag Ⓑ   na·syoh·*naa*·luh feys·dakh
The Flemish and the Walloons each have their own language, culture and government, but on 21 July everyone – well, nearly everyone – considers themselves a Belgian in the first place, if only to enjoy the extra day off! A big annual *militaire optocht* mee·lee·*tey*·ruh *op*·tokht (military parade) – also commonly known as *défilé* dey·fee·*ley* – is held in Brussels in front of the Royal Palace and is overseen by the Royal Family, who is an important symbol of unity. The date goes back to 21 July 1830, when Belgium was declared independent from France after yet another uprising and when the present-day kingdom was founded.

party on in the netherlands

Queen's Day

Koninginnedag ®   koh·ning·*khi*·nuh·dakh

In the Netherlands, everyone gets a holiday on the Queen's birthday (30 April). Funnily enough, 30 April isn't the current Queen's birthday – when she assumed the throne in 1980, Queen Beatrix stated that she wished to keep celebrating *Koninginnedag* on 30 April, the birthday of her mother, Queen Juliana. The day is marked by street parties and festivities all around the country and almost everyone wears *oranje* oh·*ran*·yuh (orange), the colour that stands for national pride and refers to the Royal Family's name – *Oranje-Nassau* oh·*ran*·yuh *na*·saw. Every year, the Queen and her family attend a few festivities in person and these visits are always broadcast on television.

Prince's Day

Prinsjesdag ®   *prin*·shus·dakh

Every third Tuesday in September, the opening of the Dutch parliamentary year is marked by a speech given by the Queen – but written by the Prime Minister and his cabinet – to the *Staten-Generaal* staa·tuhn khey·ney·*raal* (the Dutch parliament). The Queen travels from her residence to the Binnenhof bi·nuhn·hof (lit: inner courtyard) – the location of the parliament sessions – and back in the *Gouden Koets* khaw·duhn koots (Gilded Carriage), cheered on by people lining the streets. Back at the palace, she salutes the crowd from the balcony. The same day, the Minister of Finance proposes the budget, which is carried in a special suitcase marked with the words *Derde Dinsdag van September* der·duh dins·dakh van sep·*tem*·buhr (Third Tuesday of September).

How much is it?
Hoeveel kost het? — hoo·*veyl* kost huht

Can you write down the price?
Kunt u de prijs — kunt ew duh preys
opschrijven? **pol** — *op*·skhrey·vuhn

Do I have to pay?
Moet ik betalen? — moot ik buh·*taa*·luhn

I'd like to return this, please.
Ik wil dit graag — ik wil dit khraakh
retourneren. — re·toor·*ney*·ruhn

I'd like …,   *Ik wil graag …*   ik wil khraakh …
please.

my change	*mijn wisselgeld*	meyn *wi*·suhl·khelt
a receipt	*een kwitantie*	uhn kwee·*tan*·see
a refund	*mijn geld terug*	meyn khelt tuh·*rukh*

I'd like to …   *Ik wil graag …*   ik wil khraakh …

arrange a transfer	*een giro-betaling maken* ®	uhn *khee*·roh·buh·taa·ling *maa*·kuhn
	een over-schrijving doen ®	uhn oh·vuhr·skhrey·ving doon
cash a cheque	*een cheque innen*	uhn shek *i*·nuhn
change a travellers cheque	*een reischeque innen*	uhn *reys*·shek *i*·nuhn
change money	*geld wisselen*	khelt *wi*·suh·luhn
get a cash advance	*een voorschot bekomen*	uhn *vohr*·skhot buh·*koh*·muhn
get change for this note	*dit biljet wisselen in muntstukken*	dit bil·*yet wi*·suh·luhn in *munt*·stu·kuhn
withdraw money	*geld afhalen*	khelt *af*·haa·luhn

Do you accept ...?	Accepteert u ...? pol	ak·sep·teyrt ew ...
credit cards	kredietkaarten	krey·deet·kaar·tuhn
debit cards	debetkaarten	dey·bet·kaar·tuhn
travellers cheques	reischeques	reys·sheks

Where's ...?	Waar vind ik een ...?	waar vint ik uhn ...
an automated teller machine	pin-automaat ℕ geldautomaat ℬ	pin·aw·toh·maat khelt·aw·toh·maat
a foreign exchange office	wisselkantoor	wi·suhl·kan·tohr

What's the ...?	Wat is de ...?	wat is duh ...
charge	kost hiervoor	kost heer·vohr
exchange rate	wisselkoers	wi·suhl·koors

It's ...	Het is ...	huht is ...
free	gratis	khraa·tis
(12) euros	(twaalf) euro	(twaalf) eu·roh

How much is it per ...?	Hoeveel kost het per ...?	hoo·veyl kost huht puhr ...
caravan	caravan	ke·ruh·ven ℕ ka·ra·van ℬ
day	dag	dakh
game	spel	spel
hour	uur	ewr
(five) minutes	(vijf) minuten	(veyf) mee·new·tuhn
night	nacht	nakht
page	pagina	paa·khee·na
person	persoon	puhr·sohn
tent	tent	tent
vehicle	wagen	waa·khuhn
week	week	weyk

For more money-related phrases, see **banking**, page 89.

getting around

rondreizen

Note that in Belgium, the word *premetro* is used to refer to a metro line that's still part of the tram network.

Which … goes to (Amsterdam)?	*Welke … gaat naar (Amsterdam)?*	wel·kuh … khaat naar (am·stuhr·dam)
boat	*boot*	boht
bus	*bus*	bus
train	*trein*	treyn

Is this the … to (the left bank)?	*Is dit de … naar (de linkeroever)?*	is dit duh … naar (duh ling·kuhr·oo·vuhr)
ferry	*veerboot* Ⓝ	veyr·boht
	ferry Ⓑ	fe·ree
metro	*metro*	mey·troh
premetro	*premetro*	prey·mey·troh
tram	*tram*	trem/tram Ⓝ/Ⓑ

When's the … (bus)?	*Hoe laat gaat de … (bus)?*	hoo laat khaat duh … (bus)
first	*eerste*	eyr·stuh
last	*laatste*	laat·stuh
next	*volgende*	vol·khun·duh

What time does it leave?
Hoe laat vertrekt het? hoo laat vuhr·trekt huht

What time does it get to (Gouda)?
Hoe laat komt het aan in (Gouda)? hoo laat komt huht aan in (khaw·da)

How long will it be delayed?
Hoeveel vertraging is er? hoo·veyl vuhr·traa·khing is uhr

Is this seat available?
Is deze zitplaats vrij? is dey·zuh zit·plaats vrey

That's my seat.
Dat is mijn zitplaats.   dat is meyn *zit*·plaats

Please stop here.
Stop hier alstublieft. **pol**   stop heer al·stew·*bleeft*

How long do we stop here?
Hoelang houden we   hoo·*lang* haw·duhn wuh
hier halt?   heer halt

tickets

kaartjes

The word *kaartje* is the one that's most commonly used to indicate transport tickets, but you may also hear *ticket* (pronounced as in English, *ti*·kuht, or ti·*ket* in Belgium), *biljet* bil·*yet* and *vervoerbewijs* vuhr·*voor*·buh·weys.

Where do I buy a ticket/strip card?
Waar kan ik een kaartje/   waar kan ik uhn *kaar*·chuh/
strippenkaart kopen?   *stri*·puhn·kaart *koh*·puhn

Do I need to book (well in advance)?
Moet ik (lang op voorhand)   moot ik (lang op *vohr*·hant)
reserveren?   rey·ser·*vey*·ruhn

Can I get a sleeping berth?
Kan ik een slaapplaats   kan ik uhn *slaa*·plaats
hebben?   *he*·buhn

I'd like a ticket for my bike/dog.
Ik wil een kaartje voor   ik wil uhn *kaar*·chuh vohr
mijn fiets/hond kopen.   meyn feets/hont *koh*·puhn

I'd like a Train+Bike ticket.
Ik wil graag een   ik wil khraakh uhn
Trein+Fiets ticket. ®   treyn plus feets ti·*ket*

Can I pick up a rental bike at the (Leeuwarden) train station, please?
Kan ik een huurfiets   kan ik uhn *hewr*·feets
oppikken in het station   o·pi·kuhn in huht sta·*syon*
van (Leeuwarden)   van (*ley*·war·duhn)
alstublieft? **pol**   al·stew·*bleeft*

choices, choices ...

The local rail systems in the Low Countries can take you quickly to just about anywhere. A vast array of discount passes, multi-travel deals, weekend fares, seasonal specials, specific trip offers combining train travel with admission to attractions or events, and other lower-cost options are on offer. Not all options are available everywhere all the time, so always inquire about the cheapest option for your trip:

What's the cheapest way of travelling to (The Hague)?
Wat is de goedkoopste manier om naar (Den Haag) te reizen? — wat is duh khoot·*kohp*·stuh ma·*neer* om naar (duhn haakh) tuh *rey*·zuhn

Is there a special ticket deal for ...?	*Is er een speciaal kaartje voor ...?*	is uhr uhn spey·*syaal kaar*·chuh vohr ...
a day trip to (the coast)	*een dagtrip naar (de kust)*	uhn *dakh*·trip naar (duh kust)
the (Van Gogh) exhibition	*de (Van Gogh) tentoonstelling*	duh (van khokh) tuhn·*tohn*·ste·ling
families	*families*	fa·*mee*·lees
groups	*groepen*	*khroo*·puhn
a weekend trip to (Brussels)	*een weekendtrip naar (Brussel)*	uhn *wey*·kent·trip naar (*bru*·suhl)
the zoo	*de dierentuin*	duh *dee*·ruhn·töyn

A ... ticket (to Maastricht).	*Een ... (naar Maastricht) graag.*	uhn ... (naar maas·*trikht*) khraakh
one-way	*enkele reis*	*eng*·kuh·luh reys
return	*retourtje* ⓝ	ruh·*toor*·chuh
	heen- en terugreis ⓑ	*heyn*·en· tuh·*rukh*·reys

A ... ticket (to Bruges).	*Een ... kaartje (naar Brugge) graag.*	uhn ... *kaar*·chuh (naar *bru*·khuh) khraakh
1st-class	*eerste klas*	*eyr*·stuh klas
2nd-class	*tweede klas*	*twey*·duh klas

A ... ticket (to Sneek).	*Een kaartje voor ... (naar Sneek) graag.*	uhn *kaar*·chuh vohr ... (naar sneyk) khraakh
child's	*een kind*	uhn kint
seniors'	*senioren*	sey·*nyoh*·ruhn
student	*een student*	uhn stew·*dent*

transport

47

I'd like a/an …	Ik wil graag een	ik wil khraakh uhn
seat.	zitplaats …	zit-plaats …
aisle	bij het	bey huht
	gangpad	khang-pat
nonsmoking	voor	vohr
	niet-rokers	neet-roh-kuhrs
smoking	voor rokers	vohr roh-kuhrs
window	bij het raam	bey huht raam

Is there …?	Is er … aan boord?	is uhr … aan bohrt
air conditioning	aircondi-	eyr-kon-di-
	tioning	shuh-ning
a toilet	een toilet	uhn twa-let

How much is it?
Hoeveel kost het? — hoo-veyl kost huht

How long does the trip take?
Hoe lang duurt de reis? — hoo lang dewrt duh reys

Is it a direct route?
Is het een rechtstreekse — is huht uhn rekh-streyk-suh
verbinding? — vuhr-bin-ding

What time should I check in?
Hoe laat moet ik inchecken? — hoo laat moot ik in-she-kuhn

I'd like to … my	Ik wil graag	ik wil khraakh
ticket, please.	mijn kaartje …	meyn kaar-chuh …
cancel	annuleren	a-new-ley-ruhn
change	wijzigen	wey-zi-khhun
collect	afhalen	af-haa-luhn
confirm	bevestigen	buh-ves-ti-khuhn

listen for …

deze/die	dey-zuh/dee	**this/that one**
dienstregeling	deenst-rey-khuh-ling	**timetable**
geannuleerd	khuh-a-new-leyrt	**cancelled**
loket n	lo-ket	**ticket window**
perron n	pe-ron	**platform**
reisagent	reys-a-khent	**travel agent**
staking	staa-king	**strike** n
vertraagd	vuhr-traakht	**delayed**
vol	vol	**full**

luggage

bagage

Where can I find a/the ...?	*Waar vind ik ...?*	waar vint ik ...
baggage belt	*de bagage-band*	duh ba·*khaa*·zhuh·bant
baggage claim	*het bagage inleverpunt*	huht ba·*khaa*·zhuh *in*·ley·vuhr·punt
left-luggage office	*de bagage-depot*	duh ba·*khaa*·zhuh·dey·*poh*
luggage locker	*de bagage-kluizen*	duh ba·*khaa*·zhuh·*klöy*·zuhn
porter service	*de kruiersservice*	duh *kröy*·yuhr·seur·vis
trolley	*een bagage-wagentje*	uhn ba·*khaa*·zhuh·*waa*·khuhn·chuh

My luggage has been ...	*Mijn bagage is ...*	meyn ba·*khaa*·zhuh is ...
damaged	*beschadigd*	buh·*skhaa*·dikht
lost	*verloren*	vuhr·*loh*·ruhn
stolen	*gestolen*	khuh·*stoh*·luhn

Can I have some coins/tokens?
Ik wil graag enkele muntstukken/jetons.
ik wil khraakh *eng*·kuh·luh munt·stu·kuhn/zhuh·*tons*

backpack	*rugzak*	*rukh*·zak
bag	*tas*	tas
box	*doos*	dohs
cosmetic bag	*toiletzak*	twa·*let*·zak
dress bag	*tas voor een jurk/ kleed* ⑩/⑬	tas vohr uhn yurk/ kleyt
suit bag	*tas voor een pak/ kostuum* ⑩/⑬	tas vohr uhn pak/ kos·*tewm*
suitcase	*koffer*	*ko*·fuhr

doorreis	dohr·reys	transit
handbagage	hant·ba·khaa·zhuh	carry-on baggage
hersluitbare	her·slöyt·baa·ruh	resealable
doorzichtige	dohr·zikh·ti·khuh	transparent
plastic tas	ples·tik tas	plastic bag
instapkaart	in·stap·kaart	boarding pass
overvracht	oh·vuhr·vrakht	excess baggage
scherpe	skher·puh	sharp objects
voorwerpen	vohr·wer·puhn	
verzegelde tas	vuhr·zey·khul·duh tas	sealed bag
vloeistoffen	vlooy·sto·fuhn	liquids

plane

vliegtuig

Where does flight (KL1083) depart?
Waar vertrekt vlucht — waar vuhr·*trekt* vlukht
(KL1083)? — (kaa el teen *dree·en·takh*·tikh)

Where does flight (KL1082) arrive?
Waar komt vlucht — waar komt vlukht
(KL1082) aan? — (kaa el teen *twey·en·takh*·tikh) aan

Where's (the) ...?	*Waar is ...?*	waar is ...
airport shuttle	de shuttledienst	duh shu·tuhl·deenst
arrivals hall	de aankomsthal	duh aan·komst·hal
departures hall	de vertrekhal	duh vuhr·trek·hal
duty-free shop	het taxfree winkelen	huht taks·free wing·kuh·luhn
gate (12)	gate (twaalf)	geyt (twaalf)
transfer desk	de transferbalie	duh trans·fer·baa·lee

Aankomst	aan·komst	Arrival
Hellingbaan	he·ling·baan	Travelator
Naar de Platforms	naar duh plat·forms	To the Trains
Roltrap	rol·trap	Escalator
Vertrek	vuhr·trek	Departure

bus & coach

Is this a bus stop?
Is dit een bushalte?　　is dit uhn *bus*·hal·tuh

How often do buses come?
Hoe vaak komt de bus?　　hoo vaak komt duh bus

Does it stop at (Keukenhof)?
Stopt het in (Keukenhof)?　　stopt huht in (*keu*·kuhn·hof)

What's the next stop?
Welk is de volgende　　welk is duh *vol*·khuhn·duh
halte?　　*hal*·tuh

I'd like to get off at (Lisse).
Ik wil graag in (Lisse)　　ik wil khraak in (*li*·suh)
uitstappen.　　öyt·sta·puhn

bus station	*busstation* n	*bus*·sta·syon
bus stop	*bushalte*	*bus*·hal·tuh
city bus	*stadsbus*	*stats*·bus
coach	*touringcar*	*too*·ring·kar
departure bay	*vertrekplaats*	*vuhr*·trek·plaats
intercity a	*intercity*	in·tuhr·*si*·tee
local a	*plaatselijk*	*plaat*·suh·luhk
shuttle bus	*shuttle bus*	*shu*·tuhl bus
timetable	*dienstregeling*	*deenst*·rey·khuh·ling

For bus numbers, see **numbers & amounts**, page 33.

train

What's the next station?
Welk is het volgende　　welk is huht *vol*·kuhn·duh
station?　　sta·*syon*

Does it stop at (Berchem)?
Stopt het in (Berchem)?　　stopt huht in (*ber*·chuhm)

Do I need to change?
Moet ik overstappen?　　moot ik *oh*·vuhr·sta·puhn

Is it …?	Is het een …?	is huht uhn …
direct	directe	dee·rek·tuh
	verbinding	vuhr·bin·ding
express	expressdienst	eks·pres·deenst

Which carriage	Welke wagon	wel·kuh wa·khon
is for …?	is …?	is …
1st class	eerste klas	eyr·stuh klas
bicycles	voor fietsen	vohr feet·suhn
(Roosendaal)	voor (Roosendaal)	vohr (roh·zuhn·daal)

Which carriage is for dining?
Welk is de welk is duh
restauratiewagen? res·toh·raa·see·waa·khuhn

boat

boot

What's the …	In welke conditie	in wel·kuh kon·dee·see
like today?	is … vandaag?	is … van·daakh
lake	het meer	huht meyr
river	de rivier	duh ree·veer
sea	de zee	duh zey

Are there life jackets?
Zijn er zwemvesten zeyn uhr zwem·ves·tuhn
aan boord? aan bohrt

What island/beach is this?
Welk eiland/strand is dit? welk ey·lant/strant is dit

boat	boot	boht
cabin	cabine	ka·bee·nuh
captain	kapitein	ka·pee·teyn
deck	dek n	dek
ferry	veerboot/ferry ⑩/⑥	veyr·boht/fe·ree
house boat	woonboot	wohn·boht
lifeboat	reddingsboot	re·dings·boht
life jacket	zwemvest n	zwem·vest
sailing boat	zeilboot	zeyl·boht
ship	schip n	skhip

listen for ...

de volgende halte is ...	
duh *vol*·khun·duh *hal*·tuh is ...	the next stop will be ...
gedeelte/trein naar ...	
khuh·*deyl*·tuh/treyn naar ...	carriage/train to ...
we komen aan in ...	
wuh *koh*·muhn aan in ...	we're arriving at ...

taxi

taxi

I'd like a taxi ...	*Ik wil graag*	ik wil khraakh
	een taxi ...	uhn *tak*·see ...
at (9am)	*om (negen*	om (*ney*·khuhn
	uur 's ochtends)	ewr *sokh*·tuhns)
now	*nu*	new
tomorrow	*voor morgen*	vohr *mor*·khuhn

I'd like to	*Ik wil graag een*	ik wil khraakh uhn
book a ...	*... reserveren.*	... rey·ser·*vey*·ruhn
shared taxi	*deeltaxi*	*deyl*·tak·see
train taxi	*treintaxi*	*treyn*·tak·see

Where's the taxi rank?
Waar is de taxistandplaats?   waar is duh *tak*·see·stant·plaats

Is this taxi available?
Is deze taxi vrij?   is *dey*·zuh *tak*·see vrey

Please take me to (this address).
Breng me alstublieft   breng muh al·stew·*bleeft*
naar (dit adres). pol   naar (dit a·*dres*)

How much is it (to Geleen)?
Hoeveel kost het naar   hoo·*veyl* kost huht naar
(Geleen)?   (khuh·*leyn*)

How much is the flag fall/hiring charge?
Hoeveel is het   hoo·*veyl* is huht
vertrekbedrag?   vuhr·*trek*·buh·drakh

Please come back at (10 o'clock).
Kom om (tien uur) terug   kom om (teen ewr) tuh·*rukh*
alstublieft. pol   al·stew·*bleeft*

transport

53

Please slow down.
Rijd alstublieft wat   reyt al·stew·*bleeft* wat
langzamer. pol   *lang*·zaa·muhr

Please stop/wait here.
Stop/Wacht hier   stop/wakht heer
alstublieft. pol   al·stew·*bleeft*

For other useful phrases, see **directions**, page 61 and **money**, page 43.

car & motorbike

car & motorbike hire

I'd like to hire	*Ik wil graag*	ik wil khraakh
a/an ...	*een ... huren.*	uhn ... hew·ruhn
4WD	*fourwheeldrive*	*fohr*·weel·drayf
automatic/	*auto met*	*aw*·toh met
manual	*automatische /*	aw·toh·*maa*·tee·suh/
	manuele	ma·new·*wey*·luh
	versnellingen	vuhr·*sne*·ling·uhn
car	*auto*	*aw*·toh
moped	*brommer*	*bro*·muhr
motorbike	*motorfiets*	*moh*·tor·feets

with ...	*met ...*	met ...
air conditioning	*airconditioning*	*eyr*·kon·di·shuh·ning
antifreeze	*antivries*	an·tee·*vrees*
a child safety	*een*	uhn
seat	*kinderzitje*	*kin*·duhr·zi·chuh
a driver	*chauffeur*	shoh·*feur*
snow chains	*sneeuwkettingen*	sneyw·ke·ting·uhn

How much for daily/weekly hire?
Hoeveel is het per   hoo·*veyl* is huht puhr
dag/week?   dakh/weyk

Does that include insurance?
Is verzekering   is vuhr·*zey*·kuh·ring
inbegrepen?   in·buh·khrey·puhn

PRACTICAL

Does that include mileage?
Is een aantal kilometer inbegrepen?
is uhn *aan*·tal *kee*·lo·mey·tuhr in·buh·khrey·puhn

Do you have a road map?
Heeft u een wegenkaart? pol
heyft ew uhn *wey*·khuhn·kaart

on the road

What's the speed limit?
Wat is de snelheids-beperking?
wat is duh *snel*·heyts·buh·*per*·king

Is this the road to (Middelburg)?
Gaat deze weg naar (Middelburg)?
khaat *dey*·zuh wekh naar (*mi*·duhl·burkh)

Where's a petrol/gas station?
Waar is er een benzinestation?
waar is uhr uhn ben·*zee*·nuh·sta·syon

Can you check the ...?	Kunt u alstublieft ... checken? pol	kunt ew al·stew·bleeft ... che·kuhn
oil	de olie	duh oh·lee
tyre pressure	de druk in de banden	duh druk in duh ban·duhn
water	het water	huht waa·tuhr

(How long) Can I park here?
(Hoe lang) Kan ik hier parkeren? (hoo lang) kan ik heer par·key·ruhn

Do I have to pay?
Moet ik betalen? moot ik buh·taa·luhn

problems

I need a mechanic.
Ik heb een monteur/ mecanicien nodig. ⑩/® ik hep uhn mon·teur/ mey·ka·nee·sye noh·dikh

I've had an accident.
Ik heb een ongeluk gehad. ik hep uhn on·khuh·luk khuh·hat

The car/motorbike has broken down (at the traffic lights).
De auto/motorfiets staat met panne (bij de verkeerslichten). de aw·toh/moh·tor·feets staat met pa·nuh (bey duh vuhr·keyrs·likh·tuhn)

The car/motorbike won't start.
De auto/motorfiets start niet. duh aw·toh/moh·tor·feets start neet

I have a flat tyre.
Ik heb een lekke band. ik hep uhn le·kuh bant

I've lost my car keys.
Ik ben de sleutels van mijn auto kwijt. ik ben duh sleu·tuhls van meyn aw·toh kweyt

I've locked the keys inside.
Ik heb de sleutels in de gesloten auto laten zitten. ik hep duh sleu·tuhls in duh khuh·sloh·tuhn aw·toh laa·tuhn zi·tuhn

I've run out of petrol.
Ik zit zonder benzine. ik zit zon·duhr ben·zee·nuh

Can you fix it (today)?
Kunt u het (vandaag)   kunt ew huht (van·*daakh*)
herstellen? **pol**   her·*ste*·luhn

How long will it take?
Hoe lang duurt het?   hoo lang dewrt huht

bicycle

I'd like ...	*Ik wil graag ...*	ik wil khraakh ...
my bicycle	*mijn fiets*	meyn feets
repaired	*laten*	*laa*·tuhn
	herstellen	her·*ste*·luhn
to buy a bicycle	*een fiets*	uhn feets
	kopen	*koh*·puhn
to buy a bike	*een fietsslot*	uhn *feet*·slot
lock	*kopen*	*koh*·puhn
to hire a bicycle	*een fiets*	uhn feets
	huren	*hew*·ruhn

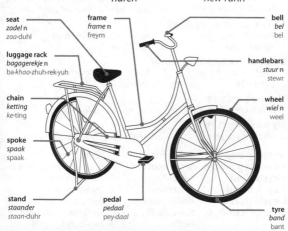

seat
zadel n
zaa·duhl

luggage rack
bagagerekje n
ba·*khaa*·zhuh·rek·yuh

chain
ketting
ke·ting

spoke
spaak
spaak

stand
staander
staan·duhr

frame
frame n
freym

pedal
pedaal
pey·*daal*

bell
bel
bel

handlebars
stuur n
stewr

wheel
wiel n
weel

tyre
band
bant

transport

57

I'd like a ... bike.	Ik wil graag een ...	ik wil khraakh uhn ...
children's	kinderfiets	kin·duhr·feets
mountain	mountain bike	maw·tuhn baayk
racing	racefiets	reys·feets
second-hand	tweedehands fiets	twey·duh·hants feets

I'd like to hire a ...	Ik wil graag een ... huren.	ik wil khraakh uhn ... hew·ruhn
basket	mandje	man·chuh
child seat	kinderzitje	kin·duhr·zi·chuh
helmet	helm	helm

How much is it per day/hour?
Hoeveel is het per dag/uur?   hoo·veyl is huht puhr dakh/ewr

Do I need a helmet?
Heb ik een helm nodig?   hep ik uhn helm noh·dikh

Are there bicycle paths?
Zijn er fietspaden?   zeyn uhr feets·paa·duhn

Is there a bicycle-path map?
Bestaat er een kaart met de fietspaden?   buh·staat uhr uhn kaart met duh feets·paa·duhn

Can we get there by bike?
Kunnen we er met de fiets heen?   ku·nuhn wuh uhr met duh feets heyn

Do you have bicycle parking?
Heeft u parking voor fietsen? pol   heyft ew par·king vohr feet·suhn

I have a puncture.
Ik heb een lekke band.   ik hep uhn le·kuh bant

My bike's been stolen.
Mijn fiets is gestolen.   meyn feets is khuh·stoh·luhn

bicycle pump	fietspomp	feets·pomp
bicycle repairman	fietsenmaker	feet·suhn·maa·kuhr
bicycle shed	fietsenhok n	feet·suhn·hok
bicycle stand	fietsenrek n	feet·suhn·rek
bicycle storage	fietsenstalling	feet·suhn·sta·ling
cycle accessories	fietsbenodigd- heden	feets·buh·noh·dikht· hey·duhn

border crossing

immigratie

I'm ...	*Ik ben ...*	ik ben ...
in transit	*op doorreis*	op *doh*·reys
on business	*op zakenreis*	op *zaa*·kuhn·reys
on holiday	*met vakantie*	met va·*kan*·see

I'm here for ...	*Ik ben hier voor ...*	ik ben heer vohr ...
(10) days	*(tien) dagen*	(teen) *daa*·khuhn
(3) weeks	*(drie) weken*	(dree) *wey*·kuhn
(2) months	*(twee) maanden*	(twey) *maan*·duhn

I'm going to (Groningen).
*Ik ben op weg naar
(Groningen).*
ik ben op wekh naar
(*khroh*·ning·uhn)

I'm staying at the (Hotel Industrie).
*Ik logeer in
(Hotel Industrie).*
ik loh·*zheyr* in
(hoh·*tel* in·du·*stree*)

The children are on this passport.
*De kinderen staan
op dit paspoort.*
duh *kin*·duh·ruhn staan
op dit *pas*·pohrt

border crossing

---

listen for ...

alleen	a·*leyn*	**alone**
familie	fa·*mee*·lee	**family**
groep	khroop	**group**
paspoort n	*pas*·pohrt	**passport**
visum n	*vee*·zum	**visa**

at customs

I have nothing to declare.
Ik heb niets aan te geven.   ik hep neets aan tuh *khey*·vuhn

I have something to declare.
Ik heb iets aan te geven.   ik hep eets aan tuh *khey*·vuhn

Do I have to declare this?
Moet ik dit aangeven?   moot ik dit *aan*·khey·vuhn

That's (not) mine.
Dat is (niet) van mij.   dat is (neet) van mey

I didn't know I had to declare it.
Ik wist niet dat ik het   ik wist neet dat ik huht
moest aangeven.   moost *aan*·khey·vuhn

Could I please have an (English) interpreter?
Mag ik alstublieft   makh ik al·stew·*bleeft*
een (Engelstalige)   uhn (*eng*·uhls·taa·li·khuh)
tolk? pol   tolk

Do you have this form in (English)?
Heeft u dit formulier   heyft ew dit for·mew·*leer*
in het (Engels)? pol   in huht (*eng*·uhls)

For phrases on payments and receipts, see **money**, page 43.

signs		
BTW teruggave	bey·tey·*wey* tuh·*rukh*·khaa·vuh	**VAT refunds**
Douane	doo·*waa*·nuh	**Customs**
Immigratie	ee·mee·*graa*·see	**Immigration**
Niets aan te Geven	neets aan tuh *khey*·vuhn	**Nothing to Declare**
Paspoortcontrole	pas·pohrt·kon·troh·luh	**Passport Control**
Quarantaine	ka·ron·*tey*·nuh	**Quarantine**
Taxfree	taks·free	**Duty-Free**

PRACTICAL

60

Where's the ...?	Waar is ...?	waar is ...
bank	de bank	duh bangk
market	de markt	duh markt

How do I get there?	Hoe kom ik er?	hoo kom ik uhr
How far is it?	Hoe ver is het?	hoo ver is huht
Can you show me (on the map)?	Kunt u het mij tonen (op de kaart)? pol	kunt ew huht mey toh·nuhn (op duh kaart)

It's ...	Het is ...	huht is ...
behind ...	achter ...	akh·tuhr ...
close	dichtbij	dikht·bey
far	ver	ver
here	hier	heer
in front of ...	voor ...	vohr ...
near ...	dicht bij ...	dikht bey ...
next to ...	naast ...	naast ...
on the corner	op de hoek	op duh hook
opposite ...	tegenover ...	tey·khuhn·oh·vuhr ...
straight ahead	rechtdoor	rekh·dohr
there	daar	daar

what's in a name?

Dutch words in street names and on signs are often combined into a single long place name which can be tricky for a foreigner to decipher (eg *Derde Leliedwarsstraat* means 'third lily-cross-street'). In bilingual Brussels, you might see something like *Rue du Marché-Aux-Herbes Graanmarkt Straat*, which is actually the French version of the street name (*Rue du Marché-Aux-Herbes*) followed by the Dutch version (*Graanmarkt Straat*), both meaning 'wheat-market street'. Note that the French *Rue* goes first and that the Dutch *Straat* is tucked onto the end (both mean 'street').

directions

61

Turn left/ right ...	Sla linksaf/ rechtsaf ...	slaa lingks·af/ rekhs·af ...
at the corner	op de hoek	op duh hook
at the traffic lights	bij de verkeerslichten	bey duh vuhr·keyrs·likh·tuhn
by bicycle	met de fiets	met duh feets
by bus	met de bus	met duh bus
by train	met de trein	met duh treyn
on foot	te voet	tuh voot
north	noord	nohrt
south	zuid	zöyt
east	oost	ohst
west	west	west
What ... is this?	Welke ... is dit?	wel·kuh ... is dit
canal	gracht	khrakht
council	gemeente	khuh·meyn·tuh
road	weg	wekh
street	straat	straat

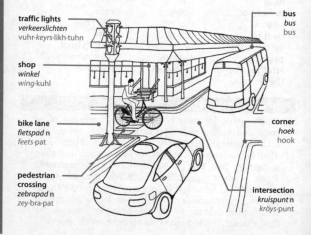

traffic lights
verkeerslichten
vuhr·*keyrs*·likh·tuhn

shop
winkel
wing·kuhl

bike lane
fietspad n
feets·pat

pedestrian crossing
zebrapad n
zey·bra·pat

bus
bus
bus

corner
hoek
hook

intersection
kruispunt n
kröys·punt

finding accommodation

accommodatie vinden

Where's a ...?	*Waar vind ik een ...?*	waar vint ik uhn ...
bed and breakfast	*gastenkamer*	*khas*·tuhn·kaa·muhr
camping ground	*camping*	*kem*·ping Ⓝ *kam*·ping Ⓑ
guesthouse	*pension*	pen·*syon*
hikers' hut	*trekkershut*	*tre*·kuhrs·hut
holiday resort	*vakantiecentrum*	va·*kan*·see·sen·trum
hotel	*hotel*	hoh·*tel*
motel	*motel*	moh·*tel*
nature campground	*natuurcamping*	na·*tewr*·kem·ping Ⓝ na·*tewr*·kam·ping Ⓑ
youth hostel	*jeugdherberg*	*yeukht*·her·berkh

Can you recommend somewhere ...?	*Kunt u iets ...* *aanbevelen?* **pol**	kunt ew eets ... *aan*·buh·vey·luhn
cheap	*goedkoops*	khoot·*kohps*
good	*goeds*	khoots
luxurious	*luxueus*	luk·sew·*weus*
nearby	*dichtbij*	dikht·*bey*
romantic	*romantisch*	roh·*man*·tees
safe for women travellers	*dat veilig is voor* *vrouwelijke* *reizigers*	dat *vey*·likh is vohr *vraw*·wuh·luh·kuh *rey*·zi·khuhrs

I want something	Ik wil iets	ik wil eets
near the …	dicht bij …	dikht bey …
beach	het strand	huht strant
city centre	het stadscentrum	huht stat·sen·trum
night life	de	duh
	uitgaansbuurt	öyt·gaans·bewrt
shops	de winkels	duh wing·kuhls
train station	het station	huht sta·syon

What's the address?
Wat is het adres?   wat is huht a·dres

For responses, see **directions**, page 61.

booking ahead & checking in

I'd like to book a room, please.
Ik wil graag een   ik wil khraakh uhn
kamer reserveren.   kaa·muhr rey·ser·vey·ruhn

I have a reservation.
Ik heb een reservatie.   ik hep uhn rey·ser·vaa·see

My name's …
Mijn naam is …   meyn naam is …

For (three) nights/weeks.
Voor (drie) nachten/   vohr (dree) nakh·tuhn/
weken.   wey·kuhn

From (2 July) to (6 July).
Van (de tweede juli)   van (duh twey·duh yew·lee)
tot (de zesde juli).   tot (duh zes·duh yew·lee)

local talk		
dive n	krot	krot
messy place	stal (lit: stable) ⓑ	stal
top spot	klassehotel	kla·suh·hoh·tel
very neat	prima in orde	pree·ma in or·duh
	(lit: excellent in order)	

PRACTICAL

64

Hoeveel nachten?	hoo·*veyl nakh*·tuhn	**How many nights?**
identiteits-	ee·den·tee·*teyts·*	**identification**
bewijs	buh·weys	
receptie	rey·*sep*·see	**reception**
sleutel	*sleu*·tuhl	**key**
vol	vol	**full**

Do I need to pay upfront?
Moet ik vooraf betalen?   moot ik *voh*·raf buh·*taa*·luhn

How much is	*Hoeveel kost*	hoo·*veyl* kost
it per ...?	*het per ...?*	huht puhr ...
night	*nacht*	nakht
person	*persoon*	puhr·*sohn*
week	*week*	weyk

Can I pay by ...?	*Kan ik met een ...*	kan ik met uhn ...
	betalen?	buh·*taa*·luhn
credit card	*kredietkaart*	krey·*deet*·kaart
travellers	*reischeque*	*reys*·shek
cheque		

Do you have	*Heeft u een ...?* pol	heyft ew uhn ...
a ... room?		
single	*éénpersoons-*	*eyn*·puhr·sohns·
	kamer	kaa·muhr
double	*tweepersoons-*	*twey*·puhr·sohns·
	kamer met een	kaa·muhr met uhn
	dubbel bed	*du*·buhl bet
twin	*tweepersoons-*	*twey*·puhr·sohns·
	kamer met	kaa·muhr met
	lits jumeaux	lee zhew·*moh*

Can I see it?
Kan ik een kijkje nemen?   kan ik uhn *keyk*·yuh *ney*·muhn

I'll take it.
Ik neem het.   ik neym huht

For other methods of payment, see **money**, page 43, and **banking**, page 89.

accommodation

65

signs

Badkamer	*bat·kaa·muhr*	**Bathroom**
Kamers vrij	*kaa·muhrs vrey*	**Vacancy**
Vol/Volzet ⑩/⑧	*vol/vol·zet*	**No Vacancy**
Wasinrichting	*was·in·rikh·ting*	**Laundry**

requests & queries

verzoeken & vragen

Is breakfast included?
Is het ontbijt   is huht ont·*beyt*
inbegrepen?   *in·*buh·khrey·puhn

When's breakfast served?
Hoe laat wordt het   hoo laat wort huht
ontbijt geserveerd?   ont·*beyt* khuh·ser·*veyrt*

Where's breakfast served?
Waar wordt het ontbijt waar wort huht ont·*beyt*
geserveerd?   khuh·ser·*veyrt*

Is there hot water all day?
Is er de hele dag   is uhr duh *hey*·luh dakh
warm water?   warm *waa*·tuhr

Please wake me at (seven).
Maak mij wakker om   maak mey *wa*·kuhr om
(zeven) uur alstublieft. **pol** (*zey*·vuhn) ewr al·stew·*bleeft*

Can I use the ...?	*Kan ik de ...*	kan ik duh ...
	gebruiken?	khuh·*bröy*·kuhn
bicycle	*fiets*	feets
kitchen	*keuken*	*keu*·kuhn
laundry	*wasinrichting*	*was*·in·rikh·ting
telephone	*telefoon*	tey·ley·*fohn*

Do you have a/an ...?	*Heeft u een ...?* pol	heyft ew uhn ...
elevator/lift	*lift*	lift
laundry service	*wasdienst*	*was*·deenst
message board	*berichtenbord*	buh·*rikh*·tuhn·bort
safe	*kluis*	klöys
sauna	*sauna*	*saw*·na
swimming pool	*zwembad*	*zwem*·bat

Could I have a ..., please?	*Kan ik een ... hebben alstublieft?* pol	kan ik uhn ... *he*·buhn al·stew·*bleeft*
bicycle	*fiets*	feets
fan	*ventilator*	ven·tee·*laa*·tor
hairdryer	*haardroger*	*haar*·droh·khuhr
receipt	*kwitantie*	kwee·*tan*·see

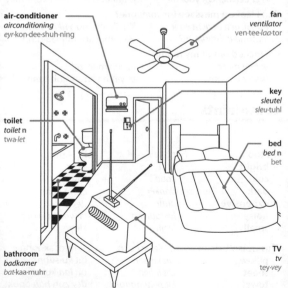

air-conditioner
airconditioning
eyr·kon·dee·shuh·ning

fan
ventilator
ven·tee·*laa*·tor

toilet
toilet n
twa·*let*

key
sleutel
sleu·tuhl

bathroom
badkamer
bat·kaa·muhr

bed
bed n
bet

TV
tv
tey·*vey*

accommodation

67

Could I have my key, please?
Kan ik mijn sleutel hebben   kan ik meyn *sleu*·tuhl *he*·buhn
alstublieft? pol   al·stew·*bleeft*

Do you have a car park?
Heeft u parking? pol   heyft ew *par*·king

Do you rent out bicycles?
Verhuurt u fietsen? pol   vuhr·*hewrt* ew *feet*·suhn

Do you arrange tours/trips here?
Organiseert u   or·kha·nee·*zeyrt* ew
rondleidingen/tochten? pol   *ront*·ley·ding·uhn/*tokh*·tuhn

Do you change money here?
Wisselt u geld hier? pol   *wi*·suhlt ew khelt heer

Is there a message for me?
Is er een bericht voor mij?   is uhr uhn buh·*rikht* vohr mey

Can I leave a message for someone?
Kan ik een bericht voor   kan ik uhn buh·*rikht* vohr
iemand achterlaten?   *ee*·mant *akh*·tuhr·laa·tuhn

I'm locked out of my room.
Ik heb mezelf   ik hep muh·*zelf*
buitengesloten.   *böy*·tuhn·khuh·sloh·tuhn

complaints

klachten

It's too ...	Het is te ...	huht is tuh ...
bright	*licht*	likht
cold	*koud*	kawt
dark	*donker*	*dong*·kuhr
expensive	*duur*	dewr
noisy	*lawaaierig*	la·*waa*·yuh·rikh
small	*klein*	kleyn

This ... isn't clean.	... is niet schoon.	... is neet skhohn
pillow	*Dit kussen*	dit *ku*·suhn
sheet	*Dit laken*	dit *laa*·kuhn
towel	*Deze handdoek*	*dey*·zuh *han*·dook

The ... doesn't work.	De ... is stuk.	duh ... is stuk
air conditioner	aircon-ditioning	eyr·kon·dee·shuh·ning
fan	ventilator	ven·tee·laa·tor
heater	verwarming	vuhr·war·ming

The toilet doesn't work.
Het toilet is stuk.   huht twa·*let* is stuk

There's no hot water.
Er is geen warm water.   uhr is kheyn warm *waa*·tuhr

Can I get another (blanket)?
Kan ik nog een (deken)   kan ik nokh uhn (*dey*·kuhn)
hebben alstublieft? pol   *he*·buhn al·stew·*bleeft*

a knock at the door ...

Who is it?	Wie is daar?	wee is daar
Just a moment, please.	Een momentje alstublieft. pol	uhn moh·*men*·chuh al·stew·*bleeft*
Come in.	Kom binnen.	kom *bi*·nuhn
Come back later, please.	Kom later terug alstublieft. pol	kom *laa*·tuhr tuh·*rukh* al·stew·*bleeft*

checking out

uitchecken

What time is checkout?
Hoe laat is het uitchecken?   hoo laat is huht öyt·che·kuhn

Can I have a late checkout?
Kan ik later uitchecken?   kan ik *laa*·tuhr öyt·che·kuhn

Can you call a taxi for me (for 11 o'clock)?
Kunt u een taxi   kunt ew uhn *tak*·see
(voor elf uur) voor mij   (vohr elf ewr) vohr mey
regelen alstublieft? pol   *rey*·khuh·luhn al·stew·*bleeft*

I'm leaving now.
Ik vertrek nu.   ik vuhr·*trek* new

Can I leave my bags here?
Kan ik mijn bagage hier laten?
kan ik meyn ba·*khaa*·zhuh heer *laa*·tuhn

There's a mistake in the bill/check.
Er zit een fout in de rekening.
uhr zit uhn fawt in duh *rey*·kuh·ning

Could I have my ..., please? *Kan ik mijn ...* *hebben alstublieft?* pol
kan ik meyn ... *he*·buhn al·stew·*bleeft*

deposit	*borg*	borkh
passport	*paspoort*	*pas*·pohrt
valuables	*waardevolle bezittingen*	*waar*·duh·vo·luh buh·*zi*·ting·uhn

I had a great stay, thanks.
Ik heb een aangenaam verblijf gehad, dank u. pol
ik hep uhn *aan*·khuh·naam vuhr·*bleyf* khuh·hat dangk ew

I'll recommend it to my friends.
Ik zal het aan mijn vrienden aanbevelen.
ik zal huht aan meyn *vreen*·duhn *aan*·buh·vey·luhn

I'll be back in (three) days.
Ik kom terug binnen (drie) dagen.
ik kom tuh·*rukh* bi·nuhn (dree) *daa*·khuhn

I'll be back on (Tuesday).
Ik kom (dinsdag) terug.
ik kom (dins·dakh) tuh·*rukh*

camping

kamperen

Do you have ...?	*Heeft u ...?* pol	heyft ew ...
electricity	*elektriciteit*	ey·lek·tree·see·*teyt*
a laundry	*een wasinrichting*	uhn *was*·in·rikh·ting
shower facilities	*douches*	*doo*·shuhs
a site	*een kampeerplaats*	uhn kam·*peyr*·plaats
tents for hire	*tenten te huur*	*ten*·tuhn tuh hewr

PRACTICAL

Who do I ask to stay here?
Aan wie kan ik vragen of ik   aan wee kan ik *vraa*·khuhn of ik
hier mag overnachten?   heer makh oh·vuhr·*nakh*·tuhn

Is it coin-operated?
Werkt het met   werkt huht met
muntstukken?   *munt*·stu·kuhn

Is the water drinkable?
Is het drinkbaar water?   is huht *dringk*·baar *waa*·tuhr

Could I borrow …?	*Kan ik … lenen?*	kan ik … *ley*·nuhn
How much is	*Hoeveel is*	hoo·*veyl* is
it per …?	*het per …?*	huht puhr …
person	*persoon*	puhr·*sohn*
vehicle	*auto*	*aw*·toh
Can I …?	*Mag ik …?*	makh ik …
camp here	*hier kamperen*	heer kam·*pey*·ruhn
park next to	*naast mijn*	naast meyn
my tent	*tent parkeren*	tent par·*key*·ruhn

renting

huren

Do you have	*Heeft u een …*	heyft ew uhn …
a/an … for rent?	*te huur?* pol	tuh hewr
apartment	*flat* ⓝ	flet
	appartement ⓑ	a·par·tuh·*ment*
cabin	*hut*	hut
house	*huis*	höys
room	*kamer*	*kaa*·muhr

Is there a bond?
Is er een borg te   is uhr uhn borkh tuh
betalen?   buh·*taa*·luhn

Are bills extra?
Zijn onkosten extra?   zeyn *on*·kos·tuhn *ek*·straa

Are pets permitted?
Zijn huisdieren   zeyn *höys*·dee·ruhn
toegelaten?   *too*·khu·laa·tuhn

a
c
c
o
m
m
o
d
a
t
i
o
n

71

furnished	gemeubileerd	khuh·meu·bee·leyrt
housing permit	woonvergunning	wohn·vuhr·khu·ning
partly furnished	gedeeltelijk	khuh·deyl·tuh·luhk
	gemeubileerd	khuh·meu·bee·leyrt
unfurnished	onge-	on·khuh·
	meubileerd	meu·bee·leyrt

staying with locals

logeren

Can I stay at your place?
Kan ik bij jou thuis   kan ik bey jaw töys
overnachten?   oh·vuhr·nakh·tuhn

Is there anything I can do to help?
Kan ik ergens mee helpen?   kan ik er·khuhns mey hel·puhn

Thanks for your hospitality.
Bedankt voor uw/je   buh·dangkt vohr ew/yuh
gastvrijheid. pol/inf   khast·vrey·heyt

I have my own ...	Ik heb mijn eigen ...	ik hep meyn ey·khuhn ...
mattress	matras	ma·tras
sleeping bag	slaapzak	slaap·zak

Can I ...?	Kan ik ...?	kan ik ...
bring anything for the meal	iets om te eten meebrengen	eets om tuh ey·tuhn mey·breng·uhn
do the dishes	de afwas doen	duh af·was doon
set/clear the table	de tafel dekken/ afruimen	duh taa·fuhl de·kuhn/ af·röy·muhn
take out the rubbish	het afval buitenzetten	huht af·val böy·tuhn·ze·tuhn

To compliment your hosts' cooking, see **eating out**, page 171.

PRACTICAL

looking for ...

Are shops open on (Queen's Day)?
Zijn de winkels open   zeyn duh *wing*·kuhls *oh*·puhn
op (Koninginnedag)?   op (koh·ning·*khi*·nuh·dakh)

What hours are shops open?
Wat zijn de   wat zeyn de
openingsuren   *oh*·puh·nings·*ew*·ruhn
voor de winkels?   vohr duh *wing*·kuhls

Where can I buy (a padlock)?
Waar kan ik (een   waar kan ik (uhn
hangslot) kopen?   *hang*·slot) *koh*·puhn

Where's a ...?	*Waar vind ik een ...?*	waar vint ik uhn ...
chocolate shop	*chocolade-winkel*	sho·koh·*laa*·duh·*wing*·kuhl
department store	*warenhuis* ⓝ *groot-warenhuis* ⓑ	*waa*·ruhn·höys *khroht*-waa·ruhn·höys
grocery shop	*kruideniers-zaak*	kröy·duh·*neers*·zaak
nightshop	*nachtwinkel*	*nakht*·wing·kuhl
supermarket	*supermarkt*	*sew*·puhr·markt

For more items and shopping locations, see the **dictionary**.

glorious chocolate

Chocolate shops are generally known as *chocoladewinkels*, but you might also come across these terms:

bonbonzaak ⓝ   bon·*bon*·zaak
chocolaterie   shoh·koh·la·*tree*
pralinewinkel ⓑ   pra·*lee*·nuh·wing·kuhl

making a purchase

I'm just looking.
Ik kijk alleen maar.   ik keyk a·*leyn* maar

I'd like to buy (an adaptor plug).
Ik wil graag een   ik wil khraakh uhn
(adapter) kopen.   (a·*dap*·tuhr) *koh*·puhn

The quality isn't good.
Het is geen goede   huht is kheyn *khoo*·duh
kwaliteit.   kwa·lee·*teyt*

How much is it?
Hoeveel kost het?   hoo·*veyl* kost huht

Can you write down the price?
Kunt u de prijs   kunt ew duh preys
opschrijven   *op*·skhrey·vuhn
alstublieft? **pol**   al·stew·*bleeft*

Do you have any others?
Heeft u nog andere? **pol**   heyft ew nokh *an*·duh·ruh

Can I look at it?
Kan ik het even zien?   kan ik huht *ey*·vuhn zeen

Is this (240) volts?
Is het (tweehonderd   is huht (twey·*hon*·duhrt
veertig) volt?   *feyr*·tikh) volt

Do you accept …?	*Accepteert u …?* **pol**	ak·sep·*teyrt* ew …
credit cards	*kredietkaarten*	krey·*deet*·kaar·tuhn
debit cards	*debetkaarten*	*dey*·bet·kaar·tuhn
travellers cheques	*reischeques*	*reys*·sheks

I'd like … please.	*Ik wil graag …*	ik wil khraakh …
my change	*mijn wisselgeld*	meyn *wi*·suhl·khelt
a receipt	*een kwitantie*	uhn kwee·*tan*·see
a refund	*mijn geld terug*	meyn khelt tuh·*rukh*

Could I have a bag, please?
Kan ik alstublieft
een draagtasje hebben? pol

kan ik al·stew·*bleeft*
uhn *draakh*·ta·shuh he·buhn

I don't need a bag, thanks.
Ik heb geen draagtasje
nodig, dank u. pol

ik hep kheyn *draakh*·ta·shuh
noh·dikh dangk ew

Could I have it wrapped?
Kunt u het inpakken? pol

kunt ew huht *in*·pa·kuhn

Does it have a guarantee?
Komt het met garantie?

komt huht met ga·*ran*·see

Can I have it sent abroad?
Kan ik het naar het
buitenland sturen?

kan ik huht naar huht
böy·tuhn·lant *stew*·ruhn

Can you order it for me?
Kunt u het voor mij
bestellen? pol

kunt ew huht vohr mey
be·*ste*·luhn

Can I pick it up later?
Kan ik het later oppikken?

kan ik huht *laa*·tuhr o·pi·kuhn

I'd like to return this, please.
Ik wil dit graag
retourneren.

ik wil dit khraakh
ruh·toor·*ney*·ruhn

---

faulty things

There are two main ways to say that something is faulty
in Dutch. For anything that needs to function, whether it's
mechanical or electronic, say:

Het is kapot.   huht is ka·*pot*   **It's faulty.**
  (meaning: it's broken)

For any defects that don't necessarily impact functioning,
eg a fault in fabric or in clothes, or a crack in the paint or
porcelain of an object, use the expression:

Er zit een fout in.   uhr zit uhn fawt in   **It's faulty.**
  (meaning: there's a mistake in it)

bargain	*koopje* n	*kohp*·yuh
bargain hunter	*koopjesjager*	*kohp*·yuhs·yaa·khur
closing-down sale	*uitverkoop*	*öyt*·vuhr·kohp
discount	*korting*	*kor*·ting
end-of-season sale	*seizoens-opruiming*	sey·*zoons*·op·röy·ming
sale (general) n	*verkoop*	vuhr·*kohp*
special offer	*aanbieding*	*aan*·bee·ding
specials	*koopjes* n pl Ⓝ	*kohp*·yuhs
	solden Ⓑ	*sol*·duhn
super bargain	*spotkoopje* n	*spot*·kohp·yuh

bargaining

afdingen

That's too expensive.
　Dat is te duur.　　　　　dat is tuh dewr

Can you lower the price?
　Kunt u wat van de　　　kunt ew wat van duh
　prijs afdoen? pol　　　　preys *af*·doon

Do you have something cheaper?
　Heeft u iets　　　　　　heyft ew eets
　goedkopers? pol　　　　khoot·*koh*·puhrs

What's your final price?
　Wat is uw beste prijs? pol　wat is ew *bes*·tuh preys

I'll give you (five) euros.
　Ik wil er (vijf) euro voor　ik wil uhr (veyf) *eu*·roh vohr
　betalen.　　　　　　　buh·*taa*·luhn

books & reading

Do you have ...?	Heeft u ...? pol	heyft ew ...
a book by	een boek van	uhn book van
(Hugo Claus)	(Hugo Claus)	(hew·khoh klaws)
an entertainment	een uitgaans-	uhn öyt·khaans·
guide	gids	khits

Is there an	Is er een	is uhr uhn
(English)-	(Engels)-	(eng·uhls)·
language ...?	talige ...?	taa·li·khuh ...
bookshop	boekhandel	book·han·duhl
section	afdeling	af·dey·ling

I'd like a/an ...	Ik wil graag een ...	ik wil khraakh uhn ...
dictionary	woordenboek	wohr·duhn·book
newspaper	(Engels-	(eng·uhls·
(in English)	talige) krant	taa·li·khuh) krant
notepad	notitieblok	noh·tee·see·blok

Can you recommend a book for me?
Kunt u mij een boek   kunt ew mey uhn book
aanbevelen? pol   aan·buh·vey·luhn

Do you have Lonely Planet guidebooks/phrasebooks?
Heeft u reisgidsen/   heyft ew reys·khit·suhn/
taalgidsen van   taal·khit·suhn van
Lonely Planet? pol   lohn·lee ple·nuht

---

listen for ...

Kan ik u helpen? pol
kan ik ew hel·puhn   **Can I help you?**

Kan ik u nog ergens anders mee helpen? pol
kan ik ew nokh er·khuns   **Anything else?**
an·duhrs mey hel·puhn

Nee, we hebben er geen.
ney wuh he·buhn uhr kheyn   **No, we don't have any.**

shopping

77

clothes

My size is (40).	*Ik heb maat (veertig).*	ik hep maat (*feyr*·tikh)
Can I try it on?	*Kan ik het passen?*	kan ik huht *pa*·suhn
It doesn't fit.	*Het past niet.*	huht past neet
small	*small*	smal
medium	*medium*	*mey*·dyum
large	*large*	larsh

For different types of clothing see the **dictionary**, and for sizes see **numbers & amounts**, page 33.

hairdressing

I'd like (a) …	*Ik wil graag …*	ik wil khraakh …
colour	*een kleuring*	uhn *kleu*·ring
foils/streaks/ highlights (with foils)	*highlights (met folies)*	*haay*·laayts (met *foh*·lees)
haircut	*mijn haar laten knippen*	meyn haar *laa*·tuhn *kni*·puhn
my beard trimmed	*mijn baard laten bijknippen*	meyn baart *laa*·tuhn *bey*·kni·puhn
my hair washed/ blow-dried	*mijn haar laten wassen/ föhnen*	meyn haar *laa*·tuhn *wa*·suhn/ *feu*·nuhn
shave (beard)	*een scheerbeurt*	uhn *skheyr*·beurt
shave (head)	*mijn hoofd laten kaal scheren*	meyn hohft *laa*·tuhn kaal *skhey*·ruhn

PRACTICAL

I'd like a trim.
Ik wil het laten bijknippen.
ik wil huht *laa*·tuhn *bey*·kni·puhn

Don't cut it too short.
Knip het niet te kort alstublieft. pol
knip huht neet tuh kort al·stew·*bleeft*

Please use a new blade.
Gebruik een nieuw mesje alstublieft. pol
khuh·*bröyk* uhn neew *me*·shuh al·stew·*bleeft*

Shave it all off! (beard)
Scheer het allemaal af!
skheyr huht *a*·luh·maal af

Shave it all off! (head)
Scheer me kaal!
skheyr muh kaal

I don't like this!
Ik vind dit niet goed!
ik vint dit neet khoot

I should never have let you near me!
Ik had jou nooit in mijn buurt mogen laten komen!
ik hat jaw noyt in meyn bewrt *moh*·khuhn *laa*·tuhn *ko*·muhn

music & DVD

muziek & dvd's

I'd like a …	*Ik wil graag een …*	ik wil khraakh uhn …
blank tape	*lege cassette*	*ley*·khuh ka·*se*·tuh
CD	*cd*	sey·*dey*
DVD	*dvd*	dey·vey·*dey*
video	*video*	vee·dey·yoh

I'm looking for something by (Deus).
Ik ben op zoek naar iets van (Deus).
ik ben op zook naar eets van (*dey*·yus)

What's their best recording?
Wat is hun beste album?
wat is hun *bes*·tuh *al*·bum

Can I listen to this?
Kan ik hier naar dit luisteren?
kan ik heer naar dit *löy*·stuh·ruhn

shopping

Will this work on any DVD player?
Werkt dit op elke   werkt dit op *el*·kuh
dvd-speler?   dey·vey·*dey*·*spey*·luhr

Is this for a (PAL/NTSC) system?
Is dit voor een (PAL/   is dit vohr uhn (pal/
NTSC) systeem?   en·tey·es·*sey*) sees·*teym*

video & photography

video & fotografie

Can you …?	*Kunt u …?* pol	kunt ew …
print digital photos	*digitale foto's afdrukken*	dee·khee·*taa*·luh *foh*·tohs *af*·dru·kuhn
develop this film	*deze film ontwikkelen*	*dey*·zuh film ont·*wi*·kuh·luhn
load my film	*mijn film laden*	meyn film *laa*·duhn
recharge the battery for my digital camera	*de batterij voor mijn digitale fototoestel opladen*	duh ba·tuh·*rey* vohr meyn dee·khee·*taa*·luh *foh*·toh·too·stel *op*·laa·duhn
transfer my photos to CD	*mijn foto's op cd zetten*	meyn *foh*·tohs op sey·*dey* ze·tuhn
Do you have (a) … for this camera?	*Heeft u … voor dit fototoestel?* pol	heyft ew … vohr dit *foh*·toh·too·stel
batteries	*batterijen*	ba·tuh·*rey*·yuhn
flash(bulb)	*een flits(lamp)*	uhn (*flits*·)lamp
(zoom) lens	*een (zoom)lens*	uhn (*zoom*·)lens
light meter	*een lichtmeter*	uhn *likht*·mey·tuhr
memory cards	*geheugen-kaarten*	khuh·*heu*·khun·kaar·tuhn

PRACTICAL

I need ... film for this camera.	Ik heb ... voor dit fototoestel nodig.	ik hep ... vohr dit foh·toh·too·stel noh·dikh
B&W	zwart-wit film	zwart·wit film
colour	kleurenfilm	kleu·ruhn·film
slide	diafilm	dee·ya·film
(200) speed	een film van (tweehonderd) ASA	uhn film van (twey·hon·duhrt) aa·sa

... camera		
digital	digitaal fototoestel	dee·khee·taal foh·toh·too·stel
disposable	wegwerp-camera	wekh·werp-kaa·mey·ra
underwater	onderwater-camera	on·duhr·waa·tuhr-kaa·mey·ra
video	video-camera	vee·dey·yoh-kaa·mey·ra

I need a cable to connect my camera to a computer.
Ik heb een kabel nodig
om mijn fototoestel
met een computer te
verbinden.

ik hep uhn *kaa*·buhl *noh*·dikh
om meyn *foh*·toh·too·stel
met uhn kom·*pyew*·tuhr tuh
vuhr·*bin*·duhn

I need a cable to recharge this battery.
Ik heb een kabel nodig
om deze batterij
op te laden.

ik hep uhn *kaa*·buhl *noh*·dikh
om *dey*·zuh ba·tuh·*rey*
op tuh *laa*·duhn

I need a video cassette for this camera.
Ik heb een video-
cassette voor deze
camera nodig.

ik hep uhn *vee*·dey·yoh-
ka·*se*·tuh vohr *dey*·zuh
kaa·mey·ra *noh*·dikh

When will it be ready?
Wanneer is het klaar?

wa·*neyr* is huht klaar

How much is it?
Hoeveel kost het?

hoo·*veyl* kost huht

I need a passport photo taken.
Ik heb paspoortfoto's
nodig.

ik hep *pas*·pohrt·foh·tohs
noh·dikh

I'm not happy with these photos.

Ik ben niet tevreden   ik ben neet tuh·*vrey*·duhn
met deze foto's.   met *dey*·zuh foh·tohs

I don't want to pay the full price.

Ik wil de volle prijs niet   ik wil duh *vo*·luh preys neet
betalen.   buh·*taa*·luhn

repairs

reparaties

Can I have my	*Kan ik mijn ... hier*	kan ik meyn ... heer
... repaired here?	*laten herstellen?*	*laa*·tuhn her·*ste*·luhn
When will my ...	*Wanneer is mijn*	wa·*neyr* is meyn
be ready?	*... klaar?*	... klaar
backpack	*rugzak*	*rukh*·zak
bag	*tas*	tas
(video)camera	*(video)-*	*(vee*·dey·yoh)·
	camera	*kaa*·mey·ra
(sun)glasses	*(zonne)bril*	*(zo*·nuh·)bril

souvenirs		
beer	*bier* n	beer
beer glasses	*bierglazen* n pl	*beer*·khlaa·zuhn
carpets	*tapijten* n pl	ta·*pey*·tuhn
cartoons	*stripverhalen* n pl	strip·vuhr·haa·luhn
cheese	*kaas*	kaas
chocolate	*chocolade*	shoh·koh·*laa*·duh
chocolates	*bonbons* ⓝ	bon·*bons*
	pralines ⓑ	pra·*lee*·nuh
(wooden) clogs	*klompen*	*klom*·puhn
delftware	*Delfts blauw* n	delfts blaw
diamonds	*diamanten*	dee·ya·*man*·tuhn
gin	*jenever*	yuh·*ney*·vuhr ⓝ
		zhuh·*ney*·vuhr ⓑ
lace	*kant*	kant
mural tapestries	*muurtapijten* n pl	mewr·ta·*pey*·tuhn
tapestry	*tappiserie*	ta·pee·suh·*ree*
Tintin	*Kuifje*	*köyf*·yuh
souvenirs	*souvenirs* n pl	soo·vuh·*neers*

the internet

het internet

Where's the local internet café?
Waar is het plaatselijk internetcafé?
waar is huht *plaat*·suh·luhk *in*·tuhr·net·ka·*fey*

I'd like to …	*Ik wil graag …*	ik wil khraakh …
burn a CD	*iets op cd zetten*	eets op sey·*dey* ze·tuhn
check my email	*mijn e-mails checken*	meyn *ee*·meyls *che*·kuhn
download my photos	*mijn foto's downloaden*	meyn *foh*·tohs *dawn*·loh·duhn
get internet access	*op het internet gaan*	op huht *in*·tuhr·net khaan
use a printer	*een printer gebruiken*	uhn *prin*·tuhr khuh·*bröy*·kuhn
use a scanner	*een scanner gebruiken*	uhn *ske*·nuhr khuh·*bröy*·kuhn

Do you have …?	*Heeft u …?* pol	heyft ew …
Macs	*Apple computers*	*e*·puhl kom·*pyoo*·tuhrs
PCs	*pc's*	pey·*seys*
a Zip drive	*een zipdrive*	uhn *zip*·draayf

How much per …?	*Hoeveel kost het per …?*	hoo·*veyl* kost huht puhr …
hour	*uur*	ewr
(five) minutes	*(vijf) minuten*	(veyf) mee·*new*·tuhn
page	*pagina*	*paa*·khee·na

83

Can I connect my ... to this computer?	Kan ik mijn ... met deze computer verbinden?	kan ik meyn ... met *dey*·zuh kom·*pyoo*·tuhr vuhr·*bin*·duhn
camera	fototoestel	*foh*·toh·too·stel
iPod	iPod	*aay*·pot
media player (MP3)	MP3speler	em·pey·*tree*·spey·luhr
portable hard drive	draagbare harde schijf	*draakh*·baa·ruh *har*·duh skheyf
PSP	psp	pey·es·*pey*
USB flash drive (memory stick)	USB memory stick	ew·es·*bey* me·moh·ree stik

How do I log on?	Hoe log ik in?	hoo lokh ik in
Stupid internet!	Stom internet!	stom *in*·tuhr·net
It's crashed.	Het is geblokkeerd.	huht is khuh·blo·*keyrt*
I've finished.	Ik ben klaar.	ik ben klaar

mobile/cell phone

I'd like a ...	Ik wil graag een ...	ik wil khraakh uhn ...
charger for my phone	lader voor mijn telefoon	*laa*·duhr vohr meyn tey·ley·*fohn*
mobile/cell phone for hire	mobiele telefoon huren ⓝ GSM huren ⓑ	moh·*bee*·luh tey·ley·*fohn* *hew*·ruhn khey·es·*em* *hew*·ruhn
prepaid mobile/cell phone	mobiele telefoon met beltegoed ⓝ GSM met beltegoed ⓑ	moh·*bee*·luh tey·ley·*fohn* met *bel*·tuh·khoot khey·es·*em* met *bel*·tuh·khoot
SIM card for your network	sim-kaart voor uw netwerk pol	sim·kaart vohr ew *net*·werk

84

What are the call rates?
Wat zijn de tarieven?   wat zeyn duh ta·*ree*·vuhn

(30c) per (30) seconds.
(Dertig cent) voor   (*der*·tikh sent) vohr
(dertig) seconden.   (*der*·tikh) suh·*kon*·duhn

phone

telefoon

What's your phone number?
Wat is uw/jouw   wat is ew/yaw
telefoonnummer? **pol/inf**   tey·ley·*fohn*·nu·muhr

Where's the nearest public phone?
Waar is de   waar is duh
dichtsbijzijnde   dikhts·bey·*zeyn*·duh
openbare telefoon?   oh·puhn·baa·ruh tey·ley·*fohn*

Can I look at a phone book?
Mag ik het telefoonboek   makh ik huht tey·ley·*fohn*·book
even inkijken?   *ey*·vuhn *in*·key·kuhn

Can I have some coins?
Kan ik enkele   kan ik *eng*·kuh·luh
muntstukken hebben?   *munt*·stu·kuhn *he*·buhn

I want to ...	*Ik wil graag ...*	ik wil khraakh ...
buy a phonecard	*een telefoon-kaart kopen*	uhn tey·ley·*fohn*·kaart *koh*·puhn
call (Ireland)	*(Ierland) bellen*	(*eer*·lant) *be*·luhn
make a (local) call	*een (lokaal) telefoon-gesprek maken*	uhn (loh·*kaal*) tey·ley·*fohn*·khuh·sprek *maa*·kuhn
reverse the charges	*dat de ontvanger betaalt*	dat duh ont·*vang*·uhr buh·*taalt*
speak for (three) minutes	*(drie) minuten spreken*	(dree) mee·*new*·tuhn *sprey*·kuhn

c
o
m
m
u
n
i
c
a
t
i
o
n
s

How much does ... cost?	*Hoeveel kost ...?*	hoo·*veyl* kost ...
a (three)-minute call	*een gesprek van (drie) minuten*	uhn khuh·*sprek* van (dree) mee·*new*·tuhn
each extra minute	*het per extra minuut*	huht puhr *ek*·stra mee·*newt*

What's the country code for (Australia)?
Wat is de prefix voor (Australië)?
wat is duh prey·*fiks* vohr (aw·*straa*·lee·yuh)

What's the area code for (Brussels)?
Wat is de prefix voor de zone (Brussel)?
wat is duh prey·*fiks* vohr duh *zoh*·nuh (*bru*·suhl)

The number is ...
Het nummer is ...
huht *nu*·muhr is ...

It's engaged.
Het is bezet.
huht is buh·*zet*

I've been cut off.
De verbinding is verbroken.
duh vuhr·*bin*·ding is vuhr·*broh*·kuhn

The connection's bad.
Het is een slechte verbinding.
huht is uhn *slekh*·tuh vuhr·*bin*·ding

---

listen for ...	
Fout/Verkeerd nummer. ⑩/⑪ fawt/vuhr·*keyrt* nu·muhr	**Wrong number.**
Met wie spreek ik? met wee spreyk ik	**Who's calling?**
Met wie wilt u spreken? **pol** met wee wilt ew *sprey*·kuhn	**Who do you want to speak to?**
Een momentje. uhn moh·*men*·chuh	**One moment.**
Hij/Zij is er niet. hey/zey is uhr neet	**He/She isn't here.**

PRACTICAL

Hello.
Hallo. — ha·*loh*

It's ...
Het is ... — huht is ...

Can I please speak to (Piet)?
Kan ik met (Piet) spreken alstublieft? **pol** — kan ik met (peet) *sprey*·kuhn al·stew·*bleeft*

Please tell him/her I called.
Zeg hem/haar alstublieft dat ik gebeld heb. **pol** — zekh hem/haar al·stew·*bleeft* dat ik khuh·*belt* hep

Can I leave a message?
Kan ik een boodschap laten? — kan ik uhn *boht*·skhap *laa*·tuhn

My number is ...
Mijn nummer is ... — meyn *nu*·muhr is ...

I don't have a contact number.
Ik heb geen contact-nummer. — ik hep kheyn kon·*takt*·nu·muhr

I'll call back later.
Ik bel later terug. — ik bel *laa*·tuhr tuh·*rukh*

What time should I call?
Hoe laat kan ik best bellen? — hoo laat kan ik best *be*·luhn

For telephone numbers, see also **numbers & amounts**, page 33.

post office

postkantoor

I want to send a ...	*Ik wil een ... sturen.*	ik wil uhn ... *stew*·ruhn
letter	*brief*	breef
parcel	*pakje*	*pak*·yuh
postcard	*ansichtkaart* ⓝ	*an*·sikht·kaart
	postkaart ⓑ	*post*·kaart

87

I want to buy	Ik wil een ...	ik wil uhn ...
a/an ...	kopen.	koh·puhn
aerogram	aerogram	aay·roh·gram
(padded)	(gewatteerde)	(khuh·wa·teyr·duh)
envelope	envelop	en·vuh·lop
stamp	postzegel	post·zey·khul

customs	douane-	doo·waa·nuh-
declaration	verklaring	vuhr·klaa·ring
mail n	post	post
PO box	postbus	post·bus
postal address	postadres n	post·a·dres
postcode	postcode	post·koh·duh

Please send it by airmail to (Australia).

Stuur het alstublieft — stewr huht al·stew·bleeft
per luchtpost naar — puhr lukht·post naar
(Australië). pol — (aw·straa·lee·yuh)

It contains (souvenirs).

Het bevat (souveniers). — huht buh·vat (soo·vuh·neers)

Where's the poste restante section?

Waar is de poste restante — waar is duh post res·tan·tuh
afdeling? — af·dey·ling

Is there any mail for me?

Is er post voor mij? — is uhr post vohr mey

Do you have public internet access here?

Heeft u hier een — heyft ew heer uhn
openbare — oh·puhn·baa·ruh
internetaansluiting? pol — in·tuhr·net·aan·slöy·ting

snail mail		
airmail	luchtpost	lukht·post
express mail	exprespost/	eks·pres·post/
	prioritair	pree·yoh·ree·teyr
registered mail	aangetekende	aan·khuh·tey·kuhn·duh
	post	post
surface mail	gewone post	khuh·woh·nuh post

banking
bij de bank

What days is the bank open?
Welke dagen is de bank open?
wel·kuh *daa*·khuhn is duh bangk *oh*·puhn

What times is the bank open?
Wat zijn de openings-uren van de bank?
wat zeyn duh *oh*·puh·nings·*ew*·ruhn van duh bangk

Where can I ...?	*Waar kan ik ...?*	waar kan ik ...
I'd like to ...	*Ik wil graag ...*	ik wil khraakh ...
arrange a transfer	*een giro-betaling maken* Ⓝ	uhn *khee*·roh·buh·taa·ling *maa*·kuhn
	een over-schrijving doen Ⓑ	uhn *oh*·vuhr·skhrey·ving doon
cash a cheque	*een cheque innen*	uhn shek *i*·nuhn
change a travellers cheque	*een reischeque innen*	uhn *reys*·shek *i*·nuhn
change money	*geld wisselen*	khelt *wi*·suh·luhn
get a cash advance	*een voorschot bekomen*	uhn *vohr*·skhot buh·*koh*·muhn
get change for this note	*dit biljet wisselen in muntstukken*	dit bil·*yet wi*·suh·luhn in *munt*·stu·kuhn
withdraw money	*geld afhalen*	khelt *af*·haa·luhn
Where's ...?	*Waar vind ik een ...?*	waar vint ik uhn ...
an automated teller machine	*pin-automaat* Ⓝ	*pin*·aw·toh·maat
	geldautomaat Ⓑ	*khelt*·aw·toh·maat
a foreign exchange office	*wisselkantoor*	*wi*·suhl·kan·tohr

banking

89

The automated teller machine took my card.
De pin-automaat/   duh *pin*-aw·toh·maat/
geldautomaat heeft   *khelt*·aw·toh·maat heyft
mijn kaart ingeslikt. Ⓝ/Ⓑ   meyn kaart *in*·khuh·slikt

I've forgotten my PIN.
Ik ben mijn pin vergeten. Ⓝ   ik ben meyn pin vuhr·*khey*·tuhn
Ik ben mijn geheime   ik ben meyn khuh·*hey*·muh
code vergeten. Ⓑ   *koh*·duh vuhr·*khey*·tuhn

Can I use my credit card to withdraw money?
Kan ik geld afhalen met   kan ik khelt *af*·haa·luhn met
mijn kredietkaart?   meyn krey·*deet*·kaart

Has my money arrived yet?
Is mijn geld al   is mijn khelt al
aangekomen?   *aan*·khuh·koh·muhn

How long will it take to arrive?
Hoe lang duurt het tot   hoo lang dewrt huht tot
mijn geld aankomt?   meyn khelt *aan*·komt

What's the …?   *Wat is de …?*   wat is duh …
  charge for that   *kost hiervoor*   kost heer·*vohr*
  exchange rate   *wisselkoers*   *wi*·suhl·koors

For other useful phrases, see **money**, page 43.

---

listen for…		
Er is een probleem.		
uhr is uhn proh·*bleym*		**There's a problem.**
Er staat geen geld meer op de rekening.		
uhr staat kheyn khelt meyr		**You have no funds left.**
op duh *rey*·kuh·ning		
We kunnen dat niet doen.		
wuh *ku*·nuhn dat neet doon		**We can't do that.**
Teken hier.		
tey·kuhn heer		**Sign here.**
identiteitsbewijs	ee·den·tee·*teyts*·	**identification**
	buh·weys	
paspoort	*pas*·pohrt	**passport**

I'd like a/an ...   *Ik wil graag een ...*   ik wil khraakh uhn ...

    audio set   *audiogids*   aw·dee·yoh·khits

    catalogue   *catalogus*   ka·taa·loh·khus

    guide (in   *gids (in het*   khits (in huht

      English)   *Engels)*   eng·uhls)

    map (building)   *plattegrond*   pla·tuh·khront

    map (town)   *kaart*   kaart

Do you have   *Heeft u informatie*   heyft ew in·for·maa·see
information   *over beziens-*   oh·vuhr buh·zeens·
on ... sights?   *waardigheden*   waar·dikh·hey·duhn
   van ... belang? pol   van ... buh·lang

    architectural   *architectuuraal*   ar·khee·tek·tew·raal

    cultural   *cultureel*   kul·tew·reyl

    historical   *historisch*   his·toh·ris

    religious   *religieus*   ruh·lee·khyeus

I'd like to see ...
Ik wil graag ... zien.   ik wil khraakh ... zeen

What's that?
Wat is dat?   wat is dat

How old is it?
Hoe oud is het?   hoo awt is huht

Who built/made/painted it?
Wie heeft het gebouwd/   wee heyft huht khuh·bawt/
gemaakt/geschilderd?   khuh·maakt/khuh·skhil·duhrt

Could you take a photo of me/us?
Kunt u een foto van   kunt ew uhn foh·toh van
mij/ons nemen   mey/ons ney·muhn
alstublieft? pol   al·stew·bleeft

Can I take a photo (of you)?
Mag ik een foto (van u)   makh ik uhn foh·toh (van ew)
nemen? pol   ney·muhn

I'll send you the photo.
Ik stuur de foto op.   ik stewr duh foh·toh op

toegang

What time does it open/close?
Hoe laat gaat het open/dicht?
hoo laat khaat huht oh·puhn/dikht

What's the admission charge?
Wat is de toegangsprijs?
wat is duh *too*·khangs·preys

Is there a discount for ...?	*Is er korting voor ...?*	is uhr *kor*·ting vohr ...
children	*kinderen*	*kin*·duh·ruhn
families	*families*	fa·*mee*·lees
groups	*groepen*	*khroo*·puhn
older people	*senioren*	sey·*nyoh*·ruhn
pensioners	*gepensioneerden*	khuh·pen·syoh·*neyr*·duhn
students	*studenten*	stew·*den*·tuhn

signs

Bezet	buh·*zet*	**Occupied**
Dames/Heren	*daa*·muhs/*hey*·ruhn	**Women/Men**
Geen Toegang	kheen *too*·khang	**No Entry**
Ingang/Uitgang	*in*·khang/*öyt*·khang	**Entrance/Exit**
Inlichtingen	*in*·likh·ting·uhn	**Information**
Niet Aanraken	neet *aan*·raa·kuhn	**No Touching**
Alstublieft	al·stew·*bleeft*	
Open/	*oh*·puhn/	**Open/**
Gesloten	khuh·*sloh*·tuhn	**Closed**
Toiletten	twa·*le*·tuhn	**Toilets/WC**
Verboden	vuhr·*boh*·duhn	**Prohibited**
Verboden te	vuhr·*boh*·duhn tuh	**No Photography**
Fotograferen	foh·toh·khra·*fey*·ruhn	
Verboden te	vuhr·*boh*·duhn tuh	**No Smoking**
Roken	*roh*·kuhn	
Warm/Koud	warm/kawt	**Hot/Cold**

tours

rondleidingen

Can you recommend a ...?	*Kunt u een ... aanbevelen?* pol	kunt ew uhn ... *aan*·buh·vey·luhn
When's the next ...?	*Wanneer is de volgende ...?*	wa·*neyr* is duh *vol*·khuhn·duh ...
boat trip	*boottocht*	*boh*·tokht
canal cruise	*kanaaltocht*	ka·*naal*·tokht
cycle tour	*fietstocht*	*feets*·tokht
day trip	*daguitstap*	*dakh*·öyt·stap
harbour cruise	*haven-rondvaart*	*haa*·vuhn·ront·vaart
tour	*rondleiding*	*ront*·ley·ding
Is ... included?	*Is ... inbegrepen?*	is ... *in*·buh·khrey·puhn
accommodation	*accommodatie*	a·koh·moh·*daa*·see
transport	*transport*	trans·*port*

English	Dutch	Pronunciation
abbey	*abdij*	ap·*dey*
almshouse	*hofje* ℕ	*hof*·yuh
	godshuis n ⓑ	*khots*·höys
battlefields	*slagvelden* n pl	*slakh*·vel·duhn
béguinage	*begijnhof* n	buh·*kheyn*·hof
belfry	*belfort* n	*bel*·fort
brewery	*brouwerij*	braw·wuh·*rey*
bulb fields	*bollenvelden* n pl	bo·luh·vel·duhn
carillon	*beiaard*	*bey*·yaart
city gate	*(stads)poort*	(*stats*·)pohrt
cloister	*klooster* n	*kloh*·stuhr
courtyard	*hofje* n	*hof*·yuh
covered market	*hallen*	*ha*·luhn
distillery	*jenever-stokerij*	zhuh·*ney*·vuhr·stoh·kuh·*rey*
drained land	*polder*	*pol*·duhr
façade	*gevel*	*khey*·vuhl
flea market	*rommelmarkt*	*ro*·muhl·markt
fortress	*burcht/slot*	burkht/slot
gable	*geveltop*	*khey*·vuhl·top
lighthouse	*vuurtoren*	vewr·*toh*·ruhn
(wind)mill	*(wind)molen*	(*wint*·)*moh*·luhn
trenches	*loopgraven* n pl	*lohp*·khraa·vuhn
war graves	*oorlogsgraven* n pl	*ohr*·lokhs·khraa·vuhn

Is food included?
Zijn maaltijden inbegrepen?
zeyn *maal*·tey·duhn *in*·buh·khrey·puhn

How long is the (tour)?
Hoe lang duurt de (rondleiding)?
hoo lang dewrt duh (*ront*·ley·ding)

What time should we be back?
Hoe laat moeten we terug zijn?
hoo laat *moo*·tuhn wuh tuh·*rukh* zeyn

I'm with them.
Ik ben met hen.
ik ben met hen

I've lost my group.
Ik ben mijn groep kwijt.
ik ben meyn khroop kweyt

I'm attending a ...	*Ik ben hier voor een ...*	ik ben heer vohr uhn ...
conference	*conferentie*	kon·fey·ren·see
course	*cursus*	kur·sus
meeting	*vergadering*	vuhr·khaa·duh·ring
trade fair	*beurs*	beurs
I'm with ...	*Ik ben hier met ...*	ik ben heer met ...
(InBev)	*(InBev)*	(in·bef)
my colleague(s)	*mijn collega('s)*	meyn ko·ley·kha(s)
(two) others	*(twee) anderen*	(twey) an·duh·ruhn

I'm alone.
Ik ben hier op mijn eentje. ik ben heer op meyn *eyn*·chuh

I have an appointment with ...
Ik heb een afspraak met ... ik hep uhn *af*·spraak met ...

I'm staying at the (Hotel Industrie), room (205).
Ik logeer in (Hotel Industrie), kamer (tweehonderd en vijf). ik loh·*zheyr* in (hoh·*tel* in·dus·*tree*) *kaa*·muhr (twey·*hon*·duhrt en veyf)

I'm here for (two) days/weeks.
Ik ben hier voor (twee) dagen/weken. ik ben heer voor (twey) *daa*·khuhn/*wey*·kuhn

Can I please have your business card?
Mag ik een visitekaartje van u? pol makh ik uhn vee·*zee*·tuh·kaar·chuh van ew

Here's my ...	Hier is mijn ...	heer is meyn ...
What's your ...?	Wat is uw/	wat is ew/
	jouw ...? pol/inf	yaw ...
address	adres	a·dres
cell/mobile	mobiel	moh·beel
number	telefoon-	tey·ley·fohn·
	nummer ⓝ	nu·muhr
	GSM-nummer ⓑ	khey·es·em·nu·muhr
email address	e-mailadres	ee·meyl·a·dres
fax number	faxnummer	faks·nu·muhr
pager number	beepernummer	bee·puhr·nu·muhr
work number	telefoon-	tey·ley·fohn·
	nummer	nu·muhr
	van het werk	van huht werk

Where's the ...?	Waar is ...?	waar is ...
business	het business-	huht bis·nis·
centre	centre	sen·tuhr
business	het	huht
district	zakencentrum	zaa·kuhn·sen·trum
conference	de conferentie	duh kon·fey·ren·see
industrial	de industrie-	duh in·dus·tree·
estate	zone	zoh·nuh
meeting	de vergade-	duh vuhr·khaa·duh·
	ring	ring

I need ...	Ik heb ... nodig.	ik hep ... noh·dikh
a computer	een computer	uhn kom·pyoo·tuhr
an internet	een internet-	uhn in·tuhr·net·
connection	aansluiting	aan·slöy·ting
an interpreter	een tolk	uhn tolk
who speaks	(die Engels	(dee eng·uhls
(English)	spreekt)	spreykt)
more business	meer visite-	meyr vee·zee·tuh·
cards	kaartjes	kaar·chus

I need space to set up.
Ik heb plaats nodig   ik hep plaats noh·dikh
om mij op te stellen.   om mey op tuh ste·luhn

I need to send a fax.
Ik moet een fax sturen.   ik moot uhn faks stew·ruhn

That went very well.
   Dat ging vlotjes.   dat khing *vlo*·chus

Thank you for your interest.
   Bedankt voor uw   be·*dangkt* vohr ew
   interesse. **pol**   in·tuh·*re*·suh

Shall we go for a drink/meal?
   Zullen we iets gaan   *zu*·luhn wuh eets khaan
   drinken/eten?   *dring*·kuhn/*ey*·tuhn

It's on me.
   Ik betaal.   ik buh·*taal*

cards on the table

Dutch businesspeople tend to be big on academic titles, at least on their business cards (rather than as a form of address). There's a vast (and often confusing) nomenclature and an even greater number of abbreviations to choose from to indicate your academic degree(s) in front of your name; there are rules and regulations, and much debate ... but in the end everyone agrees it's not all that important.

On Dutch *visitekaartjes* vee·*zee*·tuh·*kaar*·chus (business cards) you might see abbreviations like these in front of someone's name:

bc.	*baccalaureus*	**hbo degree (tertiary education outside university)**
dr.	*doctor (PhD)*	**university degree with a PhD**
drs.	*doctorandus*	**university degree**
ing.	*ingenieur*	**engineer**
ir.	*ingenieur*	**engineer (with a university degree)**
mr.	*meester*	**lawyer**

If you're the proud owner of more than one title, these will be combined following specific rules such as: *drs.* + *dr.* = *dr.* and *ing.* + *dr.* = *dr. ing.* which could lead to combinations such as *mr. ir. drs. ing.* Note that there's no specific title for a medical doctor – usually their card will read something like *Jaap Steen, arts* (*arts* arts meaning 'doctor').

business

97

Over the centuries, English has borrowed many words from Dutch – or via Dutch from other languages. Many of them are nautical terms, but there are also painting terms, food terms and so on. Here are some examples.

loanword:	origin:
booze	Middle Dutch *būsen*
boss	*baas* (master)
brandy	*brandewijn* (burnt wine)
bundle	probably Middle Dutch *bundel*
coleslaw	*koolsla* (cabbage salad)
cookie	*koekje*, diminutive of *koek* (cake)
cruise	*kruisen* (to cross)
deck	Middle Dutch *dec* (covering)
dock (nautical)	Middle Dutch *docke*
duffel	cloth named after *Duffel*, a Belgian town
easel	*ezel* (donkey)
freight	Middle Dutch *vrecht* – *vracht* (load) in present-day Dutch
landscape	from *landskip* (Dutch painting term), based on Middle Dutch *landscap* (region)
mannequin	*manneken* (little man), diminutive of *man* (man)
pickle	possibly Middle Dutch *pekel*
pump	Middle Dutch *pumpe* (pipe)
sketch	Dutch *schets*
skipper	Middle Dutch *schipper* (shipper)
slurp	Middle Dutch *slorpen* (to sip)
smuggle	*smokkelen*
snoop	*snoepen* (to eat furtively)
splinter	Middle Dutch *splinter/splinte* (splint)
split	Middle Dutch *splitten* (to cleave)
spook	*spook* (ghost)
tub	Middle Dutch *tubbe*
waffle	*wafel* (earlier *wæfel*)
wagon	*wagen* (wain, or these days, car)

senior & disabled travellers
senioren & gehandicapte reizigers

The Low Countries have done a lot lately to make public venues wheelchair-accessible, and all new buildings have ramps and/or lifts. More wheelchair-accessible buses are also popping up. Arrangements for assistance on trains can be made if you ring up the station or, in the Netherlands, the *Bureau Assistentieverlening Gehandicapten* (Bureau for assistance to disabled people), the day before your trip. In Belgium, there's also the railways' brochure *Gids voor de Reiziger met Beperkte Mobiliteit* (Guide for Travellers with Limited Mobility).

I have a disability.
Ik heb een handicap.
ik hep uhn hen·dee·kep/
han·dee·kap ⓝ/ⓑ

I need assistance.
Ik heb hulp nodig.
ik hep hulp *noh*·dikh

I'm deaf/hard of hearing.
Ik ben doof/hardhorend.
ik ben dohf/hart·*hoh*·ruhnt

I have a hearing aid.
Ik heb een hoorapparaat.
ik hep uhn *hohr*·a·pa·raat

My companion's blind.
Mijn metgezel is blind.
meyn *met*·khuh·zel is blint

What services do you have for people with a disability?
Welke voorzieningen heeft u voor personen met een handicap? pol
wel·kuh vohr·*zee*·ning·uhn
heyft ew vohr puhr·*soh*·nuhn
met uhn *hen*·dee·kep/
han·dee·kap ⓝ/ⓑ

Are there disabled parking spaces?
Zijn er parkeerplaatsen voor gehandicapten?
zeyn uhr par·*keyr*·plaat·suhn
vohr khuh·*hen*·dee·kep·tuhn/
khuh·*han*·dee·kap·tuhn ⓝ/ⓑ

Is there wheelchair access?
Is het toegankelijk voor rolstoelgebruikers?
is huht too·*khang*·kuh·luhk
vohr *rol*·stool·khuh·*bröy*·kuhrs

How wide is the entrance?
Hoe breed is de ingang?
hoo breyt is duh *in*·khang

senior & disabled travellers

Are guide dogs permitted?
Zijn geleidehonden   zeyn khuh·*ley*·duh·hon·duhn
toegelaten?   too·khuh·laa·tuhn

How many steps are there?
Hoeveel treden zijn er?   hoo·*veyl trey*·duhn zeyn uhr

Is there an elevator/lift?
Is er een lift?   is uhr uhn lift

Are there disabled toilets?
Zijn er toiletten voor   zeyn uhr twa·*le*·tuhn vohr
gehandicapten?   khuh·*hen*·dee·kep·tuhn/
   khuh·*han*·dee·kap·tuhn ⓝ/ⓑ

Are there rails in the bathroom?
Is er een reling in de   is uhr uhn *rey*·ling in duh
badkamer?   *bat*·kaa·muhr

Is there somewhere I can sit down?
Kan ik hier ergens   kan ik heer *er*·khuhns
neerzitten?   *neyr*·zi·tuhn

Could you call me a disabled taxi?
Kunt u een taxi voor   kunt ew uhn *tak*·see vohr
gehandicapten   khuh·*hen*·dee·kep·tuhn/
voor me bestellen   khuh·*han*·dee·kap·tuhn
alstublieft? pol   vohr muh buh·*ste*·luhn
   al·stew·*bleeft* ⓝ/ⓑ

Could you help me cross the street safely?
Kunt u me helpen de   kunt ew muh *hel*·puhn duh
straat veilig over te   straat *vey*·likh *oh*·vuhr tuh
steken? pol   *stey*·kuhn

guide dog (assistance dog)	*geleidehond*	khuh·*ley*·duh·hont
guide dog (seeing-eye dog)	*blinde- geleidehond*	*blin*·duh· khuh·*ley*·duh·hont
person with a disability	*persoon met een handicap*	puhr·*sohn* met uhn *hen*·dee·kep/ *han*·dee·kap ⓝ/ⓑ
ramp	*helling*	*he*·ling
senior person	*oudere persoon*	*aw*·duh·ruh puhr·*sohn*
walking frame	*looprek* n	*lohp*·rek
walking stick	*wandelstok*	*wan*·duhl·stok
wheelchair	*rolstoel*	*rol*·stool

travelling with children

Where's the nearest ...?	*Waar is de dichtsbijzijnde ...?*	waar is duh *dikhts·bey·zeyn·*duh ...
drinking fountain	*drinkwaterfontein*	*dringk·*waa·tuhr·fon·*teyn*
playground	*speeltuin*	*speyl·*töyn

Where's the nearest ...?	*Waar is het dichtsbijzijnde ...?*	waar is huht *dikhts·bey·zeyn·*duh ...
park	*park*	park
swimming pool	*zwembad*	*zwem·*bat
tap	*kraantje*	*kraan·*chuh
theme park	*pretpark*	*pret·*park

Do you sell ...?	*Verkoopt u ...?* pol	vuhr·*kohpt* ew ...
baby wipes	*babydoekjes*	*bey·*bee·dook·yuhs
disposable nappies	*wegwerpluiers*	*wekh·*werp·löy·yuhrs
painkillers for infants	*pijnstillers voor babies*	*peyn·*sti·luhrs vohr *bey·*bees

Is there a ...?	*Is er een ...?*	is uhr uhn ...
baby change room	*kamer om babies te verschonen*	*kaa·*muhr om *bey·*bees tuh vuhr·*skhoh·*nuhn
child discount	*korting voor kinderen*	*kor·*ting vohr *kin·*duh·ruhn
child-minding service	*oppasdienst*	*o·*pas·deenst
children's menu	*kindermenu*	*kin·*duhr·muh·new
child's portion	*portie voor kinderen*	*por·*see vohr *kin·*duh·ruhn
crèche	*crèche*	kresh
family ticket	*familieticket*	fa·*mee·*lee·*ti·*kuht

I need a/an …	Ik heb een … nodig.	ik hep uhn … noh·dikh
baby (car) seat	baby-autostoel	bey·bee·aw·toh·stool
(English-speaking) babysitter	babysit (die Engels spreekt)	bey·bee·sit (dee eng·uhls spreykt)
booster seat	zitting-verhoger voor de auto	zi·ting·vuhr·hoh·khuhr vohr duh aw·toh
child (bicycle) seat	kinderzitje voor de fiets	kin·duhr·zi·chuh vohr de feets
child (car) seat	kinder-autostoel	kin·duhr·aw·toh·stool
cot	wieg	weekh
highchair	kinderstoel	kin·duhr·stool
plastic bag	plastic/ plastieken tas ⓝ/ⓑ	ples·tik/ plas·tee·kuhn tas
plastic sheet	stuk plastic/ plastiek ⓝ/ⓑ	stuk ples·tik/ plas·teek
potty	potje	po·chuh
pram	kinderwagen	kin·duhr·waa·khun
pushchair/ stroller	wandel-wagen	wan·duhl·waa·khun
sick bag	papieren zak	pa·pee·ruhn zak

Are there any good places to take children around here?

Zijn er hier in de buurt goede plekken om kinderen mee naar toe te nemen?	zeyn uhr heer in duh bewrt khoo·duh ple·kuhn om kin·duh·ruhn mey naar too tuh ney·muhn

Is there space for a pram?

Is er plaats voor een kinderwagen?	is uhr plaats vohr uhn kin·duhr·waa·khuhn

Are children allowed?

Zijn kinderen toegelaten?	zeyn kin·duh·ruhn too·khuh·laa·tuhn

Where can I change a nappy?

Waar kan ik een luier verschonen?	waar kan ik uhn löy·yuhr vuhr·shoh·nuhn

Is it OK if I breast-feed here?

Kan ik hier de borst geven?   kan ik heer duh borst khey·vuhn

Could I have some paper and pencils, please?

Zou ik wat papier en enkele potloden kunnen hebben alstublieft? **pol**   zaw ik wat pa·*peer* en *eng*·kuh·luh *pot*·loh·duhn ku·nuhn *he*·buhn al·stew·*bleeft*

Is this suitable for (six)-year-old children?

Is dit geschikt voor kinderen van (zes) jaar?   is dit khuh·*skhikt* vohr *kin*·duh·ruhn van (zes) yaar

Do you know a dentist/doctor who is good with children?

Kent u een tandarts/ dokter die goed is met kinderen? **pol**   kent ew een *tan*·darts/ *dok*·tuhr dee khoot is met *kin*·duh·ruhn

If your child is sick, see **health**, page 199.

children

103

talking with children

In this section, phrases are in the informal *je* yuh (you) form only. For more details, see the box **all about you** on page 109.

What's your name?
Hoe heet je? — hoo heyt yuh

How old are you?
Hoe oud ben je? — hoo awt ben yuh

When's your birthday?
Wanneer is je verjaardag? — wa·*neyr* is yuh vuhr·*yaar*·dakh

Do you have a brother/sister?
Heb jij een broer/zus? — hep yey uhn broor/zus

Do you go to kindergarten?
Ga je naar de kleuterschool? — khaa yuh naar duh *klöy*·tuhr·skhohl

Do you go to school?
Ga je naar school? — khaa yuh naar skhohl

What grade are you in?
In welk jaar zit je? — in welk yaar zit yuh

Do you like ...?

school	*Ga je graag naar school?*	khaa yuh khraakh naar skhohl
sport	*Hou je van sport?*	haw yuh van sport
your teacher	*Vind je je juf/ meester leuk?* m/f	vint yuh yuh yuf/ *meys*·tuhr leuk

Do you learn (English)?
Leer je (Engels)? — leyr yuh (*eng*·uhls)

What do you do after school?
Wat doe je na school? — wat doo yuh naa skhohl

Who's your favourite sportsperson?
Wie is jouw favoriete sportman/sportvrouw? m/f — wee is yaw fa·voh·*ree*·tuh *sport*·man/*sport*·vraw

Are you lost?
Ben je de weg kwijt? — ben yuh duh wekh kweyt

talking about children

In this section, phrases are in the informal *je* yuh (you) form only. For more details, see the box **all about you** on page 109.

When's the baby due?
Wanneer wordt de baby verwacht?
wa·*neyr* wort duh *bey*·bee vuhr·*wakht*

What are you going to call the baby?
Welke naam heb je gekozen voor de baby?
wel·kuh naam hep yuh khuh·*koh*·zuhn vohr duh *bey*·bee

Is this your first child?
Is dit je eerste kindje?
is dit yuh *eyr*·stuh *kin*·chuh

How many children do you have?
Hoeveel kinderen heb je?
hoo·*veyl kin*·duh·ruhn hep yuh

What a beautiful child!
Wat een mooi kind!
wat uhn moy kint

Is it a boy or a girl?
Is het een jongen of een meisje?
is huht uhn *yong*·uhn of uhn *mey*·shuh

What's his/her name?
Hoe heet hij/zij?
hoo heyt hey/zey

How old is he/she?
Hoe oud is hij/zij?
hoo awt is hey/zey

Does he/she go to school?
Gaat hij/zij naar school?
khaat hey/zey naar skhohl

He/She has your eyes.
Hij/Zij heeft jouw ogen.
hey/zey heyft yaw *oh*·khun

He/She looks like you.
Hij/Zij lijkt op jou.
hey/zey leykt op yaw

You're all grown up now, so it's about time you heard the truth about Santa Claus. Did you know that the origin of this much-loved figure is *Sinterklaas* sin·tuhr·*klaas* (the word is a corruption of *St Nikolaas* sint·*nee*·koh·laas – the Dutch name for St Nicholas), patron saint of all children? Or that it was the Dutch settlers in New Amsterdam (present-day New York) who brought the tradition of Santa Claus to America?

The festival of St Nicholas is celebrated in the Low Countries on 5 and 6 December. The Catholic church officially recognises 6 December as the name day of this canonised saint, who was a historical figure – the bishop of Myra in Asia Minor in the 4th century. In the Middle Ages, St Nicholas was famous as the patron saint of *zeelieden* zey·lee·duhn (sailors) and *handelaars* han·duh·laars (merchants), and acquired high status in the Low Countries due to their maritime and trade history. Over the centuries, however, St Nicholas' other role – that of the children's patron – became more prominent.

The legend of Sinterklaas in the Low Countries paints him as an old man who lives in Spain, where during the year he takes notes on all children's behaviour. Come November, Sinterklaas, his helper *Zwarte Piet* zwar·tuh peet (Black Pete) – or various Black Petes – and his *witte paard* wi·tuh paart (white horse) arrive by boat in a Dutch port. They're welcomed by the town mayor and their parade through the town is broadcast live on TV.

During his stay, Sinterklaas visits schools, hospitals, offices and homes, leaving presents for the children. To cope with this workload, Sinterklaas relies on an army of *hulpsinterklaazen* hulp·sin·tuhr·klaa·zuhn (Sinterklaas helpers) who dress up as Sinterklaas and appear all over the country. Grown-ups and children alike make or buy *cadeautjes* ka·*doh*·tyuhs (presents), hide and disguise them and write *brieven* bree·vuhn (letters) to Sinterklaas or *gedichten* khuh·*dikh*·tuhn (poems) that go with the presents and can gently mock the recipient. The presents are opened and the poems read on St Nicholas' Eve, 5 December – aka *pakjesavond* pak·yuhs·aa·vont (evening of presents) – with *chocolade* shoh·koh·*laa*·duh (chocolate) and *pepernoten* pey·puhr·noh·tuhn (ginger-bread) on the table. In Flanders, the presents are dropped off during the night by Sinterklaas via the *schoorsteen* skhohr·steyn (chimney) and opened by children on the morning of 6 December.

SOCIAL > meeting people
mensen ontmoeten

basics

Yes.	Ja.	yaa
No.	Nee.	ney
Please.	Alstublieft. pol	al·stew·*bleeft*
	Alsjeblieft. inf	a·shuh·*bleeft*
Thank you	Dank u (wel). pol	dangk ew (wel)
(very much).	Dank je (wel). inf	dangk yuh (wel)
You're welcome.	Graag gedaan.	khraakh khuh·*daan*
Excuse me.	Excuseer mij.	eks·kew·*zeyr* mey
(to get attention)		
Excuse me.	Pardon.	par·*don*
(to get past)		
Sorry.	Sorry.	so·ree

greetings & goodbyes

groeten & afscheid nemen

It's customary to greet people with a firm handshake and often a double cheek kiss or even a triple one – except on business occasions, when you'd do away with the kissing, of course. Young people tend to greet each other with a single quick kiss on one cheek when meeting up. Both men and women can initiate the greeting and kissing.

It's good manners to say *goedendag* (good day) or *dag* (hello) upon entering a shop, and *dag* (bye) or *tot ziens* (see you later) when leaving.

Hello.	Dag./Hallo.	dakh/ha·*loh*
Hi. (colloquial)	Hoi.	hoy

meeting people

Good ...

morning	*Goedemorgen.*	khoo·duh·*mor*·khuhn
day	*Goedendag.*	khoo·duh·*dakh*
afternoon	*Goedemiddag.*	khoo·duh·*mi*·dakh
evening	*Goedenavond.*	khoo·duh·*naa*·vont
night	*Goedenacht.*	khoo·duh·*nakht*

How are you?

Hoe gaat het	hoo khaat huht
met u/jou? pol/inf	met ew/yaw

Fine. And you?

Goed.	khoot
En met u/jou? pol/inf	en met ew/yaw

What's your name?

Hoe heet u/je? pol/inf	hoo heyt ew/yuh

My name is ...

Ik heet ...	ik heyt ...

I'd like to introduce you to (Wannes).

Laat me u/je aan	laat muh ew/yuh aan
(Wannes) voorstellen. pol/inf	(*wa*·nuhs) vohr·ste·luhn

I'm pleased to meet you.

Aangenaam.	*aan*·khuh·naam

This is my ...

	Dit is mijn ...	dit is meyn ...
child	*kind*	kint
colleague	*collega*	ko·*ley*·kha
friend	*vriend* m	vreent
	vriendin f	vreen·din
husband	*man*	man
partner	*partner*	part·nuhr
(intimate)		
wife	*vrouw*	vraw

See you later.	*Tot ziens.*	tot zeens
Bye./Goodbye.	*Dag.*	dakh
Bye! (colloquial)	*Doei!*	dooy
Good night.	*Goedenacht.*	khoo·duh·*nakht*
Bon voyage!	*Goede reis!*	khoo·duh reys

addressing people

Forms of address in Dutch are simple. The three terms below are appropriate on all formal occasions and when meeting people for the first time, unless they're young. Always use these titles until the person indicates that it's OK for you to address them with their first name by saying *Je mag mij … noemen.* yuh makh mey … *noo·*muhn (You can call me …). Note that *Juffrouw* is rarely used these days: use it only if you want to be polite to a teenage girl – in all other cases it's old-fashioned.

Mr/Sir	*Meneer (Mr)*	muh·*neyr*
Ms/Mrs/Madam	*Mevrouw (Mevr)*	muh·*vraw*
Miss	*Juffrouw (Mej)*	yu·fraw

See also the box **cards on the table** on page 97.

all about you

Dutch has two forms for the English 'you' – *jij* yey and *u* ew. The polite form *u* is used when meeting people for the first time (unless they're young), with older people, people in a position of authority and for everyone you don't know well, unless they indicate that you can address them with *jij* by saying *Zeg maar jij.* zekh maar yey (meaning 'You can use the informal *jij*'). You use the informal *jij* with family, friends and anyone you know well, with children younger than you and with people of more or less your own age in informal settings (such as in pubs or when playing sport). Note that the informal *jij* (emphatic) can also appear as *je* yuh (nonemphatic). The English possessive 'your' also has two variants in Dutch: *jouw* yaw (informal) and *uw* ew (polite). For more on pronouns, see the **phrasebuilder**, page 22.

making conversation

What a beautiful day!
Wat een prachtige dag!
wat uhn *prakh*·ti·khuh dakh

Nice/Awful weather, isn't it?
Mooi/Afschuwelijk weer,
niet waar?
moy/af·*skhew*·wuh·luhk weyr
neet waar

Do you live here?
Woont u hier? pol
Woon je hier? inf
wohnt ew heer
wohn yuh heer

Where are you going?
Waar gaat u heen? pol
Waar ga je heen? inf
waar khaat ew heyn
waar khaa yuh heyn

Do you like it here?
Vind u/je het hier leuk? pol/inf
vint ew/yuh huht heer leuk

I love it here.
Ik vind het hier erg leuk.
ik vint huht heer erkh leuk

What's this called?
Hoe noem je dit?
hoo noom yuh dit

Can I take a photo (of you)?
Mag ik een foto
(van u/je) nemen? pol/inf
makh ik uhn *foh*·toh
(van ew/yuh) *ney*·muhn

I'll send you the photo.
Ik stuur de foto op.
ik stewr duh *foh*·toh op

That's (beautiful), isn't it!
Dat is (mooi), niet waar?
dat is (moy) neet waar

Are you here on holiday?
Bent u hier met vakantie? pol
Ben je hier met vakantie? inf
bent ew heer met va·*kan*·see
ben yuh heer met va·*kan*·see

---

etiquette tips

- It's OK to be a little late on social occasions (up to 15 minutes), but be punctual for all official engagements.
- Never forget someone's birthday.
- Don't inquire about a person's salary.

I'm here ...	Ik ben hier ...	ik ben heer ...
for a holiday	met vakantie	met va·*kan*·see
on business	op zakenreis	op *zaa*·kuhn·reys
to study	om te studeren	om tuh stew·*dey*·ruhn

How long are you here for?

Hoelang blijft u hier? pol	hoo·*lang* bleyft ew heer
Hoelang blijf je hier? inf	hoo·*lang* bleyf yuh heer

I'm here for (four) weeks/days.

Ik blijf hier (vier) dagen/ weken.	ik bleyf heer (veer) *daa*·khuhn/ *wey*·kuhn

nationalities

nationaliteiten

Where are you from?

Waar komt u vandaan? pol	waar komt ew van·*daan*
Waar kom je vandaan? inf	waar kom yuh van·*daan*

I'm from ...	Ik kom uit ...	ik kom öyt ...
Australia	Australië	aw·*straa*·lee·yuh
Canada	Canada	*ka*·na·da
England	Engeland	*eng*·uh·lant
South Africa	Zuid-Afrika	zöyt·*aa*·free·ka
the USA	Amerika	a·*mey*·ree·ka

age

leeftijd

How old ...?	Hoe oud ...	hoo awt ...
are you	bent u pol	bent ew
	ben je inf	ben yuh
is your	is uw/jouw	is ew/yaw
daughter	dochter pol/inf	*dokh*·tuhr
is your son	is uw/jouw	is ew/yaw
	zoon pol/inf	zohn

I'm ... years old.
Ik ben ... jaar. ik ben ... yaar

He/She is ... years old.
Hij/Zij is ... jaar. hey/zey is ... yaar

Too old!
Te oud! tuh awt

Older/Younger than you think.
Ouder/Jonger dan aw·duhr/yong·uhr dan
u/je denkt. pol/inf ew/yuh dengkt

I'm younger than I look.
Ik ben jonger dan ik ik ben yong·uhr dan ik
er uitzie. uhr öyt·zee

For your age, see **numbers & amounts**, page 33.

occupations & studies

What's your occupation?
Wat is uw/jouw beroep? pol/inf wat is ew/yaw buh·roop

I'm a ...	*Ik ben ...*	ik ben ...
businessperson	*zakenman* m	*zaa*·kuhn·man
	zakenvrouw f	*zaa*·kuhn·vraw
chef	*kok*	kok
chocolate maker	*chocolatier*	shoh·koh·la·*tye*
civil servant	*openbaar*	oh·*puhn*·baar
	ambtenaar	*amp*·tuh·naar
farmer	*boer/boerin* m/f	boor/boo·*rin*
interpreter	*tolk*	tolk
journalist	*journalist*	zhoor·na·*list*
lawyer	*advocaat*	at·voh·*kaat*
manual worker	*arbeider* m	*ar*·bey·duhr
	arbeidster f	*ar*·beyt·stuhr
student	*student*	stew·*dent*
teacher (general)	*leraar* m	*ley*·raar
	lerares f	ley·raa·*res*
translator	*vertaler*	vuhr·*taa*·luhr

SOCIAL

I work for the European Community.
Ik werk voor de   ik werk vohr duh
Europese Gemeenschap.   eu·roh·pey·suh khuh·meyn·skhap

I work in the Red Light District.
Ik werk in de rosse buurt.   ik werk in duh ro·suh bewrt

I'm self-employed.
Ik werk voor mezelf.   ik werk vohr muh·zelf

I work in ...	*Ik werk in ...*	ik werk in ...
administration	*administratie*	at·mee·nee·straa·see
health	*de gezondheids-zorg*	duh khuh·zont·heyts·zorkh
hospitality	*de horeca-sector*	duh hoh·rey·ka·sek·tor

I'm ...	*Ik ben ...*	ik ben ...
retired	*met pensioen*	met pen·syoon
unemployed	*werkloos*	werk·lohs

What are you studying?	*Wat studeert u?* pol	wat stew·deyrt ew
	Wat studeer jij? inf	wat stew·deyr yey

I'm studying ...	*Ik studeer ...*	ik stew·deyr ...
Dutch	*Nederlands*	ney·duhr·lants
humanities	*humane wetenschappen*	hew·maa·nuh wey·tuhn·skha·puhn
science	*wetenschappen*	wey·tuhn·skha·puhn

local talk		
Hey!	*He daar!*	hey daar
Great!	*Fantastisch!*	fan·tas·tis
Sure.	*Natuurlijk.*	na·tewr·luhk
Maybe.	*Misschien.*	mi·skheen
No way!	*Geen sprake van!*	kheyn spraa·kuh van
Go ahead!	*Doe maar!* Ⓝ	doo maar
	Vooruit! Ⓑ	voh·röyt
Just a minute.	*Een minuutje.*	uhn mee·new·chuh
Just joking!	*Grapje!*	khrap·yuh
It's OK.	*In orde.*	in or·duh
No problem.	*Geen probleem.*	kheyn proh·bleym
All's OK!	*Alles kits!*	a·luhs kits

family

Do you have a ...?	Heeft u een ...? pol	heyft ew uhn ...
	Heb jij een ...? inf	hep yey uhn ...
I have a ...	Ik heb een ...	ik hep uhn ...
I don't have a ...	Ik heb geen ...	ik hep kheyn ...
brother	broer	broor
daughter	dochter	dokh·tuhr
granddaughter	kleindochter	kleyn·dokh·tuhr
grandson	kleinzoon	kleyn·zohn
husband	man	man
partner (intimate)	partner	part·nuhr
sister	zus	zus
son	zoon	zohn
wife	vrouw	vraw

Are you married?
Bent u getrouwd? pol   bent ew khuh·trawt
Ben je getrouwd? inf   ben yuh khuh·trawt

I live with someone.
Ik woon samen.   ik wohn saa·muhn

I'm ...	Ik ben ...	ik ben ...
married	getrouwd	khuh·trawt
separated	gescheiden	khuh·skhey·duhn
single	vrijgezel	vrey·khuh·zel

farewells

Tomorrow is my last day here.
Morgen is het mijn   mor·khuhn is huht meyn
laatste dag hier.   laat·stuh dakh heer

If you come to (Scotland), you can stay with me.
Als je naar (Schotland)   als yuh naar (skhot·lant)
komt, dan kan je bij mij   komt dan kan yuh bey mey
logeren. inf   lo·zhey·ruhn

Keep in touch!
Laat iets van je horen! laat eets van yuh *hoh*·ruhn

It's been great meeting you.
Het was leuk u/jou te huht was leuk ew/yaw tuh
leren kennen. pol/inf *ley*·ruhn *ke*·nuhn

Here's my …	*Hier is mijn …*	heer is meyn …
What's your …?	*Wat is uw/*	wat is ew/
	jouw …? pol/inf	yaw …
address	*adres*	a·*dres*
email address	*e-mailadres*	ee·meyl·a·dres
phone number	*telefoonnummer*	tey·ley·*fohn*·nu·muhr

well-wishing

Bless you! (for sneezing)	*Gezondheid!*	khuh·*zont*·heyt
Cheers! (toast)	*Proost!*	prohst
Congratulations!	*Gefeliciteerd!*	khuh·fey·lee·see·*teyrt*
Good luck!	*Veel geluk!*	veyl khuh·*luk*
Happy birthday!	*Gefeliciteerd met je verjaardag!*	khuh·fey·lee·see·*teyrt* met yuh vuhr·*yaar*·dakh
Happy carnival!	*Prettige carnaval!*	pre·ti·khuh kar·na·*val*
Happy Easter!	*Zalig Pasen!*	*zaa*·likh *paa*·suhn
Happy festive season!	*Prettige einde- jaarsfeesten!*	pre·ti·khuh eyn·duh· yaars·feys·tuhn
Happy holidays!	*Een fijne vakantie!*	uhn *fey*·nuh va·*kan*·see
Happy New Year!	*Gelukkig nieuwjaar!*	khuh·*lu*·kikh neew·yaar
Happy travels!	*Goede reis!*	*khoo*·duh reys
Have a great Sinterklaas!	*Een fijn sinterklaasfeest!*	uhn feyn sin·tuhr·*klaas*·feyst
Merry Christmas!	*Zalig Kerstmis!*	*zaa*·likh *kerst*·mis

clowning around

They sure know how to turn it on for the *carnaval* kar·na·*val* in the Low Countries. Whatever its origin, the carnival (with Shrove Tuesday) – celebrated in February, just before Lent – was a rite of passage marking the end of winter and the rebirth of nature for the pagans, or contrasting exuberance with abstinence during fasting for Catholics. The carnival heartland lies in the south of the Netherlands and in Flanders – it's said that those north of the rivers Maas and Waal don't know how to handle this feast that's an escape from normal (ie organised) everyday life.

At carnival time, a fever grips the country and everyone lets their hair down. Revellers wear *maskers* mas·kuhrs (masks) and *verkleden zich* vuhr·*kley*·duhn zikh (wear fancy dress), and drink, dance and celebrate with friends and complete strangers alike for days and nights on end. It's OK to act silly and nothing is to be taken seriously – if you venture outside, revellers will drag you into pubs, and you might not emerge for days. Many towns put on a *carnavalstoet* kar·na·*val*·stoot (procession with floats) that carnival groups have worked on for a whole year. Every year, new carnival songs are being composed – and are commercially successful.

It's the ultimate party of nonsense, and one of the best places to witness (and take part in) this debauchery has got to be Maastricht. It's irresistible fun!

In this chapter, phrases are in the informal *je* yuh (you) form only. For more details, see the box **all about you** on page 109.

common interests

algemene interesses

What do you do in your spare time?
Wat doe je in je vrije tijd?   wat doo yuh in yuh *vrey*·yuh teyt

Do you like ...?	*Hou je van ...*	haw yuh van ...
I (don't) like ...	*Ik hou (niet) van ...*	ik haw (neet) van ...
comics	*stripverhalen*	strip·vuhr·haa·luhn
computer games	*computerspelletjes*	kom·*pyoo*·tuhr·spe·luh·chus
cooking	*koken*	*koh*·kuhn
cycling	*fietsen*	*feet*·suhn
dancing	*dansen*	*dan*·suhn
doing terraces	*terrasjes doen*	tuh·*ra*·shuhs doon
drawing	*tekenen*	*tey*·kuh·nuhn
gardening	*tuinieren*	*töy·nee*·ruhn
going out	*uitgaan*	*öyt*·khaan
hiking	*wandelen*	*wan*·duh·luhn
ice-skating	*schaatsen*	*skhaat*·suhn
music	*muziek*	mew·*zeek*
painting	*schilderen*	*skhil*·duh·ruhn
photography	*fotografie*	foh·toh·khra·*fee*
reading	*lezen*	*ley*·zuhn
shopping	*winkelen*	*wing*·kuh·luhn
surfing the internet	*op het internet surfen*	op huht *in*·tuhr·net *sur*·fuhn
travelling	*reizen*	*rey*·zuhn
watching TV	*TV kijken*	tey·*vey key*·kuhn

For types of sports, see **sport**, page 143, and the **dictionary**.

music

Do you dance?	*Dans je?*	dans yuh
Do you play	*Bespeel je*	buh·*speyl* yuh
an instrument?	*een muziek-*	uhn mew·*zeek*·
	instrument?	in·strew·ment
Do you sing?	*Zing je?*	zing yuh
What ... do	*Welke ...*	*wel*·kuh ...
you like?	*vind je leuk?*	vint yuh leuk
bands	*bands* ⑩	bents
	groepen ⑧	*khroo*·puhn
music	*muziek*	mew·*zeek*
singers	*zangers*	*zang*·uhrs
Belgian pop	*Belgische*	*bel*·khi·suh
music	*popmuziek*	*pop*·mew·zeek
classical music	*klassieke muziek*	kla·*see*·kuh mew·*zeek*
Dutch pop music	*Nederpop*	*ney*·duhr·pop
electronic	*elektronische*	ey·lek·*troh*·ni·suh
music	*muziek*	mew·*zeek*
traditional	*traditionele*	tra·dee·syoh·*ney*·luh
music	*muziek*	mew·*zeek*
West Flemish	*West-Vlaamse*	west·*vlaam*·suh
rap	*rapmuziek*	*rep*·mew·zeek
world music	*wereldmuziek*	*wey*·ruhlt·mew·zeek

Off to a concert? See **tickets**, page 46, and **going out**, page 127.

cinema & theatre

I feel like going	*Ik heb zin om naar*	ik hep zin om naar
to a/an ...	*een ... te gaan.*	uhn ... tuh khaan
ballet	*ballet*	ba·*let*
film	*film*	film
opera	*opera*	*oh*·pey·ra
play	*toneelstuk*	to·*neyl*·stuk

SOCIAL

118

Did you like (the film)?
Vond je (de film) leuk?   vont yuh (duh film) leuk

What's showing at the cinema tonight?
Welke films draaien   *wel·*kuh films *draa·*yuhn
vanavond?   va·*naa·*vont

What's showing at the theatre tonight?
Wat staat er op het   wat staat uhr op huht
theaterprogramma   tey·*yaa·*tuhr·proh·*khra·*ma
voor vanavond?   vohr va·*naa·*vont

Is it in (English)?
Is het in het (Engels)?   is huht in huht (*eng·*uhls)

Does it have (English) subtitles?
Is het met (Engelse)   is huht met (*eng·*uhl·suh)
ondertitels?   on·duhr·tee·tuhls

Is this seat taken?
Is deze plaats bezet?   is *dey·*zuh plaats buh·*zet*

Have you got tickets for ...?
Heb jij kaartjes voor ...?   hep yey *kaar·*chus vohr ...

Are there any extra tickets?
Zijn er nog meer kaartjes?   zeyn uhr nokh meyr *kaar·*chus

I'd like cheap/the best tickets.
Ik wil graag de   ik wil khraakh duh
goedkoopste/beste   khoot·*kohp·*stuh/*bes·*tuh
kaartjes.   *kaar·*chus

Is there a matinee show?
Is er een matinee-   is uhr uhn ma·tee·*ney·*
voorstelling?   vohr·ste·ling

Have you seen (*Antonia's Line*)?
Heb jij (Antonia) gezien?   heb yey (an·*toh·*nya) *khuh·*zeen

Who's in it?
Wie speelt er in mee?   wee speylt uhr in mey

It stars (*Jan Decleir*).
Het is met (Jan Decleir).   huht is met (yan duh·*kleyr*)

I thought it was ...	Ik vond het ...	ik vont huht ...
boring	saai Ⓝ	saay
	vervelend Ⓑ	vuhr·*vey*·luhnt
excellent	uitstekend	öyt·*stey*·kuhnt
funny	grappig	*khra*·pikh
interesting	interessant	in·tey·re·*sant*
nothing special	niks speciaals	niks spey·*syaals*
sad	droevig	*droo*·vikh
I (don't) like ...	Ik hou (niet) van ...	ik haw (neet) van ...
action movies	actiefilms	*ak*·see·films
animated films	tekenfilms	*tey*·kuhn·films
(Dutch/	(Nederlandse/	(*ney*·duhr·lant·suh/
Flemish)	Vlaamse)	*vlaam*·suh)
cinema	cinema	see·*ney*·ma
comedies	komedies	koh·*mey*·dees
horror movies	griezelfilms	*khree*·zuhl·films
short films	kortfilms	*kort*·films
war movies	oorlogsfilms	*ohr*·lokhs·films

great small art

The Dutch equivalent of the French *cabaret* is *kleinkunst* *kleyn*·kunst (lit: small-art), with the *luisterlied* *löy*·stuhr·leet (lit: listening-song) the equivalent of the French *chanson*. The term *kleinkunst* is said to refer to the intimate character of the art form. The *Amsterdamse Academie voor Kleinkunst* was founded in 1960. Wim Kan (1911–1983), Toon Hermans (1916–2000), Wim Sonneveld (1917–1974) and Jules de Corte (1924–1996) are much-loved legends. Other successful *kleinkunstenaars* *kleyn*·kuns·tuh·naars (*kleinkunst* artists) are Paul van Vliet, Liesbeth List, Ramses Shaffy, Boudewijn de Groot, Bram Vermeulen and Stef Bos. Pop artists such as Rob de Nijs and Thé Lau are also counted among the best in the genre.

In Flanders, the term *kleinkunst* refers to artists who perform in Dutch, accompanied by a few (usually acoustic) instruments. For a taste of Flemish *kleinkunst*, check out Wannes Van de Velde, Raymond van het Groenewoud or the band Laïs. *Kleinkunstenaars* also make part of the line-up at the annual *Dranouter Folkfestival* dra·*noo*·tuhr folk·fes·ti·val in August.

feelings & opinions
gevoelens & opinies

feelings

gevoelens

Are you ...?	*Bent u ...?* **pol**	bent ew ...
	Ben jij ...? **inf**	ben yey ...
I'm (not) ...	*Ik ben (niet) ...*	ik ben (neet) ...
annoyed	*geërgerd*	khuh·*erkh*·uhrt
disappointed	*teleurgesteld*	tuh·*leur*·khuh·stelt
embarrassed	*gegeneerd*	khuh·zhuh·*neyrt*
happy	*gelukkig*	khuh·*lu*·kikh
in a hurry	*gehaast*	khuh·*haast*
sad	*droevig*	*droo*·vikh
surprised	*verrast*	vuh·*rast*
tired	*moe*	moo
worried	*ongerust*	on·khuh·*rust*
Are you ...?	*Heeft u ...?* **pol**	heyft ew ...
	Heb jij ...? **inf**	hep yey ...
I'm (not) ...	*Ik heb (geen) ...*	ik hep (kheyn) ...
homesick	*heimwee*	*heym*·wey
hungry	*honger*	*hong*·uhr
thirsty	*dorst*	dorst

Are you hot/cold?
Heeft u het warm/koud? **pol**   heyft ew huht warm/kawt
Heb jij het warm/koud? **inf**   hep yey huht warm/kawt

I'm (not) hot/cold.
Ik heb het (niet) warm/koud.   ik hep huht (neet) warm/kawt

Are you well?
Voelt u zich goed? **pol**   voolt ew zikh khoot
Voel je je goed? **inf**   vool ye ye khoot

I'm (not) well.
Ik voel me (niet) goed.   ik vool muh (neet) khoot

If you're not feeling well, see **health**, page 199.

feelings & opinions

121

mixed feelings		
not at all	*helemaal niet*	hey·luh·*maal* neet
I don't care at all.	*Ik geef er helemaal niet om.*	ik kheyf uhr hey·luh·*maal* neet om
a little	*een beetje*	uhn *bey*·chuh
I'm a little sad.	*Ik ben een beetje droevig.*	ik ben uhn *bey*·chuh *droo*·vikh
very	*heel*	heyl
I'm very tired.	*Ik ben heel moe.*	ik ben heyl moo
extremely	*ontzettend*	ont·*ze*·tuhnt
I'm extremely worried.	*Ik ben ontzettend ongerust.*	ik ben ont·*ze*·tuhnt on·khuh·*rust*

opinions

Did you like it?
   Vond u/je het leuk? **pol/inf**   vont ew/yuh huht leuk

What do you think of it?
   Wat vond u/je er van? **pol/inf**   wat vont ew/yuh uhr van

I thought it was ...	*Ik vond het ...*	ik vont huht ...
It's ...	*Het is ...*	huht is ...
awful	*afschuwelijk*	af·*skhew*·wuh·luhk
beautiful	*prachtig*	*prakh*·tikh
boring	*saai* ⓝ	saay
	vervelend ⓑ	vuhr·*vey*·luhnt
(too) expensive	*(te) duur*	(tuh) dewr
great	*geweldig*	khuh·*wel*·dikh
interesting	*interessant*	in·tey·re·*sant*
strange	*raar*	raar

politics & social issues

Who do you vote for?
Voor wie stemt u? pol — vohr wee stemt ew
Voor wie stem je? inf — vohr wee stem yuh

I'm (Australian), but I didn't vote for ...
Ik ben (Australiër/ — ik ben (aw·*straa*·lee·yuhr/
Australische), maar ik — aw·*straa*·li·suh) maar ik
heb niet op ... gestemd. m/f — hep neet op ... khuh·*stemt*

I support the ... party.	*Ik steun de ... partij.*	ik steun duh ... par·*tey*
communist	*communistische*	ko·mew·*nis*·ti·suh
conservative	*conservatieve*	kon·ser·va·*tee*·vuh
democratic	*democratische*	dey·moh·*kraa*·ti·suh
green	*groene*	*khroo*·nuh
liberal	*liberale*	lee·bey·*raa*·luh
social	*sociaal-*	soh·*syaal*·
democratic	*democratische*	dey·moh·*kraa*·ti·shuh
socialist	*socialistische*	soh·sya·*lis*·ti·suh

Did you hear about ...?
Heeft u gehoord over ...? pol — heyft ew khuh·*hohrt* oh·vuhr ...
Heb je gehoord over ...? inf — hep yuh khuh·*hohrt* oh·vuhr ...

Do you agree with it?
Gaat u er mee akkoord? pol — khaat ew uhr mey a·*kohrt*
Ga je er mee akkoord? inf — khaa yuh uhr mey a·*kohrt*

I (don't) agree with ...
Ik ga (niet) akkoord met ... — ik khaa (neet) a·*kohrt* met ...

How do people feel about ...?
Wat denkt men hier — wat dengkt men heer
over ...? — oh·vuhr ...

How can we protest against ...?
Hoe kunnen we — hoo *ku*·nuhn wuh
protesteren tegen ...? — proh·tes·*tey*·ruhn *tey*·khuhn ...

How can we support ...?
Hoe kunnen we ... steunen? — hoo *ku*·nuhn wuh ... *steu*·nuhn

feelings & opi...

abortion	*abortus*	a·*bor*·tus
corruption	*corruptie*	ko·*rup*·see
crime	*misdaad*	*mis*·daad
drugs	*drugs*	drukhs
the economy	*de economie*	duh ey·koh·noh·*mee*
education	*onderwijs* n	on·duhr·*weys*
euthanasia	*euthanasie*	eu·ta·na·*zee*
federalism	*federalisme* n	fey·dey·ra·*lis*·muh
foreign aid	*ontwikkelingshulp*	ont·*wi*·kuh·lings·hulp
globalisation	*globalisering*	khloh·ba·lee·*zey*·ring
human rights	*mensenrechten* n pl	*men*·suh·rekh·tuhn
immigration	*immigratie*	ee·mee·graa·see
language frontier	*taalgrens*	*taal*·khrens
nationalism	*nationalisme* n	na·syoh·na·*lis*·muh
party politics	*partijpolitiek*	par·*tey*·poh·lee·teek
poverty	*armoede*	*ar*·moo·duh
privatisation	*privatisering*	pree·va·tee·*zey*·ring
prostitution	*prostitutie*	pros·tee·*tew*·see
racism	*racisme* n	ra·*sis*·muh
security	*veiligheid*	*vey*·likh·heyt
sexism	*seksisme* n	*sek*·sis·muh
social welfare	*sociale*	soh·*syaa*·luh
	zekerheid	*zey*·kuhr·heyt
taxes	*belastingen*	buh·*las*·ting·uhn
terrorism	*terrorisme* n	te·roh·*ris*·muh
unemployment	*werkloosheid*	*werk*·lohs·heyt
war in (Iraq)	*oorlog in (Irak)*	*ohr*·lokh in (ee·*rak*)

Is there help for (the) …?	*Is er hulp voor …?*	is uhr hulp vohr …
aged	*bejaarden*	buh·*yaar*·duhn
beggars	*bedelaars*	*bey*·duh·laars
homeless	*daklozen*	*dak*·loh·zuhn
street kids	*straatkinderen*	*straat*·kin·duh·ruhn

A hot topic for discussion is the so-called *gedoogbeleid* khu·*dohkh*·buh·leyt (lit: leeway-policy) – the government policy of 'condoning to a certain degree' activities prohibited by law. The notorious example of this in the Netherlands is the use of soft drugs – an illegal activity, *gedoogd* khu·*dohkht* (condoned) in a few circumstances only.

Another concept that has its origin in the Dutch desire to live independently but in harmony with each other is *verzuiling* vuhr·*zöy*·ling (pillarisation) – the practice of organising the social order according to religious and ideological lines. Although this practice is passé now, you'll still find traces of it everywhere. For instance, the various Dutch broadcasters are still linked to religious or social groups, eg AVRO (general), BNN (youth), EO (Protestant), KRO (Catholic), NCRV (Protestant), TROS (general), VARA (social-democratic) and VPRO (progressive programmes). It fits the typical Dutch way of ensuring freedom of expression, pluralism and independence – or, as the Dutch say, *leven en laten leven* ley·vuhn en *laa*·tuhn ley·vuhn (live and let live).

the environment

het milieu

Is this a protected ...?	*Is dit een ...?*	is dit uhn ...
forest	*beschermd bos*	be·*skhermt* bos
park	*beschermd park*	be·*skhermt* park
species	*beschermde soort*	be·*skherm*·duh sohrt

Is there a ... problem here?
Is er hier een probleem met ...?
is uhr heer uhn proh·*bleym* met ...

What should be done about ...?
Wat moet er gebeuren met ...?
wat moot uhr khuh·*beu*·ruhn met ...

feelings & opinions

animal rights	dierenwelzijn n	dee·ruhn·wel·zeyn
carbon dioxide emissions	koolstofdioxide-emissie	kohl·stof·dee·yok·see·duh·ey·mee·see
climate change	klimaat-verandering	klee·maat·vuhr·an·duh·ring
deforestation	ontbossing	ont·bo·sing
drought	droogte	drohkh·tuh
endangered species	bedreigde diersoort	buh·dreykh·duh deer·sohrt
energy savings	energie-besparing	ey·ner·khee·buh·spaa·ring
the environment	het milieu n	huht mil·yeu
flood risk	overstromings-gevaar n	oh·vuhr·stroh·mings·khuh·vaar
genetically modified food	genetisch gemodificeerd voedsel n	khey·ney·tis khuh·moh·dee·fee·seyrt voot·suhl
global warming	broeikaseffect n	brooy·kas·e·fekt
hydroelectricity	waterkracht-centrales	waa·tuhr·krakht·sen·traa·luhs
intensive farming	intensieve landbouw	in·ten·see·vuh lant·baw
irrigation	irrigatie	ee·ree·khaa·see
nuclear energy	atoomenergie	a·tohm·ey·ner·khee
nuclear testing	atoomtesten	a·tohm·tes·tuhn
nuclear waste	nucleair afval n	new·kley·yer af·val
overfertilisation	overbemesting	oh·vuhr·buh·mes·ting
ozone layer	ozonlaag	oh·zon·laakh
pesticides	pesticides	pes·tee·see·duhs
pollution	vervuiling	vuhr·vöy·ling
protected species	beschermde diersoort	buh·skherm·duh deer·sohrt
rising sea levels	stijgend zeeniveau n	stey·khuhnt zey·nee·voh
solar power	zonne-energie	zo·nuh·ey·ner·khee
sustainable energy	duurzame energie	dewr·zaa·muh ey·ner·khee
toxic waste	giftig afval n	khif·tikh af·val
water shortage	watertekort n	waa·tuhr·tuh·kort
water supply	watertoevoer	waa·tuhr·too·voor
wind power	windenergie	wint·ey·ner·khee

where to go

What's there to do in the evenings?
Wat is er 's avonds te doen?
wat is uhr *saa*·vonts tuh doon

What's on …?
Wat is er … te doen?
wat is uhr … tuh doon

locally	*hier*	heer
today	*vandaag*	van·*daakh*
tonight	*vanavond*	va·*naa*·vont
this weekend	*dit weekend*	dit *wey*·kent

Where can I find …?
Waar vind ik de …?
waar vint ik duh …?

(night)clubs	*(nacht)clubs*	(*nakht*·)klups
gay/lesbian venues	*homotenten*	hoh·moh·ten·tuhn
places to eat	*eetgelegenheden*	*eyt*·khuh·ley·khuhn·hey·duhn
pubs	*cafés*	ka·*feys*
	kroegen	*kroo*·khuhn

Is there a local … guide?
Is er een …?
is uhr uhn …

entertainment	*plaatselijke uitgaansgids*	*plaat*·suh·luh·kuh *öyt*·khaans·khits
film	*plaatselijk filmprogramma*	*plaat*·suh·luhk *film*·proh·khra·ma
gay/lesbian	*plaatselijke homogids*	*plaat*·suh·luh·kuh hoh·moh·khits
music	*plaatselijke muziekgids*	*plaat*·suh·luh·kuh mew·*zeek*·khits

I feel like going to a ...	Ik heb zin om naar een ... te gaan.	ik hep zin om naar uhn ... tuh khaan
ballet	balletvoorstelling	ba·*let*·vohr·ste·ling
bar	bar	bar
café	koffiehuisje ⓝ	ko·fee·höy·shuh
	brasserie ⓑ	bra·suh·*ree*
concert	concert	kon·*sert*
dance performance	dansvoorstelling	dans·vohr·ste·ling
film	film	film
karaoke bar	karaoke	ka·ra·*oh*·key
nightclub	nachtclub	nakht·klup
party	feestje/fuif ⓝ/ⓑ	fey·shuh/föyf
performance	voorstelling	vohr·ste·ling
play	toneelvoorstelling	to·*neyl*· vohr·ste·ling
pub	café/kroeg	ka·*fey*/krookh
restaurant	restaurant	res·toh·*rant*

For more on types of places to drink and eat, see the box **places to eat & drink**, page 164.

to be or to have – that's the question

Some common expressions that require the verb 'be' in English use *hebben* he·buhn (have) in Dutch:

to be hungry	honger hebben	hong·uhr he·buhn
to be in a hurry	haast hebben	haast he·buhn
to be on leave	vakantie hebben	va·kan·see he·buhn
to be right	gelijk hebben	khu·*leyk* he·buhn
to be sleepy	slaap hebben	slaap he·buhn
to be thirsty	dorst hebben	dorst he·buhn
to be unlucky	pech hebben	pekh he·buhn
to be wrong	ongelijk hebben	on·khuh·leyk he·buhn

invitations

What are you doing ...?	Wat zijn je plannen voor ...?	wat zeyn yuh pla·nuhn vohr ...
now	nu	new
tonight	vanavond	va·naa·vont
this weekend	dit weekend	dit wey·kent

Would you like to go for a ...?	Heb je zin in een ...?	hep yuh zin in uhn ...
I feel like going for a ...	Ik heb zin in een ...	ik hep zin in uhn ...
beer	biertje	beer·chuh
coffee	koffie	ko·fee
drink	drankje	drangk·yuh
meal	maaltijd	maal·teyt
walk	wandeling	wan·duh·ling

Would you like to go ...?	Heb je zin om ...?	hep yuh zin om ...
I feel like going ...	Ik heb zin om ...	ik hep zin om ...
dancing	te gaan dansen	tuh khaan dan·suhn
out somewhere	uit te gaan	öyt tuh khaan

My round.
Mijn rondje. meyn ron·chuh

Do you know a good restaurant?
Ken je een goed restaurant? ken yuh uhn khoot res·toh·rant

Do you want to come to the concert with me?
Zou je met mij naar het concert willen gaan? zaw yuh met mey naar huht kon·sert wi·luhn khaan

We're having a party.
We houden een feestje/fuif. ⓝ/ⓑ wuh haw·duhn uhn fey·shuh/föyf

You should come.
Ik hoop dat je komt. ik hohp dat yuh komt

responding to invitations

Sure!	*Natuurlijk!*	na·*tewr*·luhk
Yes, I'd love to.	*Ja, graag.*	yaa khraakh

That's very kind of you.
Dat is erg vriendelijk van u/je. pol/inf

dat is erkh *vreen*·duh·luhk van ew/yuh

Where shall we go?
Waar zullen we naar toe gaan?

waar *zu*·luhn wuh naar too khaan

No, I'm afraid I can't.
Nee, ik vrees dat ik niet kan.

ney ik vreys dat ik neet kan

Sorry, I can't sing/dance.
Sorry, maar ik kan niet zingen/dansen.

so·ree maar ik kan neet zing·uhn/*dan*·suhn

What about tomorrow?
Misschien morgen?

mi·*skheen mor*·khuhn

orange origins

Ever wondered why the supporters of Dutch national teams at sports matches invariably dress up in *oranje* oh·*ran*·yuh (orange), when the colour doesn't even appear on the Dutch flag? The answer's simple: orange is the national colour of the Netherlands because it refers to the Royal Family's name – *Oranje-Nassau* oh·*ran*·yuh na·saw. The family is known by this name because it used to own the principality of Orange in the south of France. As for the national flag, the orange colour was indeed present on it in earlier times, but it has been replaced with red. On royal birthdays, however, an orange banner is also displayed alongside the standard tricolour as a sign of people's allegiance to the Royal Family. For more on the celebration of national pride on Queen's Day – when the whole country goes orange for the festivities – see the box **party on in the netherlands** on page 42.

arranging to meet

What time will we meet?
Hoe laat spreken we af? hoo laat *sprey*·kuhn wuh af

Where will we meet?
Waar spreken we af? waar *sprey*·kuhn wuh af

Let's meet at … *We zien elkaar …* wuh zeen el·*kaar* …
  (eight) o'clock *om (acht) uur* om (akht) ewr
  the (entrance) *bij de (ingang)* bey duh (*in*·khang)

I'll pick you up. *Ik pik je op.* ik pik yuh op
Are you ready? *Ben je klaar?* ben yuh klaar
I'm ready. *Ik ben klaar.* ik ben klaar
I'll be coming later. *Ik kom later.* ik kom *laa*·tuhr
Where will you be? *Waar vind ik je?* waar vint ik yuh

If I'm not there by (nine), don't wait for me.
Wacht niet op mij als ik er wakht neet op mey als ik uhr
om (negen) uur niet ben. om (*ney*·khuhn) ewr neet ben

I'll see you then!
Tot dan! tot dan

See you later/tomorrow.
Tot later/morgen. tot *laa*·tuhr/*mor*·khuhn

I'm looking forward to it.
Ik kijk er echt naar uit. ik keyk uhr ekht naar öyt

Sorry I'm late.
Sorry dat ik laat ben. so·ree dat ik laat ben
Never mind.
Geen probleem. kheyn proh·*bleym*

131

drugs

I don't take drugs.
  Ik gebruik geen drugs.   ik khuh·*bröyk* kheyn drukhs

I take ... occasionally.
  Ik gebruik af en toe ...   ik khuh·*bröyk* af en too ...

Do you want to have a smoke?
  Wil je roken?   wil yuh *roh*·kuhn

Do you have a light?
  Heb je een vuurtje?   hep yuh uhn *vewr*·chuh

If the police are talking to you about drugs, see **police**, page 196, for useful phrases.

---

safe swearing

Dutch has many colourful – and often strong – swear words. This said, swearing in public is a definite no-no and will, at the least, be frowned upon and reflect badly on the perpetrator (even if English is their language of choice). Problems are expected to be dealt with in a calm, rational and constructive manner. When something really goes wrong, you can express your frustration in public with a number of safe and acceptable 'swear' options as long as you don't overuse them ... and continue to solve the problem without antics. The following expressions are corruptions of more heavy-handed or blasphemous swearing words.

Potverdorie!	*pot*·vuhr·doh·ree
Verdorie!	vuhr·*doh*·ree
Verdomme!	vuhr·*do*·muh

romance
romantiek

In this chapter, phrases are in the informal *je* yuh (you) form only. For more details, see the box **all about you** on page 109.

asking someone out

iemand uit vragen

Where would you like to go (tonight)?
Waar wil je (vanavond)   waar wil yuh (va·*naa*·vont)
graag heen?   khraakh heyn?

Would you like to do something (tomorrow)?
Wil je (morgen)   wil yuh (*mor*·khuhn)
iets gaan doen?   eets khaan doon

Yes, I'd love to.
Ja, graag.   yaa khraakh

Sorry, I can't.
Sorry, maar ik kan niet.   so·ree maar ik kan neet

local talk

He's a babe.	*Hij is een mooierd.*	hey is uhn *moh*·yuhrt
She's a babe.	*Zij is een schoonheid.*	zey is uhn *skhohn*·heyt
He/She is hot.	*Hij/Zij is een lekker stuk.*	hey/zey is uhn *le*·kuhr stuk
He's a bastard.	*Hij is een eikel.* (lit: he is a dickhead)	hey is uhn *ey*·kuhl
	Hij is een zak. (lit: he is a bag)	hey is uhn zak
She's a bitch.	*Zij is een teef.* (lit: she is a bitch)	zey is uhn teyf
	Zij is een heks. (lit: she is a witch)	zey is uhn heks
He/She gets around.	*Hij/Zij slaapt met iedereen.*	hey/zey slaapt met ee·duh·*reyn*

romance

pick-up lines

Would you like a drink?
Wil je iets drinken? wil yuh eets *dring*·kuhn

You look like someone I know.
Jij lijkt op iemand die ik ken. yey leykt op *ee*·mant dee ik ken

You're a fantastic dancer.
Jij danst fantastisch. yey danst fan·*tas*·tees

Do you have a light?
Mag ik een vuurtje? makh ik uhn *vewr*·chuh

Do you hate pick-up lines too?
Heb jij ook zo'n hekel hep yey ohk zohn *hey*·kuhl
aan versiertrucs? aan vuhr·*seer*·truks

I'm attracted to your phone number.
Ik voel me aangetrokken ik vool muh *aan*·khuh·tro·kuhn
tot jouw telefoonnummer. tot yaw tey·ley·*fohn*·nu·muhr

If you think you can pick me up, then you're right.
Als je denkt mij te als yuh dengkt mey tuh
kunnen versieren, dan *ku*·nuhn vuhr·*see*·ruhn dan
heb je het goed. hep yuh huht khoot

Those clothes would look great in a pile next to my bed.
Die kleding zou dee *kley*·ding zaw
geweldig staan op een khuh·*wel*·dikh staan op uhn
hoopje naast mijn bed. *hohp*·yuh naast meyn bet

Can I ...? **Mag ik ...?** makh ik ...
dance with you met je dansen met yuh *dan*·suhn
sit here hier zitten heer *zi*·tuhn
take you home je naar huis yuh naar höys
vergezellen vuhr·khuh·*ze*·luhn

rejections

I'm here with my girlfriend/boyfriend.
Ik ben hier met mijn   ik ben heer met meyn
vriendin/vriend.   vreen·*din*/vreent

Excuse me, I have to go now.
Sorry maar ik moet   *so*·ree maar ik moot
er vandoor.   uhr van·*dohr*

I'd rather not.   *Liever niet.*   *lee*·vuhr neet
No, thank you.   *Nee, dank je wel.*   ney dangk yuh wel

hard talk

The language below is very firm and only to be used if you're being badly hassled.

Donder op!	*don*·duhr op	Piss off!
Hoepel op!	*hoo*·puhl op	Piss off!
Hou je mond!	haw yuh mont	Shut up!
Laat me met rust!	laat met rust	Leave me alone!
Val dood!	val doht	Drop dead!

getting closer

I really like you.   *Ik vind je echt leuk.*   Ik vint yuh ekht leuk
You're great.   *Jij bent fantastisch.*   yey bent fan·*tas*·tees
Can I kiss you?   *Mag ik je kussen?*   makh ik yuh *ku*·suhn

Do you want to come inside for a while?
Wil je eventjes   wil yuh *ey*·vuhn·chuhs
binnen komen?   *bi*·nuhn *koh*·muhn

Would you like to stay over?
Wil je blijven slapen?   wil yuh *bley*·vuhn *slaa*·puhn

Can I stay over?
Kan ik blijven slapen?   kan ik *bley*·vuhn *slaa*·puhn

seks

Kiss me.
Kus me. kus muh

I want you.
Ik wil je. ik wil yuh

Let's go to bed.
Laten we naar bed gaan. laa·tuhn wuh naar bet khaan

Touch me here.
Raak me hier aan. raak muh heer aan

Do you like this?
Vind je dit fijn? vint yuh dit feyn

I (don't) like that.
Ik vind dat (niet) fijn. ik vint dat (neet) feyn

I think we should stop now.
Ik denk dat we er hier mee ik denk dat wuh uhr heer mey
moeten stoppen. moo·tuhn sto·puhn

Do you have a (condom)?
Heb jij een (condoom)? hep yey uhn (kon·dohm)

Let's use a (condom).
Laten we een (condoom) laa·tuhn wuh uhn (kon·dohm)
gebruiken. khuh·bröy·kuhn

I won't do it without protection.
Ik doe het niet zonder ik doo huht neet zon·duhr
voorbehoedmiddel. voor·buh·hoot·mi·duhl

It's my first time.
Het is mijn eerste keer. huht is meyn eyr·stuh keyr

It helps to have a sense of humour.
Het helpt als je een goed huht helpt als yuh uhn khoot
gevoel voor humor hebt. khuh·vool vohr hew·mor hept

Is that why you're single?
Is dat waarom je is dat waa·rom yuh
vrijgezel bent? vrey·khuh·zel bent

Oh my god!	*Hemeltje!*	*hey·muhl·chuh*
That's great.	*Dat is fantastisch!*	dat is fan·*tas*·tees
Easy tiger!	*Zachtjesaan*	*zakh*·yuhs·aan
	lekker stuk!	*le*·kuhr stuk
That was ...	*Dat was ...*	dat was ...
heavenly	*hemels*	*hey*·muhls
incredible	*ongelofelijk*	on·khuh·*loh*·fuh·luhk
romantic	*romantisch*	roh·*man*·tees
wild	*wild*	wilt

sweet nothings

engeltje	eng·uhl·*chuh*	little angel
gekkie	*khe*·kee	little fool
liefje	*leef*·yuh	little darling
mooierd	*moh*·yuhrt	beauty **m**
schatje	*skha*·chuh	little treasure
schoonheid	*skhohn*·heyt	beauty **f**
tijgertje	*tey*·khuhr·chuh	little tiger
troetelbeertje	*troo*·tuhl·beyr·chuh	little cuddly bear

love

liefde

I think we're good together.
Ik vind dat we goed bij ik vint dat wuh khoot bey
elkaar passen. el·*kaar* pa·suhn

I love you.	*Ik hou van je.*	ik haw van yuh
Will you ...?	*Wil je met ...?*	wil yuh met ...
go out with me	*me uitgaan*	muh *öyt*·khaan
marry me	*me trouwen*	muh *traw*·wuhn
meet my	*mijn ouders*	meyn *aw*·duhrs
parents	*kennismaken*	ke·nis *maa*·kuhn

romance

problems

I don't think it's working out.
Ik denk dat het niet lukt
tussen ons tweetjes.

ik dengk dat huht neet lukt
tu·suhn ons *twey*·chus

Are you seeing someone else?
Heb je iemand anders?

hep yuh *ee*·mant *an*·duhrs

He/She is just a friend.
Hij/Zij is alleen maar
een vriend/vriendin. m/f

hey/zey is a·*leyn* maar
uhn vreent/vreen·*din*

You're just using me for sex.
Je gebruikt me alleen
maar voor de seks.

yuh khuh·*bröykt* muh a·*leyn*
maar vohr duh seks

I want to call it off.
Ik wil het uitmaken.

ik wil huht öyt·maa·kuhn

I never want to see you again.
Ik wil je nooit meer zien.

ik wil yuh noyt meyr zeen

We'll work it out.
We lossen het wel op.

wuh *lo*·suhn huht wel op

leaving

I have to leave (tomorrow).
Ik moet (morgen)
vertrekken.

ik moot (*mor*·khuhn)
vuhr·*tre*·kuhn

I'll ...   *Ik zal ...*   ik zal ...
  keep in touch   *contact houden*   kon·*takt haw*·duhn
  miss you   *je missen*   yuh *mi*·suhn
  visit you   *je opzoeken*   yuh *op*·zoo·kuhn

religion

godsdienst

What's your religion?
Wat is uw/jouw godsdienst? pol/inf
wat is ew/yaw khots·deenst

I'm not religious.
Ik ben niet gelovig.
ik ben neet khuh·loh·vikh

I'm …	Ik ben …	ik ben …
agnostic	*agnostisch*	akh·nos·tees
Buddhist	*boeddhist*	boo·dist
Catholic	*katholiek*	ka·toh·leek
Christian	*christelijk*	kris·tuh·luhk
Hindu	*hindoe*	hin·doo
Jewish	*joods*	yohts
Lutheran	*luthers*	lew·tuhrs
Muslim	*moslim*	mos·lim
Protestant	*protestants*	proh·tes·tans

I (don't) believe in …	Ik geloof (niet) in …	ik khuh·lohf (neet) in …
astrology	*astrologie*	a·stroh·loh·khee
fate	*het lot*	huht lot
God	*God*	khot

Can I … here?	Kan ik hier …?	kan ik heer …
Where can I …?	Waar kan ik …?	waar kan ik …
attend a service	*een dienst bijwonen*	uhn deenst bey·woh·nuhn
attend mass	*een mis bijwonen*	uhn mis bey·woh·nuhn
pray/worship	*bidden*	bi·duhn

cultural differences

I didn't mean to do/say anything wrong.

Het was niet mijn	huht was neet meyn
bedoeling iets verkeerds	buh·*doo*·ling eets vuhr·*keyrts*
te doen/zeggen.	tuh doon/*ze*·khuhn

Is this a local or national custom?

Is dit een plaatselijk of	is dit uhn *plaat*·suh·luhk of
een algemeen gebruik?	uhn al·khuh·*meyn* khuh·*bröyk*

I don't want to offend you.

Ik wil u/je niet	ik wil ew/yuh neet
beledigen. pol/inf	buh·*ley*·di·khuhn

I'm not used to this.

Ik ben dit niet gewend.	ik ben dit neet khuh·*went*

I'd rather not join in.

Ik doe liever niet mee.	ik doo *lee*·vuhr neet mey

I'll try it.

Ik probeer het.	ik proh·*beyr* huht

I'm sorry, it's	Sorry, maar het	so·ree maar huht
against my ...	druist in tegen ...	dröyst in *tey*·khuhn ...
beliefs	*hetgeen*	huht·*kheyn*
	waarin ik geloof	waa·*rin* ik khuh·*lohf*
principles	*mijn principes*	meyn prin·*see*·puhs
religion	*mijn*	meyn
	godsdienst	*khots*·deenst

This is ...	Dit is ...	dit is ...
different	*anders*	*an*·duhrs
fun	*leuk*	leuk
interesting	*interessant*	in·tey·re·*sant*

When's the gallery open?
Wanneer is de
kunstgalerie open?
wa·*neyr* is duh
kunst·kha·luh·*ree* oh·puhn

When's the museum open?
Wanneer is het museum
open?
wa·*neyr* is huht mew·*zey*·yum
oh·puhn

What kind of art are you interested in?
In welke soort kunst ben je
geïnteresseerd?
in *wel*·kuh sohrt kunst ben yuh
khuh·in·tey·re·*seyrt*

What's in the collection?
Waaruit bestaat de
collectie?
waa·*röyt* buh·*staat* duh
koh·*lek*·see

What do you think of ...?
Wat vind je van ...?
wat vint yuh van ...

It's an exhibition of ...
Het is een
tentoonstelling van ...
huht is uhn
tuhn·*tohn*·ste·ling van ...

I'm interested in ...
Ik ben geïnteresseerd in ...
ik ben khuh·in·tey·re·*seyrt* in ...

I like the works of ...
Ik hou van het werk van ...
ik haw van huht werk van ...

It reminds me of ...
Het doet me
denken aan ...
huht doot muh
deng·kuhn aan ...

architecture	architectuur	ar·khee·tek·tewr
art	kunst	kunst
artwork	kunstwerk n	kunst·werk
curator	curator	kew·raa·tor
design (artwork) n	ontwerp n	ont·werp
etching	etsen	et·suhn
exhibit n	voorwerp n	vohr·werp
exhibition hall	zaal	zaal
graphic a	grafisch	khraa·fis
installation	installatie	in·sta·laa·see
opening (exhibition)	opening	oh·puh·ning
opening (theatre)	première	pruh·myey·ruh
painter	schilder	skhil·duh
painting (artwork)	schilderij n	skhil·duh·rey
painting (technique)	schilderkunst	skhil·duh·kunst
performance	voorstelling	vohr·ste·ling
period	periode	pey·ryoh·duh
permanent	permanente	per·ma·nen·tuh
collection	tentoonstelling	tuhn·tohn·ste·ling
print n	druk	druk
sculptor	beeldhouwer	beylt·haw·wuhr
sculpture	beeldhouwwerk n	beylt·haw·werk
statue	standbeeld n	stant·beylt
style n	stijl	steyl
technique	techniek	tekh·neek
varnishing day	vernissage	ver·nee·saa·zhuh

art through the ages

Amsterdamse School   am·stuhr·dam·suh skhohl
Amsterdam School – an architectural movement from the first half of the 20th century

de CoBrA groep   duh koh·bra khroop
the CoBrA group – a 1940s avant-garde group of artists from Copenhagen, Brussels and Amsterdam

De Stijl   duh steyl
De Stijl (lit: the style) – a group of artists, architects and designers in the Netherlands during the 1920s and 1930s

Vlaamse Primitieven   vlaam·suh pree·mee·tee·vuhn
Flemish Primitives – a group of painters from the 15th century

sporting interests

What sport do you follow/play?
Welke sport volg/
beoefen je?
wel·kuh sport volkh/
buh·oo·fuhn yuh

I follow ...	*Ik volg het ...*	ik volkh huht ...
I play ...	*Ik speel ...*	ik speyl ...
basketball	*basketball*	bas·ket·bal
football (soccer)	*voetbal*	voot·bal
hockey	*hockey*	ho·kee
tennis	*tennis*	te·nis
volleyball	*volleybal*	vo·lee·bal
I follow ...	*Ik volg ...*	ik volkh ...
athletics	*de atletiek*	duh at·ley·teek
cycling	*het wielrennen*	huht weel·re·nuhn
I do ...	*Ik ...*	ik ...
athletics	*doe aan atletiek*	doo aan at·ley·teek
ice-skating	*schaats*	skhaats
karate	*doe aan karate*	doo aan ka·raa·tey
motorcross	*doe aan motorcross*	doo aan moh·tor·kros
scuba diving	*duik*	döyk
I ...	*Ik ...*	ik ...
cycle (casual)	*fiets*	feets
cycle (competitive)	*doe aan wielrennen*	doo aan weel·re·nuhn
run	*jog*	dzhokh
ski	*ski*	skee
swim	*zwem*	zwem
walk	*wandel*	wan·duhl

For more sports, see the **dictionary**.

Korfbal korf·bal (korfball) is a cross between netball, volleyball and basketball. Two (usually mixed) teams try to score goals by passing the ball through a cane basket mounted on a pole. The baskets on each end of the court have no board for the ball to rebound off. The playing field stretches beyond the baskets, so players can shoot from every angle, including from behind the baskets.

The *duivensport* döy·vuhn·sport (pigeon racing) is popular, especially in Flanders where you'll see many houses with a *duiventil* döy·vuhn·til (pigeon loft) in the backyard and people with pigeon-filled cane baskets on their bicycles, going to the pigeon-racing club on a race day. Not only older people but also youngsters take up the sport for its social dimension and for the 'love of the pigeon'.

A Frisian sport is *fierljeppen* feer·lye·puhn (pole-vaulting across canals). Unlike in pole-vaulting of the track-and-field variety (called *polsstokspringen* pol·stok·spring·uhn in Dutch), it's the distance covered that counts, not the height. Incredible distances are achieved by climbing the pole hand-over-hand while it's in motion. The current record stands at 19.40 metres.

going to a game

naar een wedstrijd gaan

Would you like to go to a game?
| Wil je graag naar een wedstrijd gaan? | wil yuh khraakh naar uhn wet·streyt khaan |

Who are you supporting?
| Wie is je team? | wee is yuh·teem |

What's the score?
| Wat is de stand? | wat is duh stant |

Who's ...? | *Wie ...?* | wee ...
| playing | *speelt er* | speylt uhr |
| winning | *gaat er winnen* | khaat uhr wi·nuhn |

That was a ...	*Dat was een ...*	dat was uhn ...
game!	*wedstrijd!*	*wet·streyt*
bad	*slechte*	*slekh·*tuh
boring	*saaie*	*saa·*yuh
captivating	*boeiende*	*boo·*yuhn·duh
great	*fantastische*	fan·*tas·*tee·suh
nerve-wrecking	*spannende*	*spa·*nuhn·duh

cheering on

C'mon Holland!	*Hup Holland hup!*	hup *ho·*lant hup
Go (Holland)!	*Kom op (Holland)!*	kom op (*ho·*lant)
	Kom op (Oranje)!	kom op (oh·*ran·*yuh)
Go (Belgium)!	*Allez (België)!*	a·*ley* (*bel·*khee·yuh)
A goal for (the Red Devils)!	*Een goal voor (de Rode Duivels)!*	uhn khohl vohr (duh *roh·*duh *döy·*vuhls)

playing sport

aan sport doen

Do you want to play/join in?
Wil je spelen/meedoen?   wil yuh *spey·*luhn/*mey·*doon

Can I join in?
Kan ik meedoen?   kan ik *mey·*doon

I have an injury.
Ik heb een blessure.   ik hep uhn ble·*sew·*ruh

Your/My point.
Een punt voor jou/mij.   uhn punt vohr yaw/mey

Kick/Pass it to me!
Geef het aan mij!   kheyf huht aan mey

You're a good player.
Je bent een goede speler.   yuh bent uhn *khoo·*duh *spey·*luhr

Thanks for the game.
Bedankt voor de wedstrijd.   buh·*dangkt* vohr duh *wet·*streyt

Congratulations on the victory.
Gefeliciteerd met de overwinning.   khuh·*fey·*lee·see·*teyrt* met duh oh·vuhr·*wi·*ning

Where's a good place to ...?	Waar is er een goede plek om te gaan ...?	waar is uhr uhn khoo·duh plek om tuh khaan ...
fish	vissen	vi·suhn
run	joggen	dzho·khuhn
surf	surfen	sur·fuhn

Where's the nearest ...?	Waar is het dichtsbijzijnde ...?	waar is huht dikhts·bey·zeyn·duh ...
golf course	golfterrein	kholf·tuh·reyn
gym	fitnesscentrum	fit·nuhs·sen·trum
swimming pool	zwembad	zwem·bat

Do I have to be a member to attend?
Is lidmaatschap verplicht?   is lit·maat·skhap vuhr·plikht

Is there a women-only session?
Is er een tijd voor   is uhr uhn teyt vohr
vrouwen alleen?   vraw·wuhn a·leyn

Where are the changing rooms?
Waar zijn de kleedkamers?   waar zeyn duh kleyt·kaa·muhrs

What's the charge per ...?	Hoeveel kost het per ...?	hoo·veyl kost huht puhr ...
day	dag	dakh
game	spel	spel
hour	uur	ewr
visit	bezoek	buh·zook

Can I hire a ...?	Kan ik een ... huren?	kan ik uhn ... hew·ruhn
ball	bal	bal
bicycle	fiets	feets
court (basketball)	terrein	tuh·reyn
court (tennis)	(tennis)baan	(te·nis·)baan
racket	racket	re·kuht

SOCIAL

146

sports talk

What a ...!	*Wat een ...!*	wat uhn ...
goal	*goal*	gohl/khohl ⓝ/ⓑ
hit	*slag*	slakh
kick	*trap*	trap
pass	*pas*	pas
performance	*performance*	puhr·*fohr*·muhns
shot	*schot*	skhot

cycling

wielrennen

In the Low Countries, *wielrennen* weel·re·nuhn (competitive cycling) is hugely popular and has produced many successful *kampioenen* kam·pee·*yoo*·nuhn (champions). During March and April, Belgium is in the grip of the *Belgische klassiekers* bel·khi·suh kla·*see*·kuhrs (Belgian one-day classics), which include the prestigious and spectacular *Ronde van Vlaanderen* ron·duh van *vlaan*·duh·ruhn (Tour of Flanders). The main event around the same time in Holland is the Amstel Gold Race.

Where does the race start/finish?
Waar is de start/aankomst?   waar is duh start/*aan*·komst

Where does the race pass through?
Waar komt de   waar komt duh
wedstrijd door?   *wet*·streyt dohr

How many kilometres is today's stage/race?
Hoeveel kilometer is   hoo·*veyl kee*·lo·mey·tuhr is
de rit/wedstrijd   duh rit/*wet*·streyt
van vandaag?   van van·*daakh*

Who's winning?
Wie leidt?   wee leyt

My favourite cyclist is ...
Mijn favoriete   meyn fa·voh·*ree*·tuh
wielrenner is ...   *weel*·re·nuhr is ...

Which cycling team is he in?
Voor welk team rijdt hij?   vohr welk teem reyt hey

attack n	*aanval*	*aan*·val
breakaway	*ontsnapping*	ont·*sna*·ping
(mechanical) breakdown	*(materiaal)pech*	(ma·tey·*ryaal*·)pekh
chasers	*achtervolgers*	akh·tuhr·*vol*·khuhrs
climb n	*klim*	klim
cobblestones (pavé)	*kasseien*	ka·*sey*·yuhn
crash n	*val*	val
cyclist	*wielrenner*	*weel*·re·nuhr
descent	*afdaling*	*af*·daa·ling
domestique	*knecht*	knekht
drug test	*dopingcontrole*	*doh*·ping·kon·*troh*·luh
flat tyre	*lekke/platte band* ⑧/Ⓑ	*le*·kuh/*pla*·tuh bant
gear	*versnelling*	vuhr·*sne*·ling
individual time trial	*individuele tijdrit*	in·dee·vee·dew·*wey*·luh *teyt*·rit
(yellow) jersey	*(gele) trui*	(*khey*·luh) tröy
leaders	*kopgroep*	*kop*·khroop
main rider (of a team)	*kopman*	*kop*·man
mountain stage	*bergrit*	*berkh*·rit
peloton	*peloton* n	puh·luh·*ton*
rainbow jersey (world champion)	*regenboogtrui*	*rey*·khun·bohkh·tröy
ranking	*klassement* n	kla·suh·*ment*
red lantern (last cyclist in race)	*rode lantaarn*	*roh*·duh lan·*taarn*
soigneur	*verzorger*	vuhr·*zor*·khuhr
spring classics	*voorjaars- klassiekers*	*vohr*·yaars·kla·*see*·kuhrs
sprint n	*sprint*	sprint
stage (in race)	*rit*	rit
stage winner	*ritwinnaar*	*rit*·wi·naar
team car	*volgwagen*	*volkh*·waa·khun
team time trial	*ploegentijdrit*	*ploo*·khuhn·teyt·rit
winner	*winnaar*	*wi*·naar

For phrases on getting around by bike, see **transport**, page 57.

extreme sports

I'd like to go …
Ik wil graag gaan …   ik wil khraakh khaan …

I'd like to try …
Ik wil graag … proberen.   ik wil khraakh … proh·bey·ruhn

beachsailing	*strandzeilen* n	*strant*·zey·luhn
caving	*speleologie*	spey·ley·yoh·loh·*khee*
game fishing	*sportvissen* n	*sport*·vi·suhn
hang-gliding	*deltavliegen* n	*del*·ta·vlee·khuhn
parasailing	*zeilvliegen* n	*zeyl*·vlee·khuhn
rock-climbing	*rotsklimmen* n	*rots*·kli·muhn
sailing	*zeilen* n	*zey*·luhn
skydiving	*parachute-springen* n	pa·ra·*shew*·tuh·spring·uhn
white-water rafting	*wildwatervaren*	wilt·*waa*·tuhr·vaa·ruhn

Is the equipment secure?
Is deze uitrusting veilig?   is *dey*·zuh öyt·rus·ting *vey*·likh

Is this safe?
Is dit veilig?   is dit *vey*·likh

This is insane.
Dit is krankzinnig.   dit is krangk·*zi*·nikh

For words or phrases you might need while hiking or trekking, see **outdoors**, page 157, and **camping**, page 70.

ice-skating

How long is a session?
Hoe lang is een sessie?   hoo lang is uhn se·see

How much for a session?
Hoeveel kost een sessie?   hoo·*veyl* kost uhn se·see

Can I rent ice skates?
Kan ik schaatsen huren?   kan ik *skhaat*·suhn *hew*·ruhn

My size is (40).
Ik heb maat (veertig). ik hep maat (*feyr*·tikh)

I need an extra pair of socks.
Ik heb een extra paar ik hep uhn *ek*·straa paar
sokken nodig. *so*·kuhn *noh*·dikh

Can I have my ice skates sharpened?
Kan ik mijn schaatsen kan ik meyn *skhaat*·suhn
laten slijpen? *laa*·tuhn *sley*·puhn

How thick is the ice?
Hoe dik is het ijs? hoo dik is huht eys

Are there any cracks in the ice?
Zijn er barsten in het ijs? zeyn uhr *bars*·tuhn in huht eys

Will it be thawing?
Gaat het dooien? khaat huht *doh*·yuhn

Is it safe to go on this ice?
Is het veilig op dit ijs is huht *vey*·likh op dit eys
te gaan? tuh khaan

How deep is the water under this ice?
Hoe diep is het water hoo deep is huht *waa*·tuhr
onder dit ijs? *on*·duhr dit eys

Sorry, I couldn't stop.
Sorry, ik kon niet stoppen. *so*·ree ik kon neet *sto*·puhn

Are you all right?
Gaat het? khaat huht

Ouch, that hurts!
Au, dat doet pijn! aw dat doot peyn

---

listen for ...

Blijf van het ijs! bleyf van huht eys	**Stay off the ice!**
Ga niet op dat ijs! khaa neet op dat eys	**Don't go on that ice!**
Dat ijs is gevaarlijk! dat eys is khuh·*vaar*·luhk	**That ice is dangerous!**
Het gaat dooien. huht khaat *doh*·yuhn	**The thaw is setting in.**

winter fun

Travelling in the Low Countries during winter can be a lot of fun – not only will there be fewer tourists, but you'll be able to enjoy a vast array of typical winter activities. Over the festive season, many towns set up *kerstijsbanen* kerst·eys·baa·nuhn (temporary Christmas ice rinks) in the main square, often as part of their *kerstmarkt* kerst·markt (Christmas market). You can sip *glühwein* khlew·waayn (hot spiced wine) or *jenever* yuh·ney·vuhr/zhuh·ney·vuhr Ⓝ/Ⓑ (gin) with the locals while trying some typical hearty winter snacks to keep you warm. If you're lucky enough to get some snow, you might want to try *langlaufen* lang·law·fuhn (cross-country skiing) or go *sleetje rijden* sley·chuh rey·duhn (tobogganing). And if you're really lucky and the weather gets truly cold for an extended period, you might catch the Netherlands' legendary *Elfstedentocht* elf·stey·duhn·tokht (Eleven Cities Tour), a speed-skating competition as well as a leisure-skating tour – albeit gruelling – of nearly 200 kilometres through the province of Friesland, which has been held 15 times since 1909.

figure skating	kunstrijden (op de schaats) n	kunst·rey·duhn (op duh skhaats)
gloves	handschoenen	hant·skoo·nuhn
ice	ijs n	eys
ice-boating	ijszeilen n	eys·zey·luhn
ice field	ijsvlakte	eys·vlak·tuh
ice hockey	ijshockey n	eys·ho·kee
(indoor) ice rink	(overdekte) ijsbaan	(oh·vuhr·dek·tuh) eys·baan
ice skates	schaatsen	skhaat·suhn
ice-skating	schaatsen n	skhaat·suhn
ice-skating club	ijsclub	eys·klup
ice-skating competition	schaatswedstrijd	skhaats·wet·streyt
ice-skating tour	schaatstocht	skhaats·tokht
mittens	wanten	wan·tuhn
speed skating	hardrijden (op de schaats) n	hard·rey·duhn (op duh skhaats)
temporary ice rink	tijdelijke ijsbaan	tey·duh·luh·kuh eys·baan
walking on skates	klunen	klew·nuhn

icy words

have an affair
een scheve   uhn *skhey*·vuh
schaats rijden   skhaats *rey*·duhn
(lit: skate with a bent skate)

pace up and down
ijsberen   *eys*·bey·ruhn
(lit: walk like a polar bear)

a stony stare
een ijskoude blik   uhn *eys*·kaw·duh blik
(lit: an ice-cold stare)

take no risks
niet over één nacht   neet *oh*·vuhr eyn nakht
ijs gaan   eys khaan
(lit: not walk on ice that's one night old)

tread on dangerous grounds
zich op glad ijs wagen   zikh op khlat eys *waa*·khuhn
(lit: go on very slippery ice)

soccer/football

voetbal

Who plays for (PSV Eindhoven)?
Wie speelt er voor (PSV)?   wee speylt uhr vohr (pey·es·*vey*)

He's a great (player).
Hij is een fantastische   hey is uhn fan·*tas*·tee·suh
(speler).   (*spey*·luhr)

He played brilliantly in the match against (Germany).
Hij speelde een   hey *speyl*·duh uhn
fantastische wedstrijd   fan·*tas*·tee·suh *wet*·streyt
tegen (Duitsland).   *tey*·khuhn (*döyts*·lant)

Which team is at the top of the league?
Welk team staat aan de top   welk teem staat aan duh top
van de rangschikking?   van duh *rang*·skhi·king

What a great/terrible team!
Wat een fantastisch/   wat uhn fan·*tas*·tees/
slecht team!   slekht teem

attack v	aanvallen	aan·va·luhn
attacker	aanvaller	aan·va·luhr
backward pass	terugspeelbal	tuh·rukh·speyl·bal
ball	bal	bal
centre (pass) n	voorzet	vohr·zet
coach n	trainer	trey·nuhr
corner (kick) n	hoekschop	hook·skhop
defend v	verdedigen	vuhr·dey·di·khuhn
defender	verdediger	vuhr·dey·di·khuhr
dribble v	dribbelen	dri·buh·luhn
expulsion	uitsluiting	öyt·slöy·ting
fan	supporter	sew·por·tuhr
foul n	overtreding	oh·vuhr·trey·ding
free kick	vrijschop	vrey·skhop
goal (structure)	doel n	dool
goalkeeper	doelverdediger/	dool·vuhr·dey·di·khuhr/
	keeper	kee·puhr

injury time	blessuretijd	ble·sew·ruh·teyt
manager	manager	me·ne·dzhuhr
midfield	middenveld n	mi·duhn·velt
offside	buitenspel	böy·tuhn·spel
pass n	pass	paas
penalty	strafschop	straf·skhop
player	speler	spey·luhr
red card	rode kaart	roh·duh kaart
referee	scheidsrechter	skheyts·rekh·tuhr
striker	spits	spits
throw in v	ingooien	in·khoo·yuhn
yellow card	gele kaart	khey·luh kaart
wall (of players)	muurtje n	mewr·chuh

Off to see a match? Check out **going to a game**, page 144.

tennis & table tennis

I'd like to …	*Ik wil graag …*	ik wil khraakh …
book a time to play	*een tijd boeken*	uhn teyt *boo*·kuhn
play table tennis	*tafeltennissen*	taa·fuhl·te·ni·suhn
play tennis	*tennissen*	te·ni·suhn

Can we play at night?
Kunnen we 's avonds spelen wanneer het donker is?
ku·nuhn wuh *saa*·vonts *spey*·luhn wa·*neyr* huht *dong*·kuhr is

I need my racket restrung.
Ik moet mijn racket opnieuw laten besnaren.
ik moot meyn *re*·kuht op·*neew laa*·tuhn buh·*snaa*·ruhn

ace	ace	eys
advantage	voordeel n	vohr·deyl
(table tennis) bat	(tafeltennis)bat	(taa·fuhl·te·nis·)bet
clay	klei	kley
fault	overtreding	oh·vuhr·trey·ding
grass	gras n	khras
hard court	hard court	haart kohrt
net	net n	net
ping-pong ball	pingpongbal	ping·pong·bal
play doubles v	dubbelspel spelen	du·buhl·spel spey·luhn
racquet	tennisracket n	te·nis·re·kuht
serve n	opslag	op·slakh
serve v	opslaan	op·slaan
set n	set	set
table-tennis table	pingpongtafel	ping·pong·taa·fuhl
tennis ball	tennisbal	te·nis·bal

water sports

watersporten

Can I book a lesson?
Kan ik een les boeken?   kan ik uhn les *boo*·kuhn

Can I hire (a) ...	*Kan ik ... huren?*	kan ik ... *hew*·ruhn
boat	een boot	uhn boht
canoe	een kano	uhn *kaa*·noh
kayak	een kayak	uhn *ka*·yak
life jacket	een reddingsvest	uhn *re*·dings·vest
snorkelling	materiaal om	ma·teyr·*yaal* om
gear	te snorkelen	tuh *snor*·kuh·luhn
water-skis	waterskis	*waa*·tuhr·skees
wetsuit	een wetsuit	uhn *wet*·soot

Are there any ...?	*Zijn er ...?*	zeyn uhr ...
breakwaters	golfbrekers	*kholf*·brey·kuhrs
(water) hazards	gevaren	khuh·*vaa*·ruhn
reefs	rifs	rifs
rips	sterke	*ster*·kuh
	stromingen	*stroh*·ming·uhn
sandbanks	zandbanken	*zant*·bang·kuhn

buggy	zeilwagen	zeyl·waa·khun
(for the beach)		
canoeing	kanovaren	kaa·noh·vaa·ruhn
flying kites	vliegeren	vlee·khuh·ruhn
kayaking	kajakvaren	ka·yak·vaa·ruhn
land sailing/	strandzeilen	strant·zey·luhn
yachting		
motorboat	motorboot	moh·tor·boht
oars	roeispanen	rooy·spaa·nuhn
row v	roeien	roo·yuhn
sail v	zeilen	zey·luhn
sailboard	(wind)surfplank	(wint·)surf·plangk
sailboarding	windsurfen/	wint·sur·fuhn/
	plankzeilen	plangk·zey·luhn
sailing	zeilen	zey·luhn
sailing boat	zeilboot	zeyl·boht
surfboard	surfplank	surf·plangk
surfing	surfen	sur·fuhn
wave	golf	kholf

sea slang

The seafaring Dutch have enriched their language with many sayings inspired by all things nautical, like these:

One must cut one's coat according to one's cloth.
Men moet roeien met de men moot roo·yuhn met duh
riemen die men heeft. ree·muhn dee men heyft
(lit: one must row with the oars one has)

To have your cake and eat it too.
Van twee walletjes eten. van twey wa·luh·chus ey·tuhn
(lit: eat off two quays)

The best horseman is always on his feet.
De beste stuurlui staan duh bes·tuh stewr·löy staan
aan wal. aan wal
(lit: the best navigators are on shore)

To keep one's eyes peeled.
Een oogje in het zeil uhn ohkh·yuh in huht zeyl
houden. haw·duhn
(lit: keep an eye on the sail)

In this chapter, phrases are in the informal *je* yuh (you) form only. For more details, see the box **all about you** on page 109.

hiking

wandeltochten maken

Do we need a guide?
Hebben we een gids nodig?   he·buhn wuh uhn khits *noh*·dikh

Are there guided treks?
Zijn er begeleide   zeyn uhr buh·khuh·*ley*·duh
tochten?   *tokh*·tuhn

When does it get dark?
Wanneer wordt het donker?   wa·*neyr* wort huht *dong*·kuhr

How long is the trail?
Hoe lang is het pad?   hoo lang is huht pat

How long is the hike?
Hoe lang is de tocht?   hoo lang is duh tokht

Where can I go mud-flat walking?
Waar kan ik gaan   waar kan ik khaan
wadlopen?   *wat*·loh·puhn

---

wad?

A *wad* wat (plural *wadden* wa·duhn) is a mud or sand bank whose level is just between the levels of *vloed* vloot (high tide) and *eb* ep (low tide), so it gets flooded twice a day. The Dutch *Waddeneilanden* wa·duhn·ey·lan·duhn (a group of islands) lie in the *Waddenzee* wa·duhn·zey, the world's largest *waddengebied* wa·duhn·khuh·*beet* (*wad* area), near the Dutch, German and Danish coasts. It's the perfect place to go *wadlopen* wat·loh·puhn – trekking from one *wad* to another at low tide. Inform yourself about the times of the tides before setting off and make sure you take a guide.

Where can I ...?	*Waar vind ik ...?*	waar vint ik ...
find someone	*iemand die*	*ee*·mant dee
who knows this	*deze plek/*	*dey*·zuh plek/
area/region	*streek kent*	streyk kent
get a map	*een kaart*	uhn kaart

Where can I ...?	*Waar kan ik ...?*	waar kan ik ...
buy supplies	*inkopen doen*	*in*·koh·puhn doon
hire camping	*kampeer-*	kam·*peyr*·
gear	*materiaal*	ma·teyr·*yaal*
	huren	hew·ruhn
hire hiking gear	*een trekkers-*	uhn *tre*·kuhrs·
	uitrusting	öyt·*rus*·ting
	huren	hew·ruhn

Do we need	*Moeten we ...*	moo·tuhn wuh ...
to take ...?	*meenemen?*	mey·ney·muhn
bedding	*beddegoed*	*be*·duh·khoot
food	*eten*	*ey*·tuhn
water	*water*	*waa*·tuhr

Is the track ...?	*Is het pad ...?*	is huht pat ...
(well-)marked	*(goed) beweg-*	(khoot) buh·*wekh*·
	wijzerd	wey·zuhrt
open	*open*	*oh*·puhn
scenic	*schilderachtig*	*skhil*·duhr·akh·tikh

Which is the ...	*Welk is de ...*	welk is duh ...
route?	*route?*	*roo*·tuh
easiest	*gemakke-*	khuh·*ma*·kuh·
	lijkste	luhk·stuh
most	*meest*	meyst
interesting	*interessante*	in·tey·re·*san*·tuh
shortest	*kortste*	*kort*·stuh

Where's the ...?	*Waar is ...?*	waar is ...
camping	*de kamping*	duh *kem*·ping/
ground		*kam*·ping Ⓝ/Ⓑ
nearest	*het dichts-*	huht *dikhts*·
village	*bijzijnde dorp*	bey·zeyn·duh dorp

Where are the ...?	*Waar zijn de ...?*	waar zeyn duh ...
showers	*douches*	*doo*·chus
toilets	*toiletten*	twa·*le*·tuhn

Where have you come from?
Waar kom jij vandaan?   waar kom yey van·*daan*

How long did it take?
Hoe lang heb je er   hoo lang hep yuh uhr
over gedaan?   oh·vuhr khuh·*daan*

Does this path go to (Schiermonnikoog)?
Gaat dit pad naar   khaat dit pat naar
(Schiermonnikoog)?   (*skheer*·mo·nik·ohkh)

Can I go through here?
Kan ik langs hier gaan?   kan ik langs heer khaan

Is the water OK to drink?
Is het water drinkbaar?   is huht *waa*·tuhr *dringk*·baar

Is it safe?
Is het veilig?   is huht *vey*·likh

Is there a hut?
Is er een hut?   is uhr uhn hut

I'm lost.
Ik ben verdwaald.   ik ben vuhr·*dwaalt*

---

listen for ...

Pas op voor ...!	pas op vohr ...	**Be careful of the ...!**
de onder-	duh *on*·duhr·	**undertow**
stroom	strohm	
de stroming	duh *stroh*·ming	**rip**
het getij	huht khuh·*tey*	**tide**

Het is gevaarlijk!
huht is khuh·*vaar*·luhk   **It's dangerous!**

---

beach

het strand

Where's the ...	*Waar is het ...?*	waar is huht ...
beach?		
best	*beste strand*	*bes*·tuh strant
nearest	*dichtsbijzijnde*	*dikhts*·bey·zeyn·duh
	strand	strant
nudist	*naaktstrand*	*naakt*·strant

How much to rent a/an ...?	Hoeveel is de huur voor een ...?	hoo·veyl is duh hewr vohr uhn ...
chair	strandstoel	strant·stool
hut	strandcabine	strant·ka·bee·nuh
umbrella (sun)	parasol	pa·ra·sol

Is it safe to dive/swim here?
Is het veilig om hier te duiken/zwemmen? is huht *vey*·likh om heer tuh *döy*·kuhn/*zwe*·muhn

What time is high/low tide?
Hoe laat is het vloed/eb? hoo laat is huht vloot/ep

Do we have to pay?
Moeten we betalen? moo·tuhn wuh buh·*taa*·luhn

beach & pool signs		
Verboden te Duiken	vuhr·*boh*·duhn tuh *döy*·kuhn	**No Diving**
Verboden te Zwemmen	vuhr·*boh*·duhn tuh *zwe*·muhn	**No Swimming**

weather

het weer

What's the weather like?
Hoe is het weer? hoo is huht weyr

What will the weather be like tomorrow?
Wat voor weer wordt het morgen? wat vohr weyr wort huht *mor*·khuhn

It's ...	Het is ...	huht is ...
cloudy	bewolkt	buh·*wolkt*
cold	koud	kawt
foggy	mistig	*mis*·tikh
frosty	vriesweer	*vrees*·weyr
hot	zeer warm	zeyr warm
icy	glad	khlat
sunny	zonnig	*zo*·nikh
warm	warm	warm

It's ...	Het ...	huht ...
freezing	vriest	vreest
raining	regent	rey·khunt
snowing	sneeuwt	sneywt
stormy	stormt	stormt
windy	waait	waayt

Where can I buy a/an ...?	Waar kan ik een ... kopen?	waar kan ik uhn ... koh·puhn
rain jacket	regenjas	rey·khuhn·yas
umbrella (rain)	paraplu	pa·ra·plew

weather wonders

It's raining cats and dogs.
Het regent pijpestelen.   huht *rey*·khuhnt *pey*·puh·stey·luhn
(lit: it's raining pipe stems)

It's freezing hard.
Het vriest dat het kraakt.   huht vreest dat huht kraakt
(lit: it's freezing so hard that things are bursting/cracking)

flora & fauna

planten & dieren

What ... is that?	Welke ... is dat?	wel·kuh ... is dat
bird	vogel	voh·khul
flower	bloem	bloom
plant	plant	plant
tree	boom	bohm

What animal is that?
Welk dier is dat?   welk deer is dat

What's it used for?
Waarvoor wordt het gebruikt?   waar·*vohr* wort huht khuh·*bröykt*

Can you eat the fruit?
Is de vrucht eetbaar?   is duh vrukht *eyt*·baar

Is it common?
Komt het veel voor?   komt huht veyl vohr

frog land

You might hear Dutch and Flemish refer to their respective countries as *kikkerlandje* ki·kuhr·lan·chuh (lit: little-frog-land). The temperate climate is often marked by cool, changeable weather, mild summers and precipitation spread evenly throughout the year – supposedly excellent breeding conditions for frogs. However, things seem to be hotting up in the Low Countries, courtesy of the *klimaatverandering* klee·maat·vuhr·an·duh·ring (climate change). Of course, *het weer* huht weyr (the weather), and increasingly the *broeikaseffect* brooy·kas·e·fekt (global warming, literally 'hothouse effect'), are the icebreakers par excellence.

Is it …?	Is het …?	is huht …
dangerous	gevaarlijk	khuh·vaar·luhk
endangered	met uitsterven	met öyt·ster·vuhn
	bedreigd	buh·dreykht
poisonous	giftig	khif·tikh
protected	beschermd	buh·skhermt
copse	kreupelbosje n	kreu·puhl·bo·shuh
daffodil	narcis	nar·sis
heath	heide	hey·duh
mount of mud	terp	terp
nature reserve	natuurreservaat n	na·tew·rey·ser·vaat
peat	turf	turf
pine	den	den
tulip	tulp	tulp
(pollard) willow	(knot)wilg	(knot·)wilkh
cow	koe	koo
fox	vos	vos
goose/geese	gans/ganzen	khans/khan·zuhn
migratory birds	trekvogels	trek·voh·khuls
seal	zeehond	zey·hont
sea lion	zeekoe	zey·koo
sheep	schaap n	skhaap

For more geographical and agricultural terms, and names of animals and plants, see the **dictionary**.

SOCIAL

basics

essentiële uitdrukkingen

breakfast	*ontbijt* n	ont·*beyt*
lunch	*middagmaal* n/*lunch*	mi·dakh·maal/lunsh
dinner	*avondmaal* n/*diner* n	aa·vont·maal/dee·*ney*
snack	*snack/*	snek/snak ⓝ/ⓑ/
	tussendoortje	tu·suhn·*dohr*·chuh
today's special	*dagschotel*	*dakh*·skhoh·tuhl
eat v	*eten*	*ey*·tuhn
drink v	*drinken*	*dring*·kuhn
I'd like ...	*Ik wil graag ...*	ik wil khraakh ...
Please.	*Alstublieft.* pol	al·stew·*bleeft*
Thank you.	*Dank u.* pol	dangk ew

eating out

163

bruin café　　　　　　　　　　　bröyn ka·*fey*
bruine kroeg　　　　　　　　　　*bröy*·nuh krookh
'brown café' – old-style *café/kroeg* with wooden furniture, named after the generally smoke-stained walls. The atmosphere is perfect for reading and deep (and long) conversation. They usually stay open to the wee hours.

café/kroeg　　　　　　　　　　　ka·*fey*/krookh
not a café, but a pub – an establishment mainly serving beer and other types of alcohol. Coffee and soft drinks are available as a sideline. Many also serve snacks or simple meals. The 'local' around the corner is known as *stamkroeg* stam·khrookh, *stamcafé* stam·ka·fey or *buurtcafé* bewrt·ka·fey.

de muur　　　　　　　　　　　　duh mewr
'the wall' – in the Netherlands, wall-mounted rows of small coin-operated windows with warm, deep-fried snacks. They're popular as a late-night (or early-morning) snack when everything else is closed.

eetcafé　　　　　　　　　　　　*eyt*·ka·fey
café where people go not only to drink, but to have a good meal without having to fork out restaurant prices. The aim is to have a good conversation over a meal and a few drinks. The menu is often extensive and the food yummy. Local specialities and daily specials might be available.

grand café　　　　　　　　　　　*gra*·ka·fey
more spacious *café* with comfortable seating and classy furnishings – they serve alcohol as well as nonalcoholic drinks and meals. The perfect place for a stylish and relaxed lunch or brunch.

haringstand　　　　　　　　　　*haa*·ring·stant
'herring stand' – sells the best and freshest herring

koffiehuisje n　　　　　　　　　ko·fee·*höy*·shuh
'coffee house' – espresso bar or café specialising in coffee and other hot drinks (alcohol is the sideline here). They serve cakes and pastries to go with the coffee, as well as light meals. Not unlike a *theehuisje* tey·*höy*·shuh (tea room); sometimes more like an espresso bar or *broodjeszaak* broh·chus·zaak (sandwich shop).

FOOD

164

koffieshop   *ko·fee·shop*
coffee shop – café authorised to sell soft drugs such as the ubiquitous home-grown *nederwiet* *ney·duhr·weet* (meaning 'pot from the Netherlands'). They also serve coffee and cake – but inquire about the ingredients first or you'll be putting your teeth into a space cake before you know it!

pannenkoekenhuisje n   *pa·nuh·koo·kuh·höys·shuh*
pancake parlour – a Dutch institution

patatkraam/frietkot Ⓝ/Ⓑ   *pa·tat·kraam/freet·kot*
chips shop – place specialising in Flemish-style fries. It can be a simple shack or van, or a small shop (often called *frituur* *free·tewr*) dealing in take-away fries and deep-fried snacks .

praatcafé n Ⓑ   *praat·ka·fey*
pub set up and laid out specifically to promote conversation over a drink or two (of the alcoholic variety or not) – it's all about meeting up with friends and conversation here. Snacks or light meals are often available.

proeflokaal   *proof·loh·kaal*
tasting house that used to be attached to distilleries – type of café or pub offering a large variety of gins and liqueurs (or beers) and where people go specifically to taste and appreciate what's on offer. Staff can help you choose and are generally subject matter experts. In the Netherlands, they usually specialise in *jenever* yuh·*ney*·vuhr/zhuh·*ney*·vuhr Ⓝ/Ⓑ (gin). In Belgium, it's often about *bier* beer (beer), although they also have their *druppelkot* n *dru*·puhl·kot or *jeneverkot* n zhuh·*ney*·vuhr·koht (gin shack) – sometimes a shack but often a pub with a bewildering *jenever* list.

terras   tuh·*ras*
outdoor terrace – a fixture in many *cafés* and a great place to relax, watch passers-by, read the paper or catch up with friends. At the first sign of spring, people flock here to soak up the sun. Many are now covered and heated in winter.

theatercafé   tey·*yaa*·tuhr·ka·fey
café in or near a theatre district where people tend to go before and after performances. They usually attract a mix of bohemian and chic clientele; struggling artists, would-be models, treehuggers, baby-boomers, yups and business people all rub shoulder here with each other.

eating out

165

finding a place to eat

Can you recommend a bar/restaurant?

Kunt u een bar/restaurant	kunt ew uhn bar/res·toh·*rant*
aanbevelen? pol	aan·buh·vey·luhn

Where would	*Waar zou u heen*	waar zaw ew heyn
you go for ...?	*gaan voor ...?* pol	khaan vohr ...
a celebration	*een*	uhn
	feestelijke	feys·tuh·luh·kuh
	maaltijd	maal·teyt
a cheap meal	*een*	uhn
	goedkope	khoot·koh·puh
	maaltijd	maal·teyt
local	*plaatselijke*	plaat·suh·luh·kuh
specialities	*specialiteiten*	spey·sya·lee·tey·tuhn

Where would	*Waar zou u heen*	waar zaw ew heyn
you go to	*gaan om ... te*	khaan om ... tuh
taste ...?	*proeven?* pol	proo·vuhn
good	*goed*	khoot
Indonesian	*Indonesisch*	in·doh·ney·sis
food	*eten*	ey·tuhn
the local beer	*met bier*	met beer
cuisine	*bereide*	buh·rey·duh
	gerechten	khuh·rekh·tuhn

I'd like to reserve	*Ik wil graag een*	ik wil khraakh uhn
a table for ...	*tafel voor ...*	taa·fuhl vohr ...
	reserveren.	rey·ser·vey·ruhn
(two) people	*(twee)*	(twey)
	personen	puhr·soh·nuhn
(eight) o'clock	*(acht) uur*	(akht) ewr

listen for ...		
We zijn	wuh zeyn	**We're closed.**
gesloten.	khuh·sloh·tuhn	
We zitten vol.	wuh zi·tuhn vol	**We're full.**
Een momentje.	uhn moh·men·chuh	**One moment.**

Are you still serving food?
Is de keuken nog open? is duh *keu*·kuhn nokh *oh*·puhn

How long is the wait?
Hoelang moeten we hoo·*lang moo*·tuhn wuh
wachten? *wakh*·tuhn

at the restaurant

What would you recommend?
Wat kan u aanbevelen? pol wat kan ew *aan*·buh·vey·luhn

What are they having?
Wat hebben zij? wat *he*·buhn zey

What's in that dish?
Wat zit er in dat gerecht? wat zit uhr in dat khuh·*rekht*

What's it/that called?
Hoe heet het/dat? hoo heyt huht/dat

I'll have that.
Ik neem dat. ik neym dat

Does it take long to prepare?
Duurt het lang om het dewrt huht lang om huht
te bereiden? tuh buh·*rey*·duhn

Is it self-serve?
Is het zelfbediening? is huht *zelf*·buh·dee·ning

Is service included in the bill?
Is bediening is buh·*dee*·ning
inbegrepen? *in*·buh·grey·puhn

Are these complimentary?
Zijn deze gratis? zeyn *dey*·zuh *khraa*·tis

Could I please see the wine list?
Mag ik de wijnkaart? makh ik duh *weyn*·kaart

Which beers do you serve?
Welke bieren heeft u? pol *wel*·kuh *bee*·ruhn heyft ew

I'm ready to order.
Ik wil graag bestellen. ik wil khraakh be·*ste*·luhn

To call the waiter or waitress over, address them as *Meneer* muh·*neyr* (Sir) or *Mevrouw* muh·*vraw* (Miss), or *Juffrouw* *yu*·fraw (Miss, for a teenage girl only – see also page 109).

Don't ask for a doggie bag – it's just not done in the Low Countries. When paying, never ask 'to go Dutch' in a Dutch restaurant – if you're that way inclined, ask to split the bill by saying:

Kunnen we apart betalen alstublieft? pol
ku·nuhn wuh a·*part*   **Could we pay separately,**
buh·*taa*·luhn al·stew·*bleeft*   **please?**

Tips aren't compulsory or expected – but they will be appreciated, of course.

I'd like (a/the) ..., please.	*Ik wil graag ...*	ik wil khraakh ...
children's menu	*de kindermenu*	duh *kin*·duhr·muh·new
child seat	*een kinderstoel*	uhn *kin*·duhr·stool
drink list	*de drankkaart*	duh *drang*·kaart
half portion	*een halve portie*	uhn *hal*·vuh *por*·see
local speciality	*een plaatselijke specialiteit*	uhn *plaat*·suh·luh·kuh spey·sya·lee·*teyt*
menu (in English)	*een menu (in het Engels)*	uhn me·*new* (in huht *eng*·uhls)
nonsmoking	*niet-roken*	neet·*roh*·kuhn
smoking	*roken*	*roh*·kuhn
table for (five)	*een tafel voor (vijf)*	uhn *taa*·fuhl vohr (veyf)
that dish	*dat gerecht*	dat khuh·*rekht*

I'd like it with/	*Ik wil het graag*	ik wil huht khraakh
without …	*met/zonder …*	met/*zon*·duhr …
cheese	*kaas*	kaas
chilli (sauce)	*chili(saus)*	*chee*·lee(·saws)
cream	*room*	rohm
garlic	*knoflook*	*knof*·lohk
(curried) ketchup	*(curry)ketchup*	(*ku*·ree·)*ke*·chup
(tomato)	*(tomaten)*	(toh·*maa*·tuhn·)
ketchup	*ketchup*	*ke*·chup
lemon	*citroen*	see·*troon*
mayonnaise	*mayonaise*	ma·yoh·*ney*·zuh
mustard	*mosterd*	*mos*·tuhrt
nuts	*noten*	*noh*·tuhn
oil	*olie*	*oh*·lee
pepper	*peper*	*pey*·puhr
salt	*zout*	zawt
sugar	*suiker*	*söy*·kuhr
tartare sauce	*tartaarsaus*	tar·*taar*·saws
tomato sauce	*tomatensaus*	toh·*maa*·tuhn·saws
vinegar	*azijn*	a·*zeyn*

For other specific meal requests, see **vegetarian & special meals**, page 181.

For other specific meal requests, see **vegetarian & special meals**, page 181.

listen for …

Waar wilt u zitten? pol	Where would you like to sit?
waar wilt ew *zi*·tuhn	
Wilt u al bestellen? pol	Are you ready to order?
wilt ew al buh·*ste*·luhn	
Wat mag het zijn?	What can I get for you?
wat makh huht zeyn	
Houdt u van …? pol	Do you like …?
hawt ew van …	
Ik kan … aanbevelen.	I suggest the …
ik kan …	
aan·buh·*vey*·luhn	
Alstublieft. pol	Here you go!
al·*stew·bleeft*	
Eet smakelijk.	Enjoy your meal.
eyt *smaa*·kuh·luhk	

eating out

169

look for ...

Hors D'oeuvre/	hor·*döy*·vruh/	Appetisers
Hapjes	*hap*·yuhs	
Soep	soop	Soups
Voorgerechten	vohr·*khuh*·rekh·tuhn	Entrées
Salades	sa·*laa*·duhs	Salads
Hoofdgerechten	*hohft*·khuh·rekh·tuhn	Main Courses
Tussengerechten	tu·*suhn*·khuh·rekh·tuhn	Entremets
Bijgerechten/	*bey*·khuh·rekh·tuhn/	Side Dishes
Tussengerechten	tu·*suhn*·khuh·rekh·tuhn	
Desserts/	dey·*sers*/	Desserts
Nagerechten	*naa*·khuh·rekh·tuhn	
Aperitieven	a·pey·ree·*tee*·vuhn	Aperitifs
Dranken	*drang*·kuhn	Drinks
Frisdranken	*fris*·drang·kuhn	Soft Drinks
Sterke Dranken	*ster*·kuh *drang*·kuhn	Spirits
Bier	beer	Beers
Mousserende	moo·*sey*·ruhn·duh	Sparkling Wines
Wijn Ⓝ	weyn	
Schuimwijn Ⓑ	*skhöym*·weyn	Sparkling Wines
Witte Wijn	*wi*·tuh weyn	White Wines
Rode Wijn	*roh*·duh weyn	Red Wines
Dessertwijn	dey·*sert*·weyn	Dessert Wines
Likeuren	lee·*keu*·ruhn	Digestifs/
		Liqueurs

at the table

aan tafel

Please bring a/the ...	*Mag ik ...* *alstublieft?* pol	makh ik ... al·*stew*·bleeft
bill	*de rekening*	duh *rey*·kuh·ning
cutlery	*bestek*	buh·*stek*
(wine)glass	*een (wijn)glas*	uhn (*weyn*·)khlas
serviette	*een servet*	uhn ser·*vet*
tablecloth	*een*	uhn
	tafellaken	*taa*·fuhl·laa·kuhn

I didn't order this.
Ik heb dit niet besteld.   ik hep dit neet be·*stelt*

There's a mistake in the bill/check.
Er zit een fout in de   uhr zit uhn fawt in duh
rekening.   *rey*·kuh·ning

talking food

I love this dish.
Dit gerecht is erg lekker.   dit khuh·*rekht* is erkh *le*·kuhr

I love the local cuisine.
Ik vind de plaatselijke   ik vint duh *plaat*·suh·luh·kuh
keuken erg lekker.   *keu*·kuhn erkh *le*·kuhr

Delicious!
Heerlijk/Lekker!   *heyr*·luhk/*le*·kuhr

To lick thumbs and fingers!
Om de vingers bij   om duh *ving*·uhrs bey
af te likken!   af tuh *li*·kuhn

ashtray
asbak
as·bak

spoon
lepel
ley·puhl

fork
vork
vork

plate
bord n
bort

knife
mes n
mes

wineglass
wijnglas n
weyn·khlas

glass
glas n
khlas

table
tafel
taa·fuhl

My compliments to the chef.
*Mijn complimenten   meyn kom·plee·*men*·tuhn*
aan de chef.   aan duh shef

I'm full.
Ik heb genoeg gegeten. ik hep khuh·*nookh* khuh·*khey*·tuhn

This is …	*Dit is …*	dit is …
burnt	*aangebrand*	*aan*·khuh·brant
(too) cold	*(te) koud*	(tuh) kawt
off	*bedorven*	buh·*dor*·vuhn
(too) spicy	*(te) pikant*	(tuh) pee·*kant*
stale	*oudbakken*	awt·*ba*·kuhn
superb	*fantastisch*	fan·*tas*·tees

methods of preparation

bereidingswijzen

I'd like it …	*Ik wil het graag …*	ik wil huht khraakh …
I don't want it …	*Ik wil het niet …*	ik wil huht neet …
boiled	*gekookt*	khuh·*kohkt*
deep-fried	*gefrituurd*	khuh·free·*tewrt*
fried	*gebakken*	khuh·*ba*·kuhn
grilled	*gegrild*	khu·*khrilt*
mashed	*als puree*	als pew·*rey*
medium	*redelijk* Ⓝ	rey·duh·luhk
	doorbakken	dohr·*ba*·kuhn
	à point Ⓑ	a·*pwaa*
rare	*kort gebakken* Ⓝ	kort khuh·*ba*·kuhn
	saignant Ⓑ	sey·*nya*
reheated	*opgewarmd*	*op*·khuh·warmt
smoked	*gerookt*	khuh·*rohkt*
steamed	*gestoomd*	khuh·*stohmt*
well-done	*goed*	khoot
	doorbakken	dohr·*ba*·kuhn
with the dressing on the side	*met de slasaus opzij*	met duh *slaa*·saws op·*zey*
with the sauce/ mayonnaise separate	*met de saus/ mayonnaise apart*	met duh saws/ ma·yoh·*ney*·zuh a·*part*

nonalcoholic drinks

alcoholic drinks

alcoholvrije dranken

flat/still mineral water	*spa blauw* ⓝ	spa blaw
	plat water ⓑ	plat *waa*·tuhr
mineral/bottled water	*mineraal-water*	mee·ney·*raal*·waa·tuhr
sparkling mineral water	*spa rood* ⓝ	spa roht
	spuitwater ⓑ	*spöyt*·waa·tuhr
buttermilk	*karnemelk* ⓝ	*kar*·nuh·melk
	botermelk ⓑ	*boh*·tuhr·melk
(hot) chocolate milk	*(warme) chocolade-melk*	*(war*·muh) shoh·koh·*laa*·duh·melk
(orange) juice	*(sinaasappel)sap*	(see·*naas*·a·puhl·)sap
lemonade	*limonade*	lee·moh·*naa*·duh
soft drink	*frisdrank*	*fris*·drangk
(hot) water	*(warm) water*	(warm) *waa*·tuhr
(cup of)	*(een kopje)*	(uhn *kop*·yuh)
tea/coffee	*thee/koffie*	tey/*ko*·fee
with/without ...	*met/zonder ...*	met/*zon*·duhr ...
coffee milk	*koffiemelk*	*ko*·fee·melk
lemon	*citroen*	see·*troon*
milk	*melk*	melk
sugar	*suiker*	*söy*·kuhr
whipped cream	*slagroom*	*slakh*·rohm

coffee time		
black	*zwart*	zwart
decaffeinated	*decaf*	*dey*·kaf
iced	*met ijs*	met eys
strong	*sterk*	sterk
weak	*flauw*	flaw
white	*met melk*	met melk

alcoholic drinks

Vodka, whisky, rum, tequila, gin and tonic, Campari and popular cocktails such as Bloody Mary are all known by their English names, so you shouldn't have any trouble getting your order. However, you might want to delve into the local beer and gin terminology for the huge number of local varieties on offer (for beers and gin, see the **culinary reader**, page 183).

advocaat	advocaat	at·voh·kaat
beer	bier	beer
brandy	brandewijn ⓝ	bran·duh·weyn
	cognac ⓑ	koh·nyak
champagne	champagne	sham·pa·nyuh
cocktail	cocktail	kok·teyl
gin	jenever	yuh·ney·vuhr ⓝ
		zhuh·ney·vuhr ⓑ
herb-based schnapps	Beerenburg	bey·ruhn·burkh
a shot of (whisky)	een glas (whisky)	uhn khlas (wis·kee)
strong alcoholic drink	borrel	bo·ruhl
a bottle/glass of … wine	een fles/glas …	uhn fles/khlas …
dessert	dessertwijn	dey·sert·weyn
red	rode wijn	roh·duh weyn
rosé	rosé	roh·zey
sparkling	mousserende wijn ⓝ	moo·sey·ruhn·duh weyn
	schuimwijn ⓑ	skhöym·weyn
white	witte wijn	wi·tuh weyn
a … of beer	een … bier	uhn … beer
glass	glas	khlas
jug	karaf	ka·raf
large bottle	fles	fles
small bottle	flesje	fle·shuh

Additional items are in the **culinary reader**, page 183, and the **dictionary**.

FOOD

174

in the bar

Excuse me!
Excuseer mij! — ek·skew·*zeyr* mey

I'm next.
Het is mijn beurt. — huht is meyn beurt

I'll have (a lemon-flavoured gin).
Voor mij (een citroenjenever). — vohr mey (uhn see·*troon*·yuh·*ney*·vuhr/ see·*troon*·zhuh·*ney*·vuhr) ⑩/⑯

Same again, please.
Hetzelfde alstublieft. pol — huht·*zelf*·duh al·stew·*bleeft*

No ice, thanks.
Zonder ijs asltublieft. pol — *zon*·duhr eys al·stew·*bleeft*

How much alcohol does this contain?
Hoeveel alcohol zit hierin? — hoo·*veyl* al·koh·*hol* zit heer·*in*

I'll buy you a drink.
Ik trakteer je op een drankje. — ik trak·*teyr* yuh op uhn *drangk*·yuh

What would you like?
Wat wil je drinken? — wat wil yuh *dring*·kuhn

I don't drink alcohol.
Ik drink geen alcohol. — ik dringk kheyn al·koh·*hol*

It's my round.
Mijn rondje. — meyn *ron*·chuh

Do you serve meals here?
Serveert u hier maaltijden? pol — ser·*veyrt* ew heer *maal*·tey·duhn

---

not just a beer

een biertje	uhn *beer*·chuh	normal glass of lager
een fluitje	uhn *flöy*·chuh	tall narrow glass of lager
een kleintje pils ⑩	uhn *kleyn*·chuh pils	small glass of lager
een pilsje	uhn *pil*·shuh	normal glass of lager
een pintje ⑯	uhn *pin*·chuh	normal glass of lager

eating out

175

listen for ...

Wat zal het zijn?
wat zal huht zeyn
What are you having?

Ik denk dat je genoeg op hebt.
ik dengk dat yuh
khuh·*nookh* op hept
I think you've had enough.

drinking up

stevig drinken

Cheers!
Proost! — prohst

This is hitting the spot.
Dat ging recht naar — dat khing rekht naar
m'n hoofd. — muhn hohft
(lit: that went straight to my head)

I feel fantastic!
Ik voel me heerlijk! — ik vool muh *heyr*·luhk

I think I've had one too many.
Ik denk dat ik er — ik dengk dat ik uhr
eentje teveel op heb. — *eyn*·chuh tuh·*veyl* op hep

I'm feeling drunk.
Ik voel me dronken. — ik vool muh *drong*·kuhn

I feel ill.
Ik voel me ziek. — ik vool muh zeek

Where's the toilet?
Waar is het toilet? — waar is huht twa·*let*

I'm tired, I'd better go home.
Ik ben moe. — ik ben moo
Ik ga best naar huis. — ik khaa best naar höys

Can you call a taxi for me?
Kunt u een taxi — kunt ew uhn *tak*·see
voor me bellen? **pol** — vohr muh *be*·luhn

I don't think you should drive.
Je zou niet mogen — yuh zaw neet *mo*·khuhn
rijden. — *rey*·duhn

buying food

What's the local speciality?
Wat is het streekgerecht?   wat is huht *streyk*·khuh·rekht

What's the special regional beer here?
Wat is het streekbier?   wat is huht *streyk*·beer

What's that?
Wat is dat?   wat is dat

Can I taste it?
Kan ik het eens proeven?   kan ik huht eyns *proo*·vuhn

Can I have a bag, please?
Mag ik een draagtasje   makh ik uhn *draakh*·ta·shuh
alstublieft? **pol**   al·stew·*bleeft*

I don't need a bag, thanks.
Ik heb geen draagtasje   ik hep kheyn *draakh*·ta·shuh
nodig, dank u. **pol**   *noh*·dikh dangk ew

How much is (a kilo of cheese)?
Hoeveel kost   hoo·*veyl* kost
(een kilo kaas)?   (uhn *kee*·lo kaas)

food stuff

cooked (boiled)	*gekookt*	khuh·*kohkt*
cooked (prepared)	*bereid*	buh·*reyt*
cured (pickled)	*gepekeld*	khuh·*pey*·kuhlt
cured (preserved)	*ingemaakt*	*in*·khuh·maakt
dried	*gedroogd*	kuh·*drohkht*
fresh	*vers*	vers
frozen	*ingevroren*	*in*·khuh·vroh·ruhn
raw	*rauw*	raw
smoked	*gerookt*	khuh·*rohkt*

I'd like …	Ik wil graag …	ik wil khraakh …
(one) of each	(één) van elk	(eyn) van elk
(two) of those	(twee) van die soort	(twey) van dee sohrt
them mixed/ assorted	een mengeling	uhn *meng*·uh·ling
your selection	uw selectie pol	ew sey·*lek*·see

I'd like …	Ik wil graag …	ik wil khraakh …
(200) grams	(tweehonderd) gram	(twey·*hon*·duhrt) khram
half a dozen	een half dozijn	uhn half doh·*zeyn*
a dozen	een dozijn	uhn doh·*zeyn*
a quarter kilo	een half pond	uhn half pont
half a kilo	een halve kilo/ een pond	uhn *hal*·vuh *kee*·loh/ uhn pont
a kilo	een kilo	uhn *kee*·loh
(two) kilos	(twee) kilo	(twey) *kee*·loh
a bottle	een fles	uhn fles
a jar	een pot ⓝ een bokaal ⓑ	uhn pot uhn boh·*kaal*
a packet	een pak	uhn pak
a piece	een stuk	uhn stuk
(three) pieces	(drie) stuks	(dree) stuks
a slice	een plak ⓝ een snee ⓑ	uhn plak uhn sney
(six) slices	(zes) plakken ⓝ (zes) sneetjes ⓑ	(zes) *pla*·kuhn (zes) *sney*·chus
a tin	een blik	uhn blik
(just) a little	een (klein) beetje	uhn (kleyn) *bey*·chuh
more	meer	meyr
some	enkele	*eng*·kuh·luh
that one	die	dee
this one	deze	*dey*·zuh

Less.	Minder.	*min*·duhr
A bit more.	Een beetje meer.	uhn *bey*·chuh meyr
Enough.	Dat is genoeg.	dat is khuh·*nookh*

For food items, see the **culinary reader**, page 183, and the **dictionary**.

Do you have ...?	*Heeft u ...?* pol	heyft ew ...
anything	*iets*	eets
cheaper	*goedkopers*	khoot·*koh*·puhrs
other kinds	*nog andere*	nokh *an*·duh·ruh
Where can I find the ... section?	*Waar vind ik ...?*	waar vint ik ...
dairy	*de zuivel-produkten*	duh *zöy*·vuhl·proh·duk·tuhn
fish	*de visafdeling*	duh *vis*·af·dey·ling
frozen goods	*de diepvries-produkten*	duh *deep*·vrees·proh·duk·tuhn
fruit and vegetable	*de groente-en fruitafdeling*	duh *khroon*·tuh·en·*fröyt*·af·dey·ling
meat	*het vlees*	huht vleys
poultry	*het gevogelte*	huht khuh·*voh*·khul·tuh

food finds

bakery	*bakker* Ⓝ	*ba*·kuhr
	bakkerij Ⓑ	ba·kuh·*rey*
bottle shop/ liquor store	*slijterij* Ⓝ	*sley*·tuh·rey
	drankenhandel Ⓑ	*drang*·kuhn·han·duhl
butcher's shop	*slagerij*	slaa·khuh·rey
cake shop	*banketbakker* Ⓝ	bang·*ket*·ba·kuhr
	patisserie Ⓑ	pa·ti·suh·*ree*
chocolate shop	*chocolatier*	shoh·koh·la·*tye*
fishmonger	*vishandel*	*vis*·han·duhl
greengrocer	*groenteboer*	*khroon*·tuh·boor
grocery store	*kruidenier*	kröy·duh·*neer*
health-food store	*reformwinkel*	rey·*form*·wing·kuhl
market	*markt*	markt
night shop	*nachtwinkel*	*nakht*·wing·kuhl
supermarket	*supermarkt*	*sew*·puhr·markt

cooking utensils

Could I please	*Kan ik alstublieft*	kan ik al·stew·*bleeft*
borrow a ...?	*een ... lenen?* pol	uhn ... *ley*·nuhn
I need a ...	*Ik heb een ...*	ik hep uhn ...
	nodig.	*noh*·dikh
chopping board	*snijplank*	*sney*·plangk
frying pan	*koekenpan* ⓝ	*koo*·kuh·pan
	pan ⓑ	pan
knife	*mes*	mes
saucepan	*pan* ⓝ	pan
	kookpot ⓑ	*kohk*·pot

For more cooking implements, see the **dictionary**.

---

holland vs netherlands: what's the score?

You've often heard and probably even used the term 'Holland' when talking about the Netherlands. Maybe you also wondered which of the two terms is correct – a country has to have one official name, after all, even one as tolerant as the land of the Dutch obviously is, right? Rest assured – the Dutch are no more confused about their own country than, say, the British, if you take the linguistic (and political) issue of 'Great Britain' vs 'England' as a comparison.

The official name of the country is indeed *Nederland* *ney*·duhr·lant, whereas the term *Holland* ho·lant, strictly speaking, refers to the combined provinces of *Noord* nohrt (North) and *Zuid* zöyt (South) *Holland*. However, it's now a colloquial name for the whole country, since Holland (which used to be independent) united with the rest of what's now the Netherlands back in the 16th century. Likewise, both *Nederlander* *ney*·duhr·lan·duhr and *Hollander* ho·lan·duhr are words used to refer to a Dutch person, and the adjectives *Nederlands* *ney*·duhr·lants and *Hollands* ho·lants can both be used to mean 'Dutch'. On the other hand, the Dutch language is known only as *Nederlands* *ney*·duhr·lants, just like the language all this is written in is only called 'English'!

vegetarian & special meals
vegetarische & speciale maaltijden

ordering food

Is there a ...	*Is er hier een ...*	is uhr heer uhn ...
restaurant	*restaurant*	res·toh·rant
near here?	*in de buurt?*	in duh bewrt
halal	*halal*	ha·lal
kosher	*kosher*	koh·shuhr
vegetarian	*vegetarisch*	vey·khey·taa·ris

Do you have (vegetarian) food?
Heeft u (vegetarische)   heyft ew (vey·khey·taa·ri·suh)
maaltijden? pol   maal·tey·duhn

I don't eat ...
Ik eet geen ...   ik eyt kheyn ...

Is it cooked in/with ...?
Is het bereid in/met ...?   is huht buh·reyt in/met ...

Are these free-range eggs?
Zijn dit scharreleieren?   zeyn dit skha·ruhl·ey·yuh·ruhn

Could you	*Zou u een*	zaw ew uhn
prepare a meal	*maaltijd zonder*	maal·teyt zon·duhr
without ...?	*... kunnen*	... ku·nuhn
	klaarmaken? pol	klaar·maa·kuhn
butter	*boter*	boh·tuhr
eggs	*eieren*	ey·yuh·ruhn
fish	*vis*	vis
fish stock	*visbouillon*	vis·boo·yon
meat stock	*vleesbouillon*	vleys·boo·yon
oil	*olie*	oh·lee
pork	*varkensvlees*	var·kuhns·vleys
poultry	*gevogelte*	khuh·voh·khul·tuh
red meat	*rood vlees*	roht vleys

181

Is this ...?	Is het ...?	is huht ...
decaffeinated	cafeïnevrij/ decaf	ka·fey·ee·nuh·vrey/ dey·kaf
free of animal produce	zonder dierlijke producten	zon·duhr deer·luh·kuh proh·duk·tuhn
genetically modified	genetisch ge-modificeerd	khey·ney·tis khuh· moh·dee·fee·seyrt
gluten-free	glutenvrij	khlew·tuhn·vrey
low-fat	vetarm	vet·arm
low in sugar	suikerarm	söy·kuhr·arm
organic	organisch	or·khaa·nis
salt-free	zoutloos	zawt·lohs
sugar-free	suikervrij	söy·kuhr·vrey

special diets & allergies

speciale diëten & allergieën

I'm on a special diet.
Ik volg een speciaal dieet. ik volkh uhn spey·syaal dee·yeyt

I'm (a) vegan/vegetarian.
Ik ben veganist/ ik ben vey·kha·nist/
vegetariër. vey·khey·taa·ree·yuhr

I'm allergic to ...	Ik ben allergisch voor ...	ik ben a·ler·khees vohr ...
chocolate	chocolade	shoh·koh·laa·duh
dairy produce	zuivel-producten	zöy·vuhl·proh·duk·tuhn
eggs	eieren	ey·yuh·ruhn
gelatine	gelatine	zhuh·la·tee·nuh
gluten	gluten	khlew·tuhn
honey	honing	hoh·ning
MSG	MSG/ vetsin	em·es·khey/ vet·seen
nuts	noten	noh·tuhn
seafood	vis, schaal- en schelpdieren	vis skhaal en skhelp·dee·ruhn
shellfish	schaal- en schelpdieren	skhaal en skhelp·dee·ruhn

This culinary reader covers the most common ingredients and dishes in both the Netherlands and Belgium, as well as some specialities. Dishes that are known under different names have been cross-referenced. Indonesian dishes which have become commonplace in the Netherlands are indicated with Ind. We've used the symbols Ⓝ/Ⓑ for words which are different In the Netherlands and Belgium respectively. Note that we've only indicated the Dutch nouns that have neuter gender with ⓝ after the translation – the nouns which have common gender are left unmarked (for more on gender in Dutch, see the **phrasebuilder**). If it's a plural noun, you'll also see pl.

A

aardappels *aart*-a-puhls *potatoes*
— **op z'n Vlaams** op zuhn vlaams *potatoes Flemish-style – baked in onions, bay leaf & beef broth (Flanders)*
aardbeien *aart*-bey-yuhn *strawberries*
aardnoot *aart*-noht *groundnut/peanut*
abdijbier ap-*dey*-beer *abbey-style beer – produced at non-Trappist abbeys or in other breweries, some of which are associated (sometimes only in name) with abbeys; examples are Affligem, Corsendonck, Grimbergen, Leffe & Tongerlo*
abrikoos a-bree-*kohs apricot*
advocaat at-voh-*kaat a type of egg liqueur similar to eggnog*
afgeroomde melk *af*-khuh-rohm-duh melk *skim milk*
ajuin a-*yöyn onion (see also ui)*
alcoholarm beer al-koh-*hol*-arm beer *beer low in alcohol*
alcoholvrij beer al-koh-*hol*-vrey beer *nonalcoholic beer*
amandel a-*man*-duhl *almond*
amandelbroodje ⓝ a-*man*-duhl-broh-chuh *sweet roll with almond filling*
ananas *a*-na-nas *pineapple*
andalouse an-da-*loo*-zuh *Andalusian sauce – tangy sauce of mayonnaise, peppers, onion, tomato sauce & lemon juice*
andijvie an-*dey*-vee *endive*
anijs a-*neys aniseed*

ansjovis an-*sho*-vis *anchovies*
apennoot *aa*-puh-noht *groundnut/peanut*
à point a-*pwaa medium (Belgium)*
appel *a*-puhl *apple*
appelbol *a*-puhl-bol *warm, round, sweet pastry with apple*
appelflap *a*-puhl-flap *apple turnover*
appelgebak ⓝ *a*-puhl-khuh-*bak apple pie*
appeljenever *a*-puhl-yuh-ney-vuhr/ *a*-puhl-zhuh-*ney*-vuhr Ⓝ/Ⓑ *apple-flavoured gin*
appelmoes *a*-puhl-moos *apple sauce*
appelpannenkoek *a*-puhl-*pa*-nuh-kook *apple pancake with lemon juice & caramelised sugar*
appelsien a-puhl-*seen orange (Belgium)*
appeltaart *a*-puhl-taart *apple pie*
arachideolie a-ra-*khee*-duh-oh-lee *groundnut oil*
artisjok ar-tee-*shok artichoke*
asperge a-*sper*-zhuh *asparagus*
asperges op Vlaamse wijze a-*sper*-zhus op *vlaam*-suh *wey*-zuh *asparagus Flemish-style – white asparagus with a sauce of melted butter & egg*
aubergine oh-ber-*zhee*-nuh *eggplant*
augurk aw-*khurk gherkin*
avocado a-voh-*kaa*-doh *avocado*
azijn a-*zeyn vinegar*

B

baars baars *bream*
babbelut ba-buh-*lut butterscotch*

balletjes ⓝ pl *ba*-luh-chus
small meatballs (often in soup)

bami Ind *baa*-mee *noodles*
— **goreng** Ind *khoh*-reng *fried noodles with veggies, pork & shrimp; often served with a fried egg or shredded omelette*
— **hap** hap *rectangular croquette filled with noodles*
— **rames** Ind *raa*-mes
noodles covered in various condiments

banaan ba-*naan* banana

banketletter bang-*ket*-le-tuhr
almond pastry

Barbar bar-*ber*
white beer with honey (Belgium)

basilicum ba-zee-lee-kum *basil*

bataat ba-*taat* sweet potato

beenham beyn-ham *country ham*

beignet bey-*nye* fritter

belegd broodje ⓝ buh-*lekht* broh-chuh
filled sandwich (usually a half baguette)

belegen kaas buh-*ley*-khuhn kaas
cheese ripened for 16 weeks

beschuit buh-*shöyt* typical Dutch light
crisp bread (often round)

beslag ⓝ buh-*slakh* batter

bessen be-suhn *berries*

bessenjenever be-suhn-yuh-*ney*-vuhr/
be-suhn-zhuh-*ney*-vuhr ⓝ/ⓑ
berry-flavoured gin

biefstuk *beef*-stuk steak
— **tartaar** tar-*taar*
raw minced beef with eggs & spices

bier ⓝ beer *beer*

bière brut byer brewt
champagne-like sparkling beer like Brut des Flandres from the Deus brewery (Belgium)

bier op fles beer op fles *bottled beer*

bier van 't vat beer vant va *beer on tap*

bieslook bees-lohk *chives*

biet beet *beet*

(rode) bietjes ⓝ pl (*roh*-duh) bee-chus
beetroot

bitterballen *bi*-tuhr-ba-luhn *savoury crumbed & deep-fried meatballs*

blad ⓝ blat *leaf*

bladerdeeg ⓝ *blaa*-duhr-deykh *puff pastry*

bladgroenten blat-khroon-tuhn
leafy vegetables

blanche blansh *alternative (originally French) term for* **witbier** *(Belgium)*

bleekselderij bleyk-sel-duh-*rey* see **selderij**

blikgroenten blik-khroon-tuhn
canned vegetables

blinde vink *blin*-duh vingk *meat roll of veal or beef wrapped in bacon*

bloedworst *bloot*-worst *black pudding • blood sausage – also called* **beuling** *or* **pens** *in Belgium*

bloem bloom *flour • flower*

bloemkool *bloom*-kohl *cauliflower*

Blond blont *term used to refer to the amber-coloured version of beers that come both as* **Blond** *(blonde) &* **Donker** *(dark) varieties, such as some of the Trappist beers (Belgium); sometimes also used to indicate any beer of the light-coloured variety, such as* **witbier**

boeren- boo-ruhn-
farmer-style • from the farm

boerenjongens boo-ruhn-*yong*-uhns
brandy with spices & raisins

boerenkool boo-ruhn-kohl *kale*

boerenmeisjes boo-ruhn-*mey*-shus
brandy with spices & apricots

boerenomelet boo-ruhn-oh-muh-*let*
omelette with vegetables & bacon

bokbier *bok*-beer *Dutch seasonal beer – Grolsch does Lentebok (Spring Bock) & Herfstbok (Autumn Bock)*

bolleke bo-luh-kuh *'little ball' – Antwerp locals order their De Koninck Ale referring to the shape of the glass it comes in*

bolus *boh*-lus *type of (Dutch) pastry*

bonbons bon-bons *chocolates (Holland)*

bonen *boh*-nuhn *beans*

borrel bo-ruhl *alcoholic drink • aperitif*

borrelhapjes ⓝ pl bo-ruhl-*hap*-yuhs
titbits to go with alcoholic drinks

borst borst *breast (meat)*

bosbessen bos-be-suhn *blueberries*

bosuitjes ⓝ pl bos-*öy*-chus
spring onions (also called **lente-uitjes**)

boter *boh*-tuhr *butter*

boterbabbelaar boh-tuhr-ba-buh-*laar*
sweet containing butterscotch

boterham *boh*-tuhr-ham
sandwich (of sliced bread)

boterletter boh-tuhr-*le*-tuhr *pastry*

botermelk *boh*-tuhr-melk
  buttermilk (Belgium)
bouillon boo-*yon* consommé stock
bouletten boo-*le*-tuhn
  big meatballs (Flanders)
bout bawt *leg (meat)*
braambessen *braam*-be-suhn *raspberries*
Brabantse koffietafel *braa*-bant-suh
  ko-fee-taa-fuhl *buffet-style meal consist-*
  ing of various breads, cheeses, cold meats,
  savoury & sweet spreads, pies & cakes
brandewijn *bran*-duh-weyn *brandy*
brood ⓝ *broht bread*
broodje ⓝ *broh*-chuh *bread roll*
bruidstaart *bröyts*-taart *wedding cake*
bruin bier *bröyn* beer *brown beer* – *also*
  known as **oud bruin** *(lit: old brown)*
Brusselse wafel *bru*-suhl-suh *waa*-fuhl
  big, light & crispy rectangular waffle
  served on a plate with icing sugar,
  whipped cream and/or fruit
Brussels lof ⓝ *bru*-suhls lof *see* **witlof**
Bush boosh *the strongest beer at 12%*
  alcohol (not to be confused with the
  American lager Busch) – *also comes as a*
  Christmas beer, **Bush de Noël** *(Belgium)*

C

cacao ka-*kaw*/ka-ka-oh ⓝ/ⓑ *cocoa*
cake keyk *cake*
caramelpudding ka-ra-*mel*-pu-ding
  crème caramel
cashewnoot ka-shoo-*noht cashew*
champignons sham-pee-*nyons*
  button mushrooms
charcuterie shar-kut-*ree*
  prepared/cooked/cured meats
chili *chee*-lee *chilli*
chilisaus *chee*-lee-saws *chilli sauce*
chipolataworst shee-poh-*laa*-ta-worst
  long thin sausage, rolled up
chips ships *crisps*
chocolade sho-koh-*laa*-duh *chocolate*
chocoladejenever
  shoh-koh-*laa*-duh-yuh-*ney*-vuhr/
  shoh-koh-*laa*-duh-zhuh-*ney*-vuhr ⓝ/ⓑ
  chocolate-flavoured gin
chocoladereep sho-koh-*laa*-duh-reyp
  chocolate bar
chocomel *sho*-koh-mel
  bottled chocolate drink – *ask for it*
  warme *(warm)* or **koude** *(cold)*
citroen see-*troon lemon*

citroenjenever see-*troon*-yuh-*ney*/vuhr/
  see-*troon*-zhuh-*ney*-vuhr ⓝ/ⓑ
  lemon-flavoured gin
cocktailsaus kok-*teyl*-saws
  sauce of mayonnaise, ketchup, whiskey,
  pepper & salt
commiesiekaas koh-*mee*-see-kaas
  Dutch Mimolette – *a cow's milk cheese*
  with orange skin
confituur kon-fee-*tewr*
  jam • marmalade (Flanders)
courgette koor-*zhet zucchini*
crème fraîche kreym *fresh fresh whipped*
  cream (Belgium) – *more like sour cream*
  in the Netherlands
croque monsieur krok muh-*sye toasted*
  sandwich with cheese & ham – **croque**
  madame krok ma-*dam has an egg*
  added, while **croque Hawaii** krok
  ha-*way comes with a slice of pineapple*
curryworst ku-ree-worst *long, skinless,*
  deep-fried mincemeat sausage
  (Flanders) – *in Holland called* **frikandel**

D

dadel *daa*-duhl *date (fruit)*
daging Ind *da*-khing *beef*
dagschotel *dakh*-skhoh-tuhl
  dish of the day (also called **plat du jour***)*
deeg ⓝ deykh *dough*
Delirium Tremens
  dey-*lee*-ree-yuhm *trey*-mens
  bright blonde beer of 9% alcohol –
  comes in a distinctive ceramic-looking
  bottle with pink elephants (Belgium)
dessert ⓝ de-*sert*
  dessert – *also called* **nagerecht**
doner kebab deu-nuhr kuh-*bap*
  see **shoarma**
dooier *doh*-yuhr *egg yolk*
doorbakken dohr-*ba*-kuhn *well-done*
doperwten *dop*-erw-tuhn *garden peas*
droog drokh *dry*
drop drop *sweet or salty liquorice*
druiven *dröy*-vuhn *grapes* – **blauwe**
  druiven *blaw*-wuh *dröy*-vuhn *(black*
  grapes) or **witte druiven** *wi*-tuh
  dröy-vuhn *(white grapes)*
Dubbel *du*-buhl *'double'* – *Trappist or*
  abbey-style beer higher in alcohol content
  than the **Single** *but lower than the* **Tripel**
duif döyf *pigeon*

Duvel *dew*-vuhl
'devil' – a unique strong golden ale of
8.5% alcohol with a clean, firm body &
fresh & fruity hop aromas (Belgium)

E

Edammerkaas *ey·da·muhr·kaas* a small
round cheese from Edam with red or
orange skin – traditionally weighs 1.7 kg
eend *eynt* duck
ei/eieren ⓝ/ⓟ pl *ey/ey·yuh·ruhn* egg/
eggs
eierdooier *ey·yuhr·doh·yuhr* egg yolk
eierplant *ey·yuhr·plant*
eggplant (see also **aubergine**)
eiwit ⓝ *ey·*wit egg white
erwtensoep *erw·*tuhn-soop
thick pea soup with smoked sausage &
bacon (also called **snert**)
erwtjes *erw·*chus peas
escargots *es·kar·khohs* snails (Belgium)
everzwijn ⓝ *ey·vuhr·zweyn* boar
extra belegen kaas *ek·*stra buh·*ley·*khuhn
kaas cheese ripened for seven months

F

fazant fa·*zant* pheasant
filet fee·*ley* fillet
flan fla *flan*
flensje ⓝ *flen·*shuh thin pancake
flessebier ⓝ *fle·*suh-beer bottled beer
forel fo·*rel* trout
frambozen fram·*boh·*zuhn raspberries
frambozenbier ⓝ fram·*boh·*zuhn-beer
raspberry beer – the traditional ones are
based on **Lambic** (Belgium)
Friese kaas *free·*suh kaas
a hard cheese flavoured with a combina-
tion of cumin & cloves
Friese nagelkaas *free·*suh *naa·*khul-kaas
'Frisian clove cheese' – a spiced cheese
with a firm texture
friet/frieten/frites freet/*free·*tuhn/frit/
freet chips – also called **patat** in Holland
frikandel *free·*kan-*del* long, skinless, deep-
fried mincemeat sausage (Holland) –
in Flanders called **curryworst** • spicy
meatball or meat patty (Belgium)

frisdrank *fris·*drangk soft drink
fruit ⓝ *fröyt* fruit
fruitbier *fröyt·*beer fruit beer

G

gado-gado Ind *ga·*doh·*ga·*doh
steamed vegetables & a hard-boiled egg
served with peanut sauce & rice
ganache ga·*nash* a blend of chocolate,
fresh cream & cocoa butter flavoured
with coffee, cinnamon or liqueurs
gans khans goose
garnalen khar·*naa·*luhn shrimps
garnalenkroket khar·*naa·*luhn-kroh-ket
deep-fried croquette filled with (grey)
shrimps
garnering khar·*ney·*ring garnish
gazeus kha·*zeus* carbonated
gebak ⓝ khuh·*bak* cakes & pastries
gebakken khuh·*ba·*kuhn baked • fried
gebarbecued khuh·*bar·*buh-kewt
barbecued
gebraad ⓝ khuh·*braat* roast
gebraden khu·*braa·*duhn roasted
— **aan 't spit** aant·*spit* spit-roasted
gedroogd khuh·*drohkht* dried
geflambeerd khuh·*flam·*beyrt flambéed
gefrituurd khuh·*free·*tewrt deep-fried
gegratineerd khuh·*khra·*te·neyrt
browned on top with cheese (au gratin)
gegrild khuh·*khrilt* grilled
gehakt ⓝ khuh·*hakt* mincemeat
gehaktballetjes ⓝ pl
khuh·*hakt·*ba·luh-chuhs small meatballs
geit kheyt goat
geitenkaas *khey·*tuh-kaas goat's cheese
gekoeld khuh·*koolt* chilled
gekonfijt fruit ⓝ khu·kon·*feyt* fröyt
candied fruit
gekookt khuh·*kohkt* boiled
gekruid (met …) khuh·*kröyt* (met …)
seasoned (with …)
gemarineerd khuh·ma·ree·*neyrt* marinated
gember *khem·*buhr ginger
gemberpannenkoek
*khem·*buhr·*pa·*nuh·kook
pancake laced with small chunks of
ginger & ginger syrup
gemengd khuh·*mengt* assorted • mixed

186

FOOD

gemengde salade
khuh·*meng*·duh sa·*laa*·duh *mixed salad*

gepaneerd khuh·pa·*neyrt*
coated in breadcrumbs

gepocheerd khuh·po·*sheyrt poached*

geraspt khuh·*raspt grated*

gerookt khuh·*rohkt smoked*

gerookte Goudse kaas khuh·*rohk*·tuh
khawt·suh kaas *'smoked Gouda cheese' –
a sausage-shaped hard cheese that's
smoked slowly in brick ovens*

geroosterd khuh·*roh*·stuhrt *roasted*
 — **brood** ⓝ broht
toast (of bread slices)

gesauteerd khuh·soh·*teyrt sautéed*

gesmolten khuh·*smol*·tuhn *melted*

gesmoord khuh·*smohrt braised*

gesneden khuh·*sney*·duhn *cut • sliced*

gestoofd khuh·*stohft stewed*

gestoomd khu·*stohmt steamed*

getapt beer khuh·*tapt* beer *beer on tap*

gevogelte ⓝ khuh·*voh*·khuhl·tuh
fowl • poultry

gevuld khuh·*vult stuffed*

gezouten khuh·*zaw*·tuhn *salted*

gianduja zhan·*doo*·cha
a blend of chocolate & hazelnut paste

glazuur ⓝ khla·*zewr icing*

goed doorbakken khoot dohr·*ba*·kuhn
well-done

Goudse kaas *khawt*·suh kaas
'Gouda cheese' – a popular Dutch cheese

graanjenever *khraan*·yuh·ney·vuhr/
khraan·zhuh·ney·vuhr ⓝ/Ⓑ
see **jenever**

granaatappel khra·*naat*·a·puhl
pomegranate

griesmeelpudding khrees·*meyl*·pu·ding
*semolina pudding often served with a
berry sauce*

groene paprika *khroo*·nuh pa·*pree*·ka
green capsicum

groentebouillon *khroon*·tuh·boo·*yon*
vegetable broth • vegetable stock

groenten *khroon*·tuhn *vegetables*

groentenkrans *khroon*·tuh·krans
*assortment of warm vegetables served
with a meal*

Gueuze *kheu*·zuh *a blend of two or more*
 Lambic *beers, resulting in a more
sparkling variety (Belgium)*

gyros *khee*·ros *see* **shoarma**

H

Haagse bluf *haakh*·suh bluf
*egg whites beaten stiff & served with red
currant or berry juice*

haan haan *cock*

haas haas *hare*

hagelslag *haa*·khuhl·slakh
chocolate sprinkles

half doorbakken half dohr·*ba*·kuhn
medium – in Belgium à point

ham ham *ham*

hammetje ⓝ *ha*·muh·chuh
whole ham on the bone

hapjes ⓝ pl *hap*·yuhs
appetisers • snacks • titbits

harde kaas *har*·duh kaas *hard cheese*

hardgekookt ei ⓝ *hart*·khuh·kohkt ey
hard-boiled egg

haring *haa*·ring *herring*
 — **met groene bonen**
met *khroo*·nuh *boh*·nuhn *herring with
green beans, bacon & potatoes*

haringsla *haa*·ring·slaa *cold salad of
chopped herring with boiled potatoes,
other cooked vegetables & mayonnaise –
often served on a bread roll*

hartig/hartelijk
har·tikh/*har*·tuh·luhk ⓝ/Ⓑ *savoury*

havermout *haa*·vuhr·mawt *oats*

havermoutpap *haa*·vuhr·mawt·pap
milk-based oatmeal porridge

hazelnoot *haa*·zuhl·noht *hazelnut*

heet heyt *hot (temperature) • spicy*

helder *hel*·duhr *clear (eg soup)*

hersenen/hersentjes
her·suh·nuhn/*her*·suhn·chus *brains*

hert ⓝ hert *venison*

hesp hesp *ham (Belgium)*

hete bliksem *hey*·tuh *blik*·suhm
*'hot lightning' – Dutch stew of potatoes,
apples, onions & bacon*

Hollandse nieuwe ho·*lant*·suh *nee*·wuh
*filleted herring – the first catch of the
season (from late May)*

honing *hoh*·ning *honey*

hoofdgerecht ⓝ *hohft·khuh·rekht*
main course
hoorntje ⓝ *hohrn·chuh* custard-filled,
horn-shaped pastry • ice-cream cone
hutspot *huts·pot*
stew of potatoes, onions & carrots
huzarensla *hew·zaa·ruhn·slaa*
meat & potato salad

I

ijs ⓝ *eys* ice • ice cream
ingeblikt *in·khuh·blikt* canned
ingemaakt *in·khuh·maakt* preserved
— **zuur** ⓝ *zewr* pickles
inktvis *ingkt·vis* squid

J

jachtschotel *yakht·skhoh·tuhl* 'hunter's
stew' – oven dish with meat & potatoes
jam *zhem* jam
janhagel *yan·haa·khul* almond cookies
spiced with cinamon & allspice
jenever *yuh·ney·vuhr/zhuh·ney·vuhr* ⓝ/ⓑ
gin (also called **graanjenever**) – traditionally distilled from juniper berries;
comes in a variety of strengths & tastes
jeneverbessen *yuh·ney·vuhr·be·suhn/
zhuh·ney·vuhr·be·suhn* ⓝ/ⓑ
juniper berries
jong *yong* young
— **belegen kaas** *buh·ley·khuhn kaas*
cheese ripened for eight weeks
jonge jenever *yong·uh yuh·ney·vuhr/
yong·uh zhuh·ney·vuhr* ⓝ/ⓑ
young jenever
jonge kaas *yong·uh kaas* 'young cheese' –
cheese ripened for four or five weeks
jus *zhew* gravy • juice (from meat)
— **d'orange** *do·ransh*
orange juice (Holland)

K

kaas *kaas* cheese
kaasaardappelen *kaas·aart·a·puh·luhn*
baked potatoes covered with melted
cheese
kaasblokjes ⓝ pl *kaas·blok·yuhs*
cheese cubes (often served with mustard
as an accompaniment to drinks)

kaaskroketten *kaas·kroh·ke·tuhn*
deep-fried croquettes with a cheesy/
creamy filling
kaasplank *kaas·plangk* cheese board
kabeljauw *ka·buhl·yaw* cod
kalfsoesters *kalfs·oos·tuhrs* veal
kalfsvlees *kalfs·vleys* veal
kalkoen *kal·koon* turkey
kammosselen *ka·mo·suh·luhn* scallops
kaneel *ka·neyl* cinnamon
kappertjes ⓝ pl *ka·puhr·chus* capers
karakollen *ka·ra·ko·luhn* snails (Belgium)
karbonade *kar·boh·naa·duh*
chop/cutlet – also called **kotelet**
karnemelk *kar·nuh·melk* buttermilk
kastanjes *kas·tan·yus* chestnuts
kekers *key·kuhrs* see **kikkererwten**
Kernhemkaas *kern·nuhm·kaas* a soft &
supple cheese with a mild texture
kersen *ker·suhn* cherries
kerstomaatjes *kers·toh·maa·chus*
cherry tomatoes
kervel *ker·vuhl* chervil
ketchap *ke·tyap* (Indonesian) soy sauce
kibbeling *ki·buh·ling*
deep-fried cod parings
kikkerbilletjes ⓝ pl *ki·kuhr·bi·luh·chus*
frog's legs
kikkererwten *ki·kuhr·erw·tuhn* chickpeas
kip *kip* chicken
klapstuk ⓝ *klap·stuk* rib of beef
knakworst *knak·worst* frankfurter
knoedel *knoo·duhl* dumpling
knoflook *knof·lohk* garlic – also called **look**
knolraap *knol·raap* swede • Swedish turnip
knolselderij *knol·sel·duh·rey* celeriac
koek *kook* biscuit • cookie
koekje ⓝ *kook·yuh* biscuit • cookie
koenjit lnd *koon·yit* ground turmeric
koffie *ko·fee* coffee
koffiemelk *ko·fee·melk* slightly sour-
tasting cream akin to condensed milk,
served separately with coffee
koffie verkeerd *ko·fee vuhr·keyrt*
coffee with a generous serving of milk,
similar to a caffe latte
kokosnoot *koh·kos·noht* coconut
komijn *koh·meyn* cumin
kommommer *kom·ko·muhr* cucumber
konfituur *kon·fee·tewr* jam

konijn Ⓝ ko·*neyn* rabbit
— **met pruimen** met *pröy*·muhn
rabbit cooked until tender in a sauce spiked with prunes (Flanders)

koninginnehapje Ⓝ
koh·ning·*khi*·nuh·hap·yuh vol-au-vent
(Flanders) – also see **pasteitje**

kool kohl *cabbage*

koolrabi kohl·*raa*·bee *kohlrabi*

kopstoot *kop*·stoht
'head butt' – **jenever** *with a beer chaser*

korst korst *crust*

korstdeeg Ⓝ korst·deykh *short pastry*

kort gebakken kort khuh·*ba*·kuhn
rare – see also **saignant**

kotelet ko·tuh·*let* see **karbonade**

koud kawt *cold*
— **buffet** Ⓝ bew·*fet*
buffet/smorgasbord of cold dishes

koude voorgerechten Ⓝ pl *kaw*·duh
vohr·khuh·rekh·tuhn *cold starters*

kraanwater/kraantjeswater Ⓝ Ⓝ/Ⓑ
kraan·waa·tuhr/*kraan*·chus·waa·tuhr
tap water

krab krap *crab*

kreeft kreyft *lobster*

krenten *kren*·tuhn *currants*

krentenbrood Ⓝ *kren*·tuh·broht
bread with currants

krentewegge *kren*·tuh·we·khuh
raisin roll traditionally served with coffee

Kriek kreek *cherry beer – the traditional ones are based on* **Lambic** *& also known as* **Oude Kriek** *(old Kriek) or Kriek Lambic*

krieken *kree*·kuhn *sour cherries*

kroepoek Ind *kroo*·pook
shrimp/prawn crackers

krokant kroh·*kant* crisp

kroket kroh·*ket* croquette *(often filled with meat or cheese & eaten as a snack)*

kroketjes Ⓝ pl kroh·*ke*·chus
deep-fried potato croquettes

kropsla *krop*·slaa *lettuce*

kruiden *kröy*·duhn *herbs & spices*

kruidenkaas *kröy*·duhn·kaas
cheese with spices

kruidenpannenkoek
kröy·duhn·*pa*·nuh·kook
pancake with (green) herbs & spices

kruidenthee *kröy*·duh·tey *herbal tea*

kruidnagels *kröyt*·naa·khuls *cloves*

kruimeldeeg Ⓝ *kröy*·muhl·deykh
shortcrust pastry

kruisbessen *kröys*·be·suhn *gooseberries*

krulsla *krul*·slaa *curly-leaved lettuce*

kuiken Ⓝ *köy*·kuhn *spring chicken*

Kwak kwak *amber beer of 8% alcohol with earthy aromas, probably more famous for its round-bottomed glass and stirrup-like holder than for its content (Belgium)*

kwark kwark *quark*

kwarktaart kwark·taart
cheesecake made with **kwark**

kwartel *kwar*·tuhl *quail*

kweepeer kwey·peyr *quince*

L

lam Ⓝ lam *lamb*

Lambic lam·*beek* an almost wine-like beer
from the Brussels region, brewed with wild yeast; the Belle-Vue, Lindemans, Timmermans & Mort Subite (lit: sudden death) breweries are among the best-known ones

Leerdammerkaas leyr·da·muhr·kaas
a firm cheese with cherry-sized holes & a mild, nut-like flavour (also called **Maasdammerkaas**)

Leidse kaas *leyt*·suh kaas
'Leyden cheese' – a mild, hard cheese spiced with cumin or caraway seeds

lekkerbekje Ⓝ le·kuhr·*bek*·yuh
deep-fried fish fillet

lende *len*·duh *loin*

lendebiefstuk *len*·duh·beef·stuk
eye fillet • rump steak

lente-uitjes Ⓝ *len*·tuh·öy·chus
spring onions (also called **bosuitjes**)

lever *ley*·vuhr *liver*

levertjes Ⓝ pl *ley*·vuhr·chus
small livers (eg from chicken)

licht likht *light* • *low-fat*
— **beer** beer *light beer – low-alcohol beer (for those who are driving)*

likeur lee·*keur* liqueur

limoen lee·*moon* lime

linzen *lin*·zuhn *lentils*

loempia Ind *loom*·pee·ya *large spring roll (the smaller ones are called* **mini-loempias** mee·nee·loom·pee·yas)

look lohk *garlic*

Luikse wafel *löyk*·suh *waa*·fuhl
heavy, sweet, sugary waffle, eaten warm

M

Maasdammerkaas *maas*-da-muhr-kaas
*a firm cheese with cherry-sized holes &
a mild, nut-like flavour (also called
Leerdammerkaas)*

maatjes ⓝ pl maa-chus
'little friends' – type of herring

magere melk *maa*-khu-ruh melk *skim milk*

makreel mak-*reyl mackerel*

maïs maays/ma-*yees* ⓝ/Ⓑ *sweet corn*

marmelade mar-muh-*laa*-duh *marmalade*

marsepein mar-suh-*peyn marzipan*

mayonaise ma-yoh-*ney*-suh *mayonnaise*

Mechelse asperges *me*-khuhl-suh
as-*per*-khus *white asparagus –
a speciality of the Belgian town of
Mechelen*

medaillon ⓝ *me*-da-*yon a piece of food,
usually meat, cut into a small, thin,
round or oval shape*

melk melk *milk*

meloen muh-*loon cantaloupe • melon*

met ... met *... with ...*

met koolzuur/prik met kohl-zewr/prik
carbonated

mie Ind mee *noodles*

mierikswortel *mee*-riks-wor-tuhl
horseradish

moerbei *moor*-bey *mulberry*

moorkop *mohr*-kop *éclair (Holland)*

mosselen *mo*-suh-luhn
*mussels, usually cooked in white wine,
accompanied by chips*

mosterd *mos*-tuhrt *mustard*

(gestampte) muisjes ⓝ pl
(khuh-*stamp*-tuh) *möy*-shuhs
(ground) sugar-coated aniseed

munt munt *mint*

muntthee *munt*-tey *mint tea*

N

nagerecht ⓝ pl *naa*-khuh-rekht *dessert*

nasi Ind *na*-see *rice*
— **goreng** Ind *khoh*-reng
*fried rice with onions, pork, shrimp &
spices, often served with a fried egg or
shredded omelette on top*
— **rames** Ind *raa*-muhs
*a plate of boiled rice covered with vari-
ous vegetable & meat dishes*

niertjes ⓝ *neer*-chus *kidneys*

noedels *noo*-duhls *noodles*

noordzeegarnalen
noort-zey-khar-*naa*-luhn *small grey
shrimp with a distinctive taste, found
in the North Sea only – buy them fresh
from the fish market, peel them yourself
& wash them down with a glass of beer*

noot noht *nut*

nootmuskaat noht-mus-*kaat nutmeg*

nougatine noo-kha-*teen*
*pliable paste of sugar, syrup, crushed or
ground almonds or hazelnuts*

O

oester *oos*-tuhr *oyster*

olie *oh*-lee *oil*

oliebol *oh*-lee-bol *dough fritter*

olienoot *oh*-lee-noht *groundnut/peanut*

olijf o-*leyf olive*

olijfolie o-*leyf*-oh-lee *olive oil*

omelet oh-muh-*let omelette*

ontbijtgranen ont-*beyt*-khraa-nuhn *cereal*

ontbijtkoek ont-*beyt*-kook
*gingerbread-style honey cake – called
peperkoek in Belgium*

ossehaas *o*-suh-haas
carpaccio-style fillet of beef

ossestaart *o*-suh-staart *oxtail*

ossetong *o*-suh-tong *oxtongue*

oud awt *matured • old*

oud bruin awt bröyn *'old brown' –
brown beer (see also bruin beer)*

oude jenever *aw*-duh yuh-*ney*-vuhr/
aw-duh zhuh-*ney*-vuhr ⓝ/Ⓑ
old jenever

oude kaas *aw*-duh kaas
cheese ripened for at least a year

P

paard paart *horse*

paardefilet *paar*-duh-fee-ley *fillet of horse*

paddestoelen *pa*-duh-stoo-luhn
mushrooms

paling *paa*-ling *eel*
— **in 't groen** int khroon *'green eels' –
eel in spinach sauce (Flanders)*

Palm palm
*typical Belgian-style ale, tasty & amber
in colour – look out for the horse logo*

pannenkoek *pa*-nuh-kook *pancake*
(rode/groene) paprika
  (roh-duh/khroo-nuh) *pa*-pree-ka
  (red/green) capsicum
parelhoen *paa*-ruhl-hoon *guinea fowl*
passievrucht *pa*-see-vrukht *passionfruit*
pasteitje *pa*-stey-chuh *vol-au-vent –*
  in Belgium called **koninginnehapje**
patat *pa*-tat *French fries (Holland)*
patrijs *pa*-treys *partridge*
pedis Ind puh-dees *hot (spicy)*
peer peyr *pear*
pens pens *see* **bloedworst**
peper *pey*-puhr *(cracked) pepper*
peperkoek *pey*-puhr-kook *see* **ontbijtkoek**
pepernoten *pey*-puhr-noh-tuhn
  crunchy ginger biscuits
perzik *per*-zik *peach*
peterselie *pey*-tuhr-sey-lee *parsley*
peultjes pl *peul*-chus *sugar peas*
peulvrucht *peul*-vrukht *legume*
pide *pee*-dey *Turkish pizza*
pikant pee-*kant* *spicy*
pils pils *lager – the best-selling Stella*
  Artois from Leuven is known worldwide,
  but other equally good pilsners include
  Maes, Primus & Jupiler; in Holland,
  there's Heineken of course, but also
  Amstel, Grolsch & Oranjeboom
pinda *pin*-da *groundnut/peanut*
pindasaus *pin*-da-saws *peanut sauce*
pisang Ind *pee*-sang *banana*
pistachenoot pees-*tash*-noht *pistachio*
pita *pee*-ta *stuffed pitta bread sandwiches,*
  Middle-Eastern style
pitabrood *pee*-ta-broht *pitta bread*
plak plak *slice (Holland)*
plat du jour plat dew zhoor
  French for **dagschotel**
poffert *po*-fuhrt
  a Dutch version of Gugelhoph – a small,
  round raisin cake served with coffee
poffertjes pl po-fuhr-chuhs
  small puffed-up pancakes served with
  butter & icing sugar (Holland)
pompoen pom-*poon* *pumpkin*
portie *por*-see *portion/serve*
  — gemengd khuh-*mengt*
  plate with mixed titbits, often cheese,
  salami, olives, etc

pralines pra-*lee*-nuh *chocolates*
prei prey *leek*
prinsesseboontjes pl
  prin-*se*-suh-bohn-chus *haricot beans*
pruimen *pröy*-muhn *plums • prunes*
puree pew-*rey* *mash*
puur pewr *pure/straight (alcohol)*

R

raap/rapen raap/*raa*-puhn *turnip(s)*
rabarber ra-*bar*-buhr *rhubarb*
radijs ra-*deys* *radish*
rauw raw *raw*
redelijk gebakken
  rey-duh-luhk khu-*ba*-kuhn *medium*
ree(bout) *rey*(-bawt) *venison*
reep (chocolade)
  reyp (shoh-koh-*laa*-duh) *(chocolate) bar*
ribstuk *rip*-stuk *rib steak*
rijp reyp *ripe*
rijst reyst *rice*
rijstebrij/rijstpap Ⓝ/Ⓑ
  reys-tuh-brey/*reyst*-pap *sweet rice pud-*
  ding, usually served with brown sugar
rijsttafel *reys*-taa-fuhl
  'rice table' – an array of savoury Indone-
  sian dishes, like braised beef, pork satay
  & ribs served with white rice
rijstvla *reyst*-vlaa *a tart filled with sweet,*
  creamy rice pudding
rivierkreeft ree-veer-kreyft *crayfish*
rode biet *roh*-duh beet *beetroot*
rode kool *roh*-duh kohl *red cabbage*
rode paprika *roh*-duh pa-*pree*-ka
  red capsicum
roerei *roo*-rey *scrambled eggs*
rog rokh *ray*
roggebrood *ro*-khuh-broht
  pumpernickel • rye bread
rollade ro-*laa*-duh
  rolled slices of meat held together with
  string & slow-cooked in the oven
rolmops *rol*-mops *rollmop*
romig *roh*-mikh *creamy*
rood roht *rare – in Belgium* **saignant**
roodbaars *roht*-baars *red mullet*
rood bier roht beer *red beer – wine-like in*
  colour, like Rodenbach (Belgium)
rookkaas *roh*-kaas *smoked cheese*
room rohm *cream*
roomijs *rohm*-eys *ice cream*

menu decoder

191

roomkaas rohm·kaas cream cheese
roti kip roh·tee kip curried chicken served with potatoes, long beans, bean sprouts & a chickpea-flour pancake (Suriname)
rozijnen ro·zey·nuhn raisins • sultanas
rund ⓝ runt beef
Russisch ei ⓝ ru·sis ey sliced egg served with a vegetable mix

S

saignant sey·nya rare – also called **kort gebakken**
salade sa·laa·duh salad
sambal Ind sam·bal red chilli paste
— **badjak** Ind ba·dzhak dark brown, onion-based chilli paste with a mild & sweet flavour
— **oelek** Ind oo·lek hot red chilli paste
sap ⓝ sap juice
sardientjes ⓝ pl sar·deen·chus sardines
saté sa·tey 'satay' – pieces of barbecued beef, chicken or pork on small skewers (sometimes covered in peanut sauce)
saucijs saw·seys sausage (Holland)
saucijzebroodje ⓝ saw·sey·zuh·broh·chuh sausage roll – in Belgium called **worstebrood**
saus saws sauce
savooikool sa·voy·kohl savoy cabbage
schaal- en schelpdieren ⓝ pl skhaal en skhelp·dee·ruhn crustaceans & shellfish
schaap ⓝ skhaap mutton • sheep
schelvis skhel·vis haddock
schenkel skheng·kuhl shank
schimmelkaas skhi·muhl·kaas blue cheese
schol skhol plaice
schorsenelen skhor·suh·ney·luhn black salsify
schouderstuk ⓝ skhaw·duhr·stuk shoulder (meat)
selderij sel·duh·rey celery
shoarma shoo·war·ma Lebanese & Turkish pitta bread filled with sliced lamb from a vertical spit (also known as gyros or doner kebab)
sinaasappel see·naas·a·puhl orange
Single sing·uhl 'single' – Trappist or abbey-style beer most modest in alcohol

siroop see·rohp sirup
sjalotjes ⓝ pl sha·lo·chus shallots
sla slaa lettuce • salad
slaatje slaa·chuh salad
slagroom slakh·rohm whipped cream
slakken sla·kuhn snails – in Belgium called **escargots**
slasaus slaa·saws dressing • vinaigrette
smeerkaas smeyr·kaas spreadable cheese
snee sney slice
snert snert see **erwtensoep**
snijbonen sney·boh·nuhn haricot beans
snoep snoop candy • lollies • sweets
soep soop soup
soesjes ⓝ pl soo·shuhs profiteroles
sojamelk soh·ya·melk soy milk
sojasaus soh·ya·saws soy sauce – salty (zout) or sweet (zoet)
sojascheuten soh·ya·skheu·tuhn see **taugé**
Spaanse pepers spaan·suh pey·puhrs 'Spanish peppers' – chillies
spa blauw spa blaw still mineral water
spa rood spa roht fizzy mineral water
specerijen spey·suh·rey·yuhn spices
speculaas/speculoos spey·ku·laas/ spey·ku·lohs cinnamon-flavoured biscuit
speenvarken ⓝ speyn·var·kuhn suckling pig
spek ⓝ spek bacon
spekpannenkoek spek·pa·nuh·kook crispy & aromatic bacon pancake
sperziebonen sper·zee·boh·nuhn green beans
spiegelei ⓝ spee·khul·ey fried egg, sunny side up
spinazie spee·naa·zee spinach
spruitjes ⓝ pl sprǒy·chus Brussels sprouts
spuitwater ⓝ spǒyt·waa·tuhr sparkling mineral water (soda water)
stamppot stam·pot mashed potatoes & vegetables – in Belgium called **stoemp**
sterk sterk strong (of flavour)
sterke dranken ster·kuh drang·kuhn spirits
steurgarnaal steur·khar·naal prawn
St Jacobsschelp sint·yaa·kops·skhelp scallop

stoemp stoomp *Flemish-style mashed potatoes, see* **stamppot**
— **met prei** met prey *creamy mashed potatoes with leeks & onion*
stokbrood ⓝ stok-broht *baguette*
stokvis stok-vis *dried cod*
stoofschotel stohf-skhoh-tuhl *casserole*
stoofvlees ⓝ stohf-vleys
beef stew traditionally served with fries – also called **Vlaamse stoofkarbonade**
strandgapers strant-khaa-puhrs *clams*
strooppannenkoek strohp-pa-nuh-kook
pancake with a light-brown syrup derived from the sugar beet
suiker söy-kuhr *sugar*

T

taart taart *pie • tart*
tahoe taa-hoo *tofu*
taptemelk tap-tuh-melk *skim milk*
tartaarsaus tar-taar-saws *tartare sauce*
taugé taw-zhey *bean sprouts – in Belgium called* **sojascheuten**
thee tey *tea*
— **met citroen** met see-troon
tea with lemon
timbaaltje ⓝ tim-baal-chuh
small round mould for the preparation of puddings, puréed vegetables etc • all dishes prepared in such a mould
tofoe toh-foo *tofu*
tomaten toh-maa-tuhn *tomatoes*
tompoes tom-poos *custard slice with icing*
tong tong *sole • tongue*
tonijn toh-neyn *tuna*
toost tohst *toast*
tosti tos-tee *toasted sandwich – in Belgium called* **croque monsieur**
Trappist tra-pist *Trappist beer (Belgium has six Trappist breweries – Achel, Chimay, Orval, Rochefort, Westmalle & Westvleteren; Holland has one – La Trappe)*
Tripel tri-puhl *'triple' – golden Trappist beer or abbey-style beer with a high alcohol content (refermented in the bottle)*
truffels tru-fuhls *truffles – subterranean fungi that are a highly prized delicacy*
tuin- töyn- *from the garden*

tuinbonen töyn-boh-nuhn *broad beans*
tuinkers töyn-kers *cress*

U

ui/uien öy/öy-yuhn
onion/onions (also see **ajuin***)*
uitsmijter öyt-smey-tuhr
sliced bread with cold meat covered with fried eggs & served with a garnish

V

van 't schap vant skhap
'from the shelf' – the phrase to order a beer at room temperature (Belgium)
varkenshaasje ⓝ var-kuhns-haa-shuh
pork tenderloin
varkenspoot var-kuhns-poht *pig's trotter*
varkensvlees ⓝ var-kuhns-vleys *pork*
veenbes veyn-bes *cranberry*
venkel veng-kuhl *fennel*
venusschelpen vey-nus-skhel-puhn
clams • pipis
Verboden Vrucht vuhr-boh-duhn vrukht
'forbidden fruit' – dark, strong beer from the Hoegaarden family of beers (Belgium)
verjaardagstaart vuhr-yaar-dakhs-taart
birthday cake
verloren brood ⓝ vuhr-loh-ruhn broht
'lost bread' – Flemish for **wentelteefjes**
vermicelli ver-mee-she-lee
thin noodles, often added to soup
vers vers *fresh*
vetsin vet-seen *MSG*
vijg veykh *fig*
vis vis *fish*
vla vlaa *custard*
vlaai vlaay *sweet tart/cake/pie – can contain fruit, cream, custard or chocolate*
Vlaams/Vlaamse vlaams/vlaam-suh
Flemish • Flemish-style
Vlaamse frites vlaam-suh freet
fries/chips made from the whole potato & smothered in mayonnaise
Vlaamse stoofkarbonade vlaam-suh
stohf-kar-boh-naa-duh *see* **stoofvlees**
vlammetjes ⓝ pl vla-muh-chus
spicy spring rolls
vlees ⓝ vleys *meat*

vleeswaren *vleys-waa-ruhn*
 cooked/prepared meats – also called
 charcuterie *in Belgium*
vogelnestje ⓝ *voh-khuhl-ne-shuh*
 'bird's nest' – meat loaf with egg inside
volkorenbrood ⓝ *vol-koh-ruhn-broht*
 wholemeal bread
voorgerecht ⓝ *vohr-khuh-rekht starter*
vruchten-/fruit-... *vrukh-tuhn-/fröyt-...*
 ... with fruit
vruchtenvlaai *vrukh-tuhn-vlaay*
 *a fruit flan from the Limburg region filled
 with fruits like cherries & strawberries*

W

wafel *waa-fuhl waffle*
walnoten *wal-noh-tuhn walnuts*
warm *warm hot (temperature)*
 — buffet ⓝ *bew-fet
 buffet/smorgasbord of hot dishes*
warme chocolade *war-muh
 shoh-koh-laa-duh hot chocolate (drink)*
warme voorgerechten ⓝ pl *war-muh
 vohr-khuh-rekh-tuhn warm starters*
water ⓝ *waa-tuhr water*
waterkers *waa-tuhr-kers watercress*
watermeloen *waa-tuhr-muh-loon
 watermelon*
waterzooi *waa-tuhr-zoy
 creamy meal soup with potatoes, vegetables & chicken or fish (Flanders)*
wentelteefjes ⓝ pl *wen-tuhl-teyf-yuhs
 bread slices soaked in a mixture of milk,
 egg, cinnamon & sugar & fried in an
 oiled pan – also called* **verloren brood**
 in Flanders
wijn *weyn wine*
wijngaardslakken *weyn-khaart-sla-kuhn
 see* **slakken**
wild ⓝ *wilt game*
witbier *wit-beer
 the original Belgian wheat beer – try
 Hoegaarden as a refreshment*

witlofsla *wit-lof-slaa salad of raw* **witloof**
witlof/witloof *wit-lof
 chicory – also called* **Brussels lof**
 — met kaas en ham *met kaas en ham*
 witloof *wrapped in ham & baked in the
 oven in a creamy cheese sauce – traditionally served with mashed potatoes*
witteke *wi-tuh-kuh term used to indicate
 pure* **jenever** *(as opposed to the ones
 that have fruits added)*
witte kool *wi-tuh kohl white cabbage*
worst *worst sausage*
worstebrood ⓝ *wor-stuh-broht
 see* **saucijzebroodje**
worstjes ⓝ pl *wor-shus small sausages*
wortel *wor-tuhl carrot*

Z

zacht *zakht mild • soft*
zachte kaas *zakh-tuh kaas soft cheese*
zachtgekookt ei ⓝ *zakht-khuh-koht ey
 soft-boiled egg*
zalm *zalm salmon*
zandgebak/zanddeeg ⓝ
 zant-khuh-bak/zant-deykh shortbread
zeebaars *zey-baars sea bass*
zeebrasem *zey-braa-suhm sea bream*
zeeduivel *zey-döy-vuhl monkfish*
zeewier ⓝ *zey-weer seaweed*
zoet *zoot sweet*
zoetzuur *zoot-zewr sweet & sour*
zonder ... *zon-duhr ... without ...*
zout ⓝ *zawt salt*
zure bom *zew-ruh bom
 big pickled gherkin*
zure haring *zew-ruh haa-ring
 pickled herring – also see* **rolmops**
zure room *zew-ruh rohm sour cream*
zuur *zewr sour*
zuurkool *zewr-kohl sauerkraut*
zwezeriken *zwey-zuh-ri-kuhn
 thymus (gland in chest of animals) –
 usually from veal*

SAFE TRAVEL > essentials

het belangrijkste

emergencies

noodgevallen

Help!	Help!	help
Stop!	Stop!	stop
Go away! (general)	Ga weg!	khaa wekh
Go away! (stronger)	Rot op!	rot op
Thief!	Dief!	deef
Fire!	Brand!	brant
Watch out!	Kijk uit!	keyk öyt
Careful!	Pas op!	pa·zop
Call ...!	Bel ...!	bel ...
an ambulance	een ambulance	uhn am·bew·lans
a doctor	een dokter	uhn dok·tuhr
the police	de politie	duh poh·leet·see

signs

Politiebureau	poh·leet·see·bew·roh	Police Station
Spoedafdeling	spoot·af·dey·ling	Emergency Department
Ziekenhuis	zee·kuhn·höys	Hospital

It's an emergency.
Het is een noodgeval.
huht is uhn noht·khuh·val

There's been an accident.
Er is een ongeluk gebeurd.
uhr is uhn on·khuh·luk khuh·beurt

Could you please help?
Kunt u alstublieft helpen? pol
kunt ew al·stew·bleeft hel·puhn

Can I use your phone?
Kan ik uw telefoon gebruiken? pol
kan ik ew tey·ley·fohn khuh·bröy·kuhn

essentials

195

He/She is having a/an ...	*Hij/Zij heeft een ...*	hey/zey heyft uhn ...
allergic reaction	*allergische reactie*	a·*ler*·khee·suh rey·*yak*·see
asthma attack	*aanval van astma*	*aan*·val van *ast*·ma
epileptic fit	*aanval van epilepsie*	*aan*·val van ey·pee·lep·*see*
heart attack	*hartaanval*	*hart*·aan·val

She's having a baby.
Zij krijgt een baby.   zey kreykht uhn *bey*·bee

I'm lost.
Ik ben verdwaald.   ik ben vuhr·*dwaalt*

Where are the toilets?
Waar zijn de toiletten?   waar zeyn duh twa·*le*·tuhn

Is it safe at night?
Is het 's nachts veilig?   is huht snakhts *vey*·likh

Is it safe on your own?
Is het veilig op je eentje?   is huht *vey*·likh op yuh *eyn*·chuh

Is it safe for ...?	*Is het veilig voor ...?*	is huht *vey*·likh vohr ...
gay people	*homo- sexuelen*	hoh·moh· sek·sew·*wey*·luhn
travellers	*reizigers*	*rey*·zi·khurs
women	*vrouwen*	*vraw*·wuhn

police

Where's the police station?
Waar is het politiebureau?   waar is huht poh·*leet*·see·bew·*roh*

I want to report an offence. (minor/serious)
Ik wil aangifte doen van een overtreding/misdrijf.   ik wil *aan*·khif·tuh doon van uhn oh·vuhr·*trey*·ding/*mis*·dreyf

It was him/her.
Hij/Zij was het.   hey/zey was huht

I have insurance.
Ik heb verzekering.   ik hep vuhr·*zey*·kuh·ring

the police may say ...

U wordt beschuldigd van ... pol	ew wort buh-*skhul*-dikht van ...	**You're charged with ...**
aanranding	*aan*-ran-ding	**assault**
diefstal	*deef*-stal	**theft**
het bezitten van drugs	huht buh-*zi*-tuhn van drukhs	**possession of illegal substances**
openbare zedenschennis	*oh*-puhn-baa-ruh *zey*-duhn-skhe-nis	**indecent exposure**
verstoring van de openbare orde	vuhr-*stoh*-ring van duh *oh*-puhn-baa-ruh or-duh	**disturbing the peace**
winkeldiefstal	*wing*-kuhl-deef-stal	**shoplifting**
U wordt ervan beschuldigd ... pol	ew wort uhr-*van* buh-*skhul*-dikht ...	**You're charged with ...**
geen (geldig) visum te hebben	kheyn (*khel*-dikh) *vee*-zum tuh *he*-buhn	**not having a (valid) visa**
langer te zijn gebleven dan het visum toelaat	*lang*-uhr tuh zeyn khuh-*bley*-vuhn dan huht *vee*-zum *too*-laat	**overstaying a visa**
Het is een ...	huht is uhn ...	**It's a ... fine.**
boete voor een snelheids- overtreding	*boo*-tuh vohr uhn *snel*-heyts- oh-vuhr-*trey*-ding	**speeding**
parkeerboete	par-*keyr*-boo-tuh	**parking**

I've been ...	*Ik ben ...*	ik ben ...
He/She has been ...	*Hij/Zij is ...*	hey/zey is ...
assaulted	*aangevallen*	*aan*-khuh-va-luhn
raped	*verkracht*	vuhr-*krakht*
robbed	*bestolen*	buh-*stoh*-luhn
He/She tried to ... me.	*Hij/Zij probeerde me ...*	hey/zey proh-*beyr*-duh muh ...
assault	*aan te vallen*	aan tuh *va*-luhn
rape	*te verkrachten*	tuh vuhr-*krakh*-tuhn
rob	*te bestelen*	tuh buh-*stey*-luhn

essentials

197

| My ... was stolen. | Mijn ... is gestolen. | meyn ... is khuh·*stoh*·luhn |
| I've lost my ... | Ik heb mijn ... verloren. | ik hep meyn ... vuhr·*loh*·ruhn |

backpack	rugzak	*rukh*·zak
bag	tas	tas
credit card	kredietkaart	krey·*deet*·kaart
handbag	handtas	*han*·tas
money	geld	khelt
passport	paspoort	*pas*·pohrt
wallet	portemonnee	por·tuh·mo·*ney*

Could I please have an (English) interpreter?
Mag ik alstublieft makh ik al·stew·*bleeft*
een (Engelstalige) uhn (*eng*·uhls·*taa*·li·khuh)
tolk? pol tolk

What am I accused of?
Waar word ik van waar wort ik van
beschuldigd? be·*skhul*·dikht

I didn't realise I was doing anything wrong.
Ik was er mij niet van ik was uhr mey neet van
bewust dat ik iets buh·*wust* dat ik eets
verkeerd deed. ver·*keyrt* deyt

I didn't do it.
Ik heb het niet gedaan. ik hep huht neet khuh·*daan*

I want to contact my embassy/consulate.
Ik wil contact opnemen ik wil kon·*takt* op·*ney*·muhn
met mijn ambassade/ met meyn am·ba·*saa*·duh/
consulaat. kon·sew·*laat*

Can I have a lawyer (who speaks English)?
Mag ik alstublieft makh ik al·stew·*bleeft*
een (Engelstalige) uhn (*eng*·uhls·*taa*·li·khuh)
advocaat? pol at·voh·*kaat*

This drug is for personal use.
Deze drugs zijn voor *dey*·zuh drukhs zeyn vohr
persoonlijk gebruik. puhr·*sohn*·luhk khuh·*bröyk*

I have a prescription for this drug.
Ik heb een recept/ ik hep uhn rey·*sept*/
voorschrift voor *vohr*·skhrift vohr
deze medicatie. Ⓝ/Ⓑ *dey*·zuh mey·dee·*kaa*·see

SAFE TRAVEL

doctor

bij de dokter

Where's the nearest ...?	Waar is de dichts-bijzijnde ...?	waar is duh *dikhts*-bey·zeyn·duh ...
dentist	tandarts	*tan*·darts
doctor	dokter	*dok*·tuhr
emergency department	spoedafdeling	*spoot*·af·dey·ling
optometrist	opticien	op·tee·*sye*
(night) pharmacist	(nacht)apotheek	(*nakht*·)a·poh·*teyk*

Where's the nearest ...?	Waar is het dichts-bijzijnde ...?	waar is huht *dikhts*-bey·zeyn·duh ...
hospital	ziekenhuis	*zee*·kuhn·höys
medical centre	medisch centrum	*mey*·dis *sen*·trum

I need a doctor (who speaks English).
Ik heb een dokter nodig (die Engels spreekt).
ik hep uhn *dok*·tuhr *noh*·dikh (dee *eng*·uhls spreykt)

Could I see a female doctor?
Zou ik een vrouwelijke dokter kunnen zien?
zaw ik uhn *vraw*·wuh·luh·kuh *dok*·tuhr *ku*·nuhn zeen

Could the doctor come here?
Kan de dokter naar hier komen?
kan duh *dok*·tuhr naar heer *koh*·muhn

Is there an after-hours emergency number?
Is er een noodnummer voor buiten de normale uren?
is uhr uhn *noht*·nu·muhr vohr *böy*·tuhn duh nor·*maa*·luh *ew*·ruhn

I've run out of my medication.
Mijn medicijnen zijn op.
meyn mey·dee·*sey*·nuhn zeyn op

This is my usual medicine.
Dit zijn mijn normale medicijnen.
dit zeyn meyn nor·*maa*·luh mey·dee·*sey*·nuhn

My child weighs (20 kilos).
Mijn kind weegt (twintig) kilo.
meyn kint weykht (*twin*·tikh) *kee*·loh

What's the correct dosage?
Wat is de juiste dosering?
wat is duh *yöy*·stuh doh·*zey*·ring

I don't want a blood transfusion.
Ik wil geen bloedtransfusie.
ik wil kheyn *bloot*·trans·few·zee

Please use a new syringe.
Gebruik alstublieft een nieuwe injectiespuit. **pol**
khuh·*bröyk* al·stew·*bleeft* uhn *nee*·wuh in·*yek*·see·spöyt

I have my own syringe.
Ik heb mijn eigen injectiespuit.
ik hep meyn *ey*·khuhn in·*yek*·see·spöyt

I've been vaccinated against …	*Ik ben ingeënt tegen …*	ik ben *in*·khuh·ent *tey*·khuhn …
He/She has been vaccinated against …	*Hij/Zij is ingeënt tegen …*	hey/zey is *in*·khuh·ent *tey*·khun …
hepatitis A/B/C	hepatitis A/B/C	hey·paa·*tee*·tees aa/bey/sey
tetanus	tetanus	*tey*·ta·nus
typhoid	typhus	*tee*·fus

I need new …	*Ik heb … nodig.*	ik hep … *noh*·dikh
contact lenses	nieuwe contactlenzen	*nee*·wuh kon·*takt*·len·zuhn
glasses	een nieuwe bril	uhn *nee*·wuh bril

My prescription is …
Mijn recept/voorschrift is … ⓝ/ⓑ
meyn rey·*sept*/*vohr*·skhrift is …

How much will it cost?
Hoeveel kost het?
hoo·*veyl* kost huht

Can I have a receipt for my insurance?

Kan ik een kwitantie   kan ik uhn kwee·*tan*·see
hebben voor mijn   *he*·buhn vohr meyn
verzekering?   vuhr·*zey*·kuh·ring

---

the doctor may say ...

Wat is het probleem?
  wat is huht pro·*bleym*   **What's the problem?**

Waar doet het pijn?
  waar doot huht peyn   **Where does it hurt?**

Heeft u koorts? pol
  heyft ew kohrts   **Do you have a temperature?**

Hoe lang heeft u dit al? pol
  hoo lang heyft ew   **How long have you been**
  dit al   **like this?**

Heeft u dat nog ooit gehad? pol
  heyft ew dat nokh   **Have you had this before?**
  oyt khuh·*hat*

Drinkt u? pol dringkt ew   **Do you drink?**
Gebruikt u khuh·*bröykt* ew   **Do you take**
  drugs? pol drukhs   **drugs?**
Rookt u? pol rohkt ew   **Do you smoke?**

Bent u ergens allergisch voor? pol
  bent ew *er*·khuhns   **Are you allergic**
  a·*ler*·khees vohr   **to anything?**

Neemt u medicijnen? pol
  neymt ew   **Are you on**
  mey·dee·*sey*·nuhn   **medication?**

Bent u seksueel actief? pol
  bent ew sek·sew·*weyl*   **Are you sexually active?**
  ak·*teef*

Heeft u onbeschermde seks gehad? pol
  heyf ew   **Have you had**
  on·buh·skherm·duh   **unprotected sex?**
  seks khuh·*hat*

Voor hoelang bent u op reis? pol
  vohr hoo·*lang* bent   **How long are you**
  ew op reys   **travelling for?**

Ik verwijs u door naar een specialist. pol
ik vuhr·*weys* ew dohr naar
uhn spey·sya·*list*
**I'm referring you to
a specialist.**

U moet in het ziekenhuis opgenomen worden. pol
ew moot in huht
zee·kuhn·höys
op·khuh·noh·muhn *wor*·duhn
**You need to be admitted
to hospital.**

U moet het laten onderzoeken wanneer u weer thuis bent. pol
ew moot huht *laa*·tuhn
on·duhr·*zoo*·kuhn wa·*neyr*
ew weyr töys bent
**You should have it
checked when you
go home.**

U moet naar huis gaan voor de behandeling. pol
ew moot naar höys khaan
vohr duh be·*han*·duh·ling
**You should return home
for treatment.**

U bent een hypochonder! pol
ew bent uhn
hee·poh·*khon*·duhr
You're a hypochondriac!

symptoms & conditions

symptomen & aandoeningen

I'm sick.
Ik ben ziek.
ik ben zeek

It hurts here.
Hier doet het pijn.
heer doot huht peyn

My child is (very) sick.
Mijn kind is (erg) ziek.
meyn kint is (erkh) zeek

I've been injured.
Ik ben gewond.
ik ben khuh·*wont*

He/She has been injured.
Hij/Zij is gewond.
hey/zey is khuh·*wont*

I've been vomiting.
Ik heb overgegeven.
ik hep oh·vuhr·khuh·*khey*·vuhn

He/She has been vomiting.
*Hij/Zij heeft
overgegeven.*
hey/zey heyft
oh·vuhr·khuh·*khey*·vuhn

I feel ...	Ik voel me ...	ik vool muh ...
better	beter	bey·tuhr
depressed	gedeprimeerd	khuh·dey·pree·meyrt
nauseous	misselijk	mi·suh·luhk
shivery	rillerig	ri·luh·rikh
strange	raar	raar
stressed	gestresseerd	khuh·stre·seyrt
weak	zwak	zwak
worse	slechter	slekh·tuhr

I feel anxious/dizzy.
Ik ben angstig/duizelig.   ik ben *ang*·stikh/*döy*·zuh·likh

I feel hot and cold.
Ik heb het koud en warm.   ik hep huht kawt en warm

I'm dehydrated.
Ik ben gedehydrateerd.   ik ben khuh·dey·hee·dra·teyrt

I can't sleep.
Ik kan niet slapen.   ik kan neet *slaa*·puhn

I fainted.
Ik ben flauw gevallen.   ik ben flaw khuh·*va*·luhn

I think it's the medication I'm on.
Ik denk dat het aan mijn   ik denk dat huht aan meyn
medicijnen ligt.   mey·dee·*sey*·nuhn likht

I'm on medication for ...
Ik neem medicijnen   ik neym mey·dee·*sey*·nuhn
voor ...   vohr ...

He/She is on medication for ...
Hij/Zij neemt   hey/zey neymt
medicijnen voor ...   mey·dee·*sey*·nuhn vohr ...

I have (a/an) ...
Ik heb (een) ...   ik hep (uhn) ...

He/She has (a/an) ...
Hij/Zij heeft (een) ...   hey/zey heyft (uhn) ...

I've recently had (a/an) …
Ik heb onlangs (een)   ik hep on·*langs* (uhn)
… gehad.   … khuh·*hat*

He/She has recently had (a/an) …
Hij/Zij heeft onlangs   hey/zey heyft on·*langs*
(een) … gehad.   (uhn) … khuh·*hat*

asthma	*astma*	*ast·*ma
backache	*rugpijn*	*rukh·*peyn
bronchitis	*bronchitis*	bron·*khee·*tis
cold n	*kou*	kaw
constipation	*constipatie*	kon·stee·*paa·*see
cough n	*hoest*	hoost
diabetes	*diabetes/*	dee·ya·*bey·*tes/
	suikerziekte	*söy·*kuhr·zeek·tuh
diarrhoea	*diarree*	dee·ya·*rey*
eczema	*eczema*	ek·*zey·*ma
epilepsy	*epilepsie*	ey·pee·lep·*see*
fever	*koorts*	kohrts
flu	*griep*	khreep
food	*voedsel-*	*voot·*suhl·
poisoning	*vergiftiging*	vuhr·*khif·*ti·khing
fracture	*breuk*	breuk
gastritis	*maagontsteking*	*maakh·*ont·stey·king
headache	*hoofdpijn*	*hohft·*peyn
heart attack	*hartaanval*	*hart·*aan·val
heart condition	*hartkwaal*	*hart·*kwaal
high/low blood	*hoge/lage*	*hoh·*khuh/*laa·*khuh
pressure	*bloeddruk*	*bloo·*druk
infection	*ontsteking*	ont·*stey·*king
nausea	*misselijkheid*	*mi·*suh·luhk·heyt
pain n	*pijn*	peyn
pneumonia	*longontsteking*	*long·*ont·stey·king
rash	*huiduitslag*	*höyt·*öyt·slakh
sore throat	*keelpijn*	*keyl·*peyn
sprain	*verstuiking*	vuhr·*stöy·*king
stomachache	*maagpijn*	*maakh·*peyn
toothache	*kiespijn* ℕ	*kees·*peyn
	tandpijn ℬ	*tant·*peyn

Gebruikt u een anticonceptiemiddel? pol
  khu·*bröykt* ew uhn
  an·tee·kon·*sep*·see·mi·duhl   **Are you using
contraception?**

Bent u ongesteld? pol
  bent ew on·khuh·*stelt*   **Are you menstruating?**

Bent u zwanger? pol
  bent ew *zwang*·uhr   **Are you pregnant?**

Wanneer was u laatst ongesteld? pol
  wa·*neyr* was ew laatst
  on·khuh·*stelt*   **When did you last have
your period?**

U bent zwanger. pol
  ew bent *zwang*·uhr   **You're pregnant.**

women's health

gynaecologie

| I'm pregnant. | *Ik ben zwanger.* | ik ben *zwang*·uhr |
| I'm on the pill. | *Ik neem de pil.* | ik neym duh pil |

I think I'm pregnant.
  Ik denk dat ik zwanger ben.   ik dengk dat ik *zwang*·uhr ben

I haven't had my period for (six) weeks.
  Ik ben al (zes) weken   ik ben al (zes) *wey*·kuhn
  niet ongesteld geweest.   neet on·khuh·*stelt* khuh·*weyst*

I've noticed a lump here.
  Ik heb hier een   ik hep heer uhn
  gezwel gevoeld.   khu·*zwel* khuh·*voolt*

Do you have something for (period pain)?
  Heeft u iets tegen   heyft ew eets *tey*·khuhn
  (menstruatiepijn)? pol   (men·strew·*waa*·see·peyn)

I have (a) ...	*Ik heb een ...*	ik hep uhn ...
cystitis	*blaasontsteking*	*blaas*·ont·stey·king
urinary tract infection	*infectie van de urine-wegen*	in·*fek*·see van duh ew·*ree*·nuh·wey·khuhn
yeast infection	*schimmelinfectie*	*skhi*·muhl·in·fek·see

health

205

I need (a/the) ...	*Ik heb ... nodig.*	ik hep ... *noh*·dikh
contraception	*een anticon-*	uhn an·tee·kon·
	ceptiemiddel	*sep*·see·mi·duhl
morning-after	*de morning*	duh *mohr*·ning
pill	*after pil*	*aaf*·tuhr pil
pregnancy test	*een zwanger-*	uhn *zwang*·uhr·
	schapstest	skhaps·test

allergies

I'm allergic	*Ik ben allergisch*	ik ben a·*ler*·khees
to ...	*voor ...*	vohr ...
He/She is allergic	*Hij/Zij is allergisch*	hey/zey is a·*ler*·khees
to ...	*voor ...*	vohr ...
antibiotics	*anti-*	an·tee·
	biotica	bee·*yoh*·tee·ka
anti-	*ontstekings-*	ont·*stey*·kings·
inflammatories	*remmende*	*re*·muhn·duh
	medicijnen	mey·dee·*sey*·nuhn
aspirin	*aspirine*	as·pee·*ree*·nuh
bees	*bijen*	*bey*·yuhn
codeine	*codeine*	koh·dey·*ee*·nuh
penicillin	*penicilline*	pey·nee·see·*lee*·nuh
pollen	*pollen*	*po*·luhn
sulphur-based	*zwavel-*	*zwaa*·vuhl·
drugs	*houdende*	*haw*·duhn·duh
	medicijnen	mey·dee·*sey*·nuhn
I have a skin	*Ik heb een*	ik hep uhn
allergy.	*huidallergie.*	*höyt*·a·ler·khee
antihistamines	*anti-*	an·tee·
	histaminica	his·ta·*mee*·nee·ka
inhaler	*inhalator*	in·haa·*laa*·tor
injection	*injectie*	in·*yek*·see

For some food-related allergies, see **special diets & allergies**, page 182.

parts of the body

My ... hurts.
Mijn ... doet pijn.   meyn ... doot peyn

I can't move my ...
Ik kan mijn ...   ik kan meyn ...
niet bewegen.   neet buh·*wey*·khuhn

I have a cramp in my ...
Ik heb kramp in mijn ...   ik hep kramp in meyn ...

My ... is swollen.
Mijn ... is gezwollen.   meyn ... is khu·*zwo*·luhn

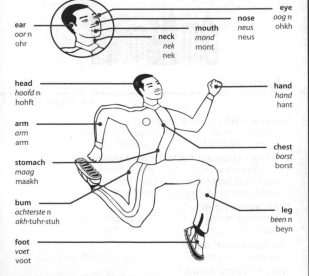

ear
oor n
ohr

eye
oog n
ohkh

nose
neus
neus

mouth
mond
mont

neck
nek
nek

head
hoofd n
hohft

hand
hand
hant

arm
arm
arm

chest
borst
borst

stomach
maag
maakh

bum
achterste n
akh·tuhr·stuh

leg
been n
beyn

foot
voet
voot

For other parts of the body, see the **dictionary**.

health

207

alternative treatments

I don't use (Western medicine).
Ik gebruik geen   ik khuh·*bröyk* kheyn
(Westerse geneeskunde).   (*wes*·tuhr·suh khuh·*neys*·kun·duh)

I prefer ...	*Ik verkies ...*	ik vuhr·*kees* ...
Can I see	*Kan ik iemand*	kan ik *ee*·mant
someone who	*zien die aan*	zeen dee aan
practises ...?	*... doet?*	... doot
acupuncture	*acupunctuur*	a·kew·punk·*tewr*
naturopathy	*natuur-*	na·*tewr*·
	geneeskunde	khuh·neys·kun·duh
reflexology	*reflexologie*	rey·flek·soh·loh·*khee*

pharmacist

I need something for (a headache).
Ik heb iets nodig   ik hep eets *noh*·dikh
tegen (hoofdpijn).   *tey*·khuhn (*hohft*·peyn)

Do I need a prescription for (antihistamines)?
Heb ik een recept/   hep ik uhn rey·*sept*/
voorschrift nodig voor   *vohr*·skhrift *noh*·dikh vohr
(antihistaminica)? Ⓝ/Ⓑ   (an·tee·his·ta·*mee*·nee·ka)

I have a prescription.
Ik heb een recept/   ik hep uhn rey·*sept*/
voorschrift. Ⓝ/Ⓑ   *vohr*·skhrift

How many times a day?
Hoeveel keer per dag?   hoo·*veyl* keyr puhr dakh

Will it make me drowsy?
Word ik er loom van?   wort ik uhr lohm van

Twee/Drie keer per dag.
twey/dree keyr puhr dakh   **Twice/Three times a day.**

Voor/Met/Na het eten.
vohr/met/na huht *ey*·tuhn   **Before/With/After food.**

Heeft u dit al eerder ingenomen? pol
heyft ew dit al *eyr*·duhr   **Have you taken this**
in·khuh·noh·muhn   **before?**

U moet deze medicijnen nemen tot ze op zijn. pol
ew moot *dey*·zuh   **You must complete**
mey·dee·*sey*·nuhn   **the course.**
ney·muhn tot zuh op zeyn

antiseptic n	*ontsmettend*	ont·*sme*·tuhnt
	middel n	*mi*·duhl
bandage	*verband* n	vuhr·*bant*
contraceptives	*anticonceptie-*	an·tee·kon·*sep*·see·
	middelen n pl	mi·duh·luhn
diarrhoea	*middel tegen*	*mi*·duhl *tey*·khuhn
medicine	*diarree* n	dee·ya·*rey*
insect repellent	*insectverdrijvend*	in·sekt·vuhr·*drey*·vuhnt
	middel n pl	*mi*·duhl
laxatives	*laxeermiddelen* n pl	lak·*seyr*·mi·duh·luhn
painkillers	*pijnstillers*	*peyn*·sti·luhrs
rehydration	*rehydratatie-*	rey·hee·dra·*taa*·see·
salts	*oplossing*	op·lo·sing
sleeping pills	*slaappillen*	*slaa*·pi·luhn

For more pharmaceutical items, see the **dictionary**.

dentist

bij de tandarts

I have a ...	*Ik heb ...*	ik hep ...
broken tooth	*een gebroken*	uhn khuh·*broh*·kuhn
	tand	tant
cavity	*een gaatje*	uhn *khaa*·chuh
toothache	*kiespijn* Ⓝ	*kees*·peyn
	tandpijn Ⓑ	*tant*·peyn

I've lost a filling.
*Ik heb een vulling
verloren.*
ik hep uhn *vu*·ling
vuhr·*loh*·ruhn

My dentures are broken.
*Ik heb mijn kunstgebit
gebroken.*
ik hep meyn *kunst*·khuh·bit
khuh·*broh*·kuhn

My gums hurt.
Mijn tandvlees doet pijn.
meyn *tant*·vleys doot peyn

I don't want it extracted!
*Ik wil niet dat hij
getrokken wordt!*
ik wil neet dat hey
khuh·*tro*·kuhn wort

Ouch!
Au!
aw

I need (a/an) ...   *Ik heb een ...
nodig.*
ik hep uhn ...
no·dikh
    anaesthetic   *verdoving*   vuhr·*doh*·ving
    filling   *vulling*   *vu*·ling

the dentist may say ...

Doe je mond ver open.
  doo yuh mont ver *oh*·puhn   **Open wide.**

Dit doet helemaal geen pijn.
  dit doot hey·luh·*maal*
  kheyn peyn   **This won't hurt a bit.**

Bijt hierop.
  beyt *hee*·rop   **Bite down on this.**

Niet bewegen.
  neet buh·*wey*·khuhn   **Don't move.**

Spoelen alsjeblieft.
  spoo·luhn a·shuh·*bleeft*   **Rinse.**

Kom terug, ik ben nog niet klaar!
  kom tuh·*rukh*
  ik ben nokh neet klaar   **Come back,
I haven't finished!**

DICTIONARY > english–dutch

In this dictionary, words are marked as n (noun), a (adjective), v (verb), adv (adverb), prep (preposition), pron (pronoun), sg (singular), pl (plural), inf (informal) and pol (polite) where necessary. Note that we've only indicated Dutch nouns which have neuter gender with ⓝ after the translation – the nouns which have common gender are left unmarked. Where a word has different masculine and feminine forms, both options are given and indicated with ⓜ/ⓕ (for more on gender in Dutch, see the **phrasebuilder**). If it's a plural noun, you'll also see pl. We've used the symbols Ⓝ/Ⓑ for words which are different in the Netherlands and Belgium respectively. For more food terms, see the **culinary reader**.

A

aboard *aan boord* aan bohrt
abortion *abortus* a·bor·tus
about (approximately) *ongeveer* on·khuh·veyr
about (relating to) *aangaande* aan·khaan·duh
above *boven* boh·vuhn
abroad *in het buitenland* in huht böy·tuhn·lant
accident *ongeval* ⓝ on·khuh·val
accommodation *accommodatie* a·koh·moh·daa·see
account (bill) n *rekening* rey·kuh·ning
across *tegenover* tey·khuhn·oh·vuhr
actor *acteur/actrice* ⓜ/ⓕ ak·teur/ak·tree·suh
acupuncture *acupunctuur* a·kew·punk·tewr
adaptor *adapter* a·dap·tuhr
addiction *verslaving* vuhr·slaa·ving
address n *adres* ⓝ a·dres
administration *administratie* at·mee·nee·straa·see
administrator *bestuurder* buh·stewr·duhr
admission (price) *toegangsprijs* too·khangs·preys
admit (let in) v *toelaten* too·laa·tuhn
adult n *volwassene* vol·wa·suh·nuh
advertisement *advertentie* at·vuhr·ten·see
advice *advise* ⓝ at·vees
aeroplane *vliegtuig* ⓝ vleekh·töykh

after *na* naa
afternoon *middag/namiddag* Ⓝ/Ⓑ mi·dakh/naa·mi·dakh
again *opnieuw* op·neew
age n *leeftijd* leyf·teyt
(three days) ago *(drie dagen) geleden* (dree daa·khuhn) khuh·ley·duhn
agree *overeenkomen* oh·vuhr·eyn·koh·muhn
agriculture *landbouw* lant·baw
ahead (clock/distance) *voorop* vohr·op
ahead (in the future) *in de toekomst* in duh too·komst
air n *lucht* lukht
air-conditioned *met airconditioning* met eyr·kon·di·shuh·ning
airline *luchtvaartmaatschappij* lukht·vaart·maat·skha·pey
airmail *luchtpost* lukht·post
airplane *vliegtuig* ⓝ vleekh·töykh
airport *luchthaven* lukht·haa·vuhn
airport tax *luchthavenbelasting* lukht·haa·vuhn·buh·las·ting
aisle (on plane) *gangpad* ⓝ khang·pat
alarm clock *wekker* we·kuhr
all *alle* a·luh
allergy *allergie* a·ler·khee
almond *amandel* a·man·duhl
almost *bijna* bey·naa
alone *alleen* a·leyn
already *al* al
also *ook* ohk
altar *altaar* ⓝ al·taar
altitude *hoogte* hohkh·tuh
always *altijd* al·teyt**

ambassador *ambassadeur/ambassadrice* ⓜ/ⓕ am·ba·sa·*deur*/am·ba·sa·*dree*·suh
ambulance *ambulance* am·bew·*lans*
anaemia *bloedarmoede* bloot·ar·*moo*·duh
ancient *oud* awt
adventure ⓝ *avontuur* ⓝ a·von·*tewr*
and *en* en
angry *boos* bohs
animal *dier* ⓝ deer
ankle *enkel* *eng*·kuhl
another *een andere* uhn *an*·duh·ruh
answer n *antwoord* ⓝ *ant*·wohrt
answer v *antwoorden* ant·*wohr*·duhn
ant *mier* meer
antibiotics *antibiotica* ⓝ pl an·tee·bee·yo·tee·ka
antinuclear *antinucleair* an·tee·nu·kley·*yer*
antique n *antiek* an·*teek*
antiseptic a *ontsmettend* ont·*sme*·tuhnt
any *enige* *ey*·ni·khuh
apartment *flat/appartement* ⓝ ⓝ/ⓑ flet/a·par·tuh·*ment*
apple *appel* *a*·puhl
appointment *afspraak* *af*·spraak
apricot *abrikoos* a·bree·*kohs*
archaeological *archeologisch* ar·khey·oh·*loh*·khis
architecture *architectuur* ar·khee·tek·*tewr*
argue (a point) *argumenteren* ar·khew·men·*tey*·ruhn
argue (with someone) *ruzie maken* *rew*·zee maa·kuhn
arm (body) *arm* arm
arrest v *arresteren* a·res·*tey*·ruhn
arrivals *aankomst* *aan*·komst
arrive *aankomen* *aan*·koh·muhn
art *kunst* kunst
art gallery *kunstgalerie* kunst·kha·luh·*ree*
artist *artiest* ar·*teest*
ashtray *asbak* *as*·bak
Asia *Azië* aa·zee·yuh
ask v *vragen* *vraa*·khun
asparagus *asperge* a·*sper*·khuh
aspirin *aspirine* as·pee·*ree*·nuh
asthma *astma* *ast*·ma
at *bij* bey
athletics *atletiek* at·ley·*teek*
atmosphere *atmosfeer* at·mos·*feyr*
attractive *aantrekkelijk* aan·*tre*·kuh·luhk
aunt *tante* *tan*·tuh
Australia *Australië* aw·*straa*·lee·yuh
ATM *pin-automaat/geldautomaat* ⓝ/ⓑ *pin*·aw·toh·maat/*khelt*·aw·toh·maat

autumn *herfst* herfst
avenue *laan* laan
awful *verschrikkelijk* vuhr·*skhri*·kuh·luhk

B

B&W (film) *zwart-wit (film)* zwart·*wit* (film)
baby food *babyvoeding* *bey*·bee·voo·ding
baby powder *talkpoeder* ⓝ *talk*·poo·duhr
back (body) *rug* rukh
back (position) *achterkant* *akh*·tuhr·kant
backpack *rugzak* *rukh*·zak
bacon *spek* ⓝ spek
bad *slecht* slekht
bag *tas* tas
baggage *bagage* ba·*khaa*·zhuh
baggage allowance *toegestane hoeveelheid bagage* too·khuh·*staa*·nuh hoo·*veyl*·heyt ba·*khaa*·zhuh
baggage claim *bagage-inleverpunt* ⓝ/ *bagage band* ba·*khaa*·zhuh·in·ley·vuhr·punt/ba·*khaa*·zhuh bant
bakery *bakker/bakkerij* ⓝ/ⓑ *ba*·kuhr/ba·kuh·*rey*
balance (account) *saldo* ⓝ *sal*·doh
balcony *balkon* ⓝ bal·*kon*
ball (sport) *bal* bal
banana *banaan* ba·*naan*
band (music) *band/groep* ⓝ/ⓑ bent/khroop
bandage *verband* ⓝ vurh·*bant*
Band-Aid *pleister* *pley*·stuhr
bank n *bank* bangk
bank account *bankrekening* *bangk*·rey·kuh·ning
banknote *bankbiljet* ⓝ *bangk*·bil·yet
baptism *doopsel* ⓝ *dohp*·suhl
bar n *bar* bar
bar of chocolate *reep chocolade* reyp shoh·koh·*laa*·duh
barber *barbier* bar·*beer*
bar work *werk als barbediende* ⓝ werk als *bar*·buh·deen·duh
basket *mand* mant
bath n *bad* ⓝ bat
bathing suit *zwempak* ⓝ *zwem*·pak
bathroom *badkamer* *bat*·kaa·muhr
battery (car) *accu* a·kew
battery (general) *batterij* ba·tuh·*rey*
battlefield *slagveld* ⓝ *slakh*·velt
be *zijn* zeyn
beach *strand* strant
bean *boon* bohn

bean sprouts *taugé/sojascheuten* Ⓝ/Ⓑ
taw·*zhey*/soh·ya·skheu·tuhn
beard *baard* baart
beautician *schoonheidsspecialiste*
skhohn·heyt·spey·sya·*lis*·tuh
beautiful *mooi* moy
beauty salon *schoonheidssalon*
skhohn·heyt·sa·*lon*
because *omdat* om·*dat*
bed *bed* Ⓝ bet
bed linen *beddegoed* Ⓝ be·duh·khoot
bedroom *slaapkamer* slaap·kaa·muhr
bee *bij* bey
beef *rundvlees* Ⓝ runt·vleys
beer *bier* Ⓝ beer
beer on tap *getapt bier* Ⓝ khuh·*tapt* beer
beetroot *rode biet* roh·duh beet
before *voor* vohr
beggar *bedelaar/bedelares* Ⓜ/Ⓕ
bey·duh·laar/bey·duh·laa·*res*
behind *achter* akh·tuhr
Belgian *Belgisch* bel·khis
Belgian person *Belg* belkh
Belgium *België* bel·khee·yuh
below *onder* on·duhr
berth (ship) n *hut* hut
berth (train) n *couchette* koo·*shet*
beside *naast* naast
best *beste* bes·tuh
bet n *weddenschap* we·duhn·skhap
bet v *wedden* we·duhn
better *beter* bey·tuhr
between *tussen* tu·suhn
bicycle *fiets* feets
big *groot* khroht
bigger *groter* khroh·tuhr
biggest *grootst* khrohtst
bike *fiets* feets
bike chain *fietsketting* feets·ke·ting
bike lock *fietsslot* Ⓝ feet·slot
bike path *fietspad* Ⓝ feets·pat
bike shop *fietsenwinkel* feet·suhn·wing·kuhl
bilingual *tweetalig* twey·taa·likh
bill (restaurant) n *rekening* rey·kuh·ning
binoculars *verrekijker* ve·ruh·key·kuhr
bird *vogel* voh·khul
birth certificate *geboorteakte* Ⓝ
khuh·*bohr*·tuh·ak·tuh
birthday *verjaardag* vuhr·yaar·dakh
biscuit *koekje* Ⓝ kook·yuh
bite (dog/insect) n *beet* beyt
bitter *bitter* bi·tuhr
black *zwart* zwart

black market *zwarte markt* zwar·tuh markt
bladder *blaas* blaas
blanket *deken* dey·kuhn
blind a *blind* blint
blister n *blaar* blaar
blocked (drain) *verstopt* vuhr·stopt
blocked (access/road) *afgesloten*
af·khuh·sloh·tuhn
blood *bloed* Ⓝ bloot
blood group *bloedgroep* bloot·khroop
blood pressure *bloeddruk* bloo·druk
blood test *bloedtest* bloo·test
blouse *bloes* bloos
blue *blauw* blaw
board (plane, ship) v *aan boord gaan*
aan bohrt khaan
boarding house *pension* Ⓝ pen·*syon*
boarding pass *instapkaart* in·stap·kaart
boat *boot* boht
boat trip *rondvaart* ront·vaart
body *lichaam* Ⓝ *li*·khaam
boiled *gekookt* khuh·*kohkt*
bone *bot* Ⓝ bot
book n *boek* Ⓝ book
book (make a booking) v *reserveren*
rey·ser·vey·ruhn
booked out *volgeboekt* vol·khuh·bookt
book shop *boekhandel* book·han·duhl
boot (footwear) *laars* laars
boots (footwear) *laarzen* pl *laar*·zuhn
border n *grens* khrens
bored *verveeld* vuhr·*veylt*
boring *saai/vervelend* Ⓝ/Ⓑ
saay/vuhr·*vey*·luhnt
borrow *lenen* ley·nuhn
botanic garden *botanische tuin*
boh·*taa*·ni·suh töyn
both *beide* bey·duh
bottle *fles* fles
bottle opener *flesopener* fles·oh·puh·nuhr
bottle shop *slijterij/drankenhandel* Ⓝ/Ⓑ
sley·tuh·*rey*/drang·kuhn·han·duhl
bottom (body) *achterwerk* Ⓝ
akh·tuhr·werk
bottom (position) *onderaan* on·duhr·aan
bowl (plate) n *kom* kom
box n *doos* dohs
boxing *boksen* Ⓝ *bok*·suhn
box of chocolates *doos bonbons/pralines*
Ⓝ/Ⓑ dohs bon·*bons*/pra·*lee*·nuh
boy *jongen* yong·uhn
boyfriend *vriend* vreent
bra *beha* bey·haa
brakes *remmen* re·muhn

brandy *brandewijn/cognac* Ⓝ/Ⓑ
  bran·duh·weyn/ko·*nyak*
brave *moedig* moo·dikh
bread *brood* Ⓝ broht
bread roll *broodje* Ⓝ *broh*·chuh
break v *breken* brey·kuhn
break down v *het begeven*
  huht buh·*khey*·vuhn
breakfast *ontbijt* Ⓝ ont·*beyt*
breast (body) *borst* borst
breathe *ademen* aa·duh·muhn
bribe n *omkoperij* om·koh·puh·*rey*
bribe v *omkopen* om·*koh*·puhn
bridge (structure) n *brug* brukh
briefcase *aktetas* ak·tuh·tas
bring *brengen* breng·uhn
broken *gebroken* khuh·*broh*·khun
broken down *stuk* stuk
brother *broer* broor
brown *bruin* bröyn
bruise n *kneuzing* kneu·zing
brush n *borstel* bor·stuhl
bucket *emmer* e·muhr
bug n *insect* Ⓝ *in*·sekt
build v *bouwen* baw·uhn
builder *aannemer* aa·ney·muhr
building *gebouw* Ⓝ khuh·*baw*
bum bag *heuptasje* Ⓝ *heup*·ta·shuh
burn n *branden* bran·duhn
burnt *verbrand* vuhr·*brant*
bus (city) *stadsbus* stats·bus
bus (intercity) *bus* bus
business n *zaken* zaa·kuhn
businessperson *zakenman/zakenvrouw*
  Ⓜ/Ⓕ *zaa*·kuhn·man/*zaa*·kuhn·vraw
business trip *zakenreis* zaa·kuhn·reys
busker *straatmuzikant*
  straat·mew·zee·kant
bus station *busstation* Ⓝ bus·sta·syon
bus stop *bushalte* bus·hal·tuh
busy (person) *bezig* bey·zikh
busy (phone) *bezet* buh·*zet*
busy (place) *druk* druk
but *maar* maar
butcher *slager* slaa·khuhr
butcher's shop *slagerij* slaa·khuh·*rey*
butter n *boter* boh·tuhr
butterfly *vlinder* vlin·duhr
button n *knoop* knohp
buy v *kopen* koh·puhn

C

cabbage *kool* kohl
cable car *cabine van een kabelbaan*
  ka·bee·nuh van uhn *kaa*·buhl·baan
café *koffiehuisje* Ⓝ/*brasserie* Ⓝ/Ⓑ
  ko·fee·höy·shuh/bra·suh·*ree*
cake shop *banketbakker/patisserie* Ⓝ/Ⓑ
  bang·ket·ba·kuhr/pa·tee·suh·*ree*
calculator *rekenmachine*
  rey·kuhn·ma·shee·nuh
calendar *kalender* ka·*len*·duhr
call (phone) n *telefoongesprek* Ⓝ
  tey·luh·fohn·khuh·sprek
camera (film/video) *camera* kaa·mey·ra
camera (photos) *fototoestel* Ⓝ
  foh·toh·too·stel
camera shop *fotozaak* foh·toh·zaak
camp v *kamperen* kam·pey·ruhn
camping ground *camping*
  kem·ping/kam·ping Ⓝ/Ⓑ
camping store *kampeerwinkel*
  kam·peyr·wing·kuhl
camp site *kampeerplaats* kam·peyr·plaats
can n *blik* Ⓝ blik
can (be able) *kunnen* ku·nuhn
can (have permission) *mogen* moh·khuhn
canal (general) *kanaal* Ⓝ ka·*naal*
canal (in town) *gracht* khrakht
canalside house *grachtenhuis* Ⓝ
  khrakh·tuhn·höys
cancel *annuleren* a·new·ley·ruhn
cancer *kanker* kang·kuhr
candle *kaars* kaars
candy *snoep* snoop
can opener *blikopener* blik·oh·puh·nuhr
cantaloupe *meloen* muh·*loon*
capsicum *peper* pey·puhr
captain *kapitein* ka·pee·teyn
car *wagen/auto* waa·khuhn/*aw*·toh
caravan *caravan* ke·ruh·ven/ka·ra·van Ⓝ/Ⓑ
carbon dioxide *koolstofdioxide*
  kohl·stof·dee·yok·*see*·duh
carbon dioxide emissions
  koolstofdioxide-emissie
  kohl·stof·dee·yok·see·duh·ey·*mee*·see
cardiac arrest *hartstilstand* hart·stil·stant
cards (playing) *speelkaarten*
  speyl·kaar·tuhn
care (for a sick person) v *(iemand)*
  verzorgen (ee·mant) vuhr·*zor*·khuhn
care (have feelings for) v *(om iemand)*
  geven (om ee·mant) khey·vuhn

car hire *autoverhuur* aw·toh·vuhr·hewr
car park *parking* par·king
carpenter *timmerman* ti·muhr·man
carpet *kleed* ⓝ/*tapijt* ⓝ/ⓑ kleyt/ta·peyt
car registration *inschrijvingsbewijs* ⓝ
  in·skhrey·vings·buh·weys
carrot *wortel* wor·tuhl
carry *dragen* draa·khuhn
cash n *baar geld* ⓝ baar khelt
cash (a cheque) v *(een cheque) innen*
  (uhn shek) i·nuhn
cashew *cashewnoot* ka·shoo·noht
cashier *kassier/kassierster* ⓜ/ⓕ
  ka·seer/ka·seer·stuhr
cash register *kassa* ka·sa
castle *kasteel* ⓝ kas·teyl
casual work
  tijdelijke baan ⓝ/*interimwerk* ⓝ ⓑ
  tey·duh·luh·kuh baan/in·tuh·rim·werk
cat *kat* kat
cathedral *katedraal* ka·tey·draal
cauliflower *bloemkool* bloom·kohl
cave n *grot* khrot
CD *cd* sey·dey
celebration *viering* vee·ring
cell phone *mobiele telefoon* ⓝ/*gsm* ⓑ
  moh·bee·luh tey·ley·fohn/khey·es·em
cemetery *kerkhof* ⓝ kerk·hof
centre n *centrum* ⓝ sen·trum
ceramics *keramiek* key·ra·meek
cereal (breakfast) *ontbijtgranen* ⓝ pl
  ont·beyt·khraa·nuhn
certificate *certificaat* ⓝ ser·tee·fee·kaat
chain n *ketting* ke·ting
chair n *stoel* stool
chairperson *voorzitter* vohr·zi·tuhr
chairlift (skiing) *stoeltjeslift* stool·chuhs·lift
championships *kampioenschap* ⓝ
  kam·pee·yoon·skhap
chance n *kans* kans
change (general) n *verandering*
  vuhr·an·duh·ring
change (loose coins) n *kleingeld* ⓝ
  kleyn·khelt
change (money given back) n
  wisselgeld ⓝ wi·suhl·khelt
change (money) v *(geld) wisselen*
  (khelt) wi·suh·luhn
changing room (shop) *paskamer*
  pas·kaa·muhr
changing room (sport, individual)
  kleedhokje ⓝ kleyt·hok·yuh

changing room (sport, communal)
  kleedkamer kleyt·kaa·muhr
charming *charmant* shar·mant
chat up v *opvrijen* op·vrey·yuhn
cheap *goedkoop* khoot·kohp
cheat (at games) n *valsspeler* val·spey·luhr
cheat (in business) n *oplichter* op·likh·tuhr
check (banking) n *cheque* shek
check (bill) n *rekening* rey·kuh·ning
check v *controleren* kon·troh·ley·ruhn
check-in (desk) *incheckbalie* in·shek·ba·lee
checkpoint *controlepost* kon·troh·luh·post
cheese *kaas* kaas
cheese shop *kaaswinkel* kaas·wing·kuhl
chef *chef-kok* shef·kok
chemist (pharmacist)
  apotheker/apothekeres ⓜ/ⓕ
  a·poh·tey·kuhr/a·poh·tey·kuh·res
chemist (pharmacy) *apotheek* a·poh·teyk
cheque (banking) *cheque* shek
cherry *kers* kers
chess *schaakspel* ⓝ skhaak·spel
chessboard *schaakbord* ⓝ skhaak·bort
chest (body) *borst* borst
chestnut *hazelnoot* haa·zuhl·noht
chewing gum *kauwgom* kaw·khom
chicken *kip* kip
chicken pox *windpokken* wint·po·kuhn
chickpeas *kekers/kikkererwten* ⓝ/ⓑ
  key·kuhrs/ki·kuhr·erw·tuhn
child *kind* ⓝ kint
child-minding service *kinderoppasdienst*
  kin·duhr·o·pas·deenst
children *kinderen* ⓝ pl kin·duh·ruhn
child seat *kinderzitje* ⓝ kin·duhr·zi·chuh
chilli sauce *chilisaus* chee·lee·saws
chiropractor *chiropractor* chee·roh·prak·tor
chocolate *chocolade* shoh·koh·laa·duh
chocolate bar *chocoladereep*
  shoh·koh·laa·duh·reyp
choose *kiezen* kee·zuhn
chopping board *snijplank* sney·plangk
chopsticks *eetstokjes* ⓝ pl eyt·stok·yuhs
Christmas *Kerstmis* kerst·mis
Christmas Day *kerstdag* kerst·dakh
Christmas Eve *kerstavond* kerst·aa·vont
church *kerk* kerk
cigar *sigaar* see·khaar
cigarette *sigaret* see·kha·ret
cigarette lighter *aansteker* aan·stey·kuhr
cinema *bioscoop* bee·yos·kohp
citizenship *staatsburgerschap* ⓝ
  staats·bur·khuhr·skhap

city *stad* stat
city centre *stadscentrum* ⓝ *stat·sen·trum*
civil rights *burgerrechten*
 bur·khuh·rekh·tuhn
class (category) n *klas/klasse* klas/*kla·*suh
classical *klassiek* kla·*seek*
class system *klassesysteem* ⓝ
 kla·suh·sees·*teym*
clean a *schoon/proper* ⓝ/ⓑ
 skhohn/*proh·*puhr
clean v *schoonmaken* skhohn·*maa·*kuhn
cleaning *schoonmaak* skhohn·maak
client *klant* klant
cliff *rotswand* rots·want
climate change *klimaatverandering*
 klee·*maat·*vuhr·an·*duh·*ring
climb v *klimmen* kli·muhn
cloakroom *garderobe/vestiaire*
 khar·duh·roh·buh/ves·*tyer*
clock n *klok* klok
clogs *klompen* klom·puhn
close a *dichtbij* dikht·*bey*
close v *sluiten* slöy·tuhn
closed *gesloten* khuh·*sloh·*tuhn
clothesline *waslijn* was·leyn
clothing *kleding* kley·ding
clothing store *kledingzaak* kley·ding·zaak
cloud n *wolk* wolk
cloudy *bewolkt* buh·*wolkt*
clutch (car) *koppeling* ko·puh·ling
coach (bus) n *touringcar* too·ring·kar
coach v *coachen* koh·chuhn
coast n *kust* kust
coat n *jas/mantel* yas/*man·*tuhl
coat hanger *kleerhanger* kleyr·hang·uhr
cobblestones *kasseien* ka·*sey·*yuhn
cockroach *kakkerlak* ka·kuhr·lak
coconut *kokosnoot* koh·kos·noht
coffee *koffie* ko·fee
coins *muntstukken* munt·stu·kuhn
cold (illness) n *kou* kaw
cold (weather) n *kou/koude* kaw/*kaw·*duh
cold a *koud* kawt
colleague *collega* ko·ley·kha
collect call *gesprek voor rekening*
 van de ontvanger khuh·*sprek* vohr
 *rey·kuh·ning van duh ont·*vang·uhr
college *college* ⓝ ko·*ley·*zhuh
colour n *kleur* kleur
comb n *kam* kam
come *komen* koh·muhn
comedy *komedie* ko·mey·dee
comfortable *comfortabel* kom·for·*taa·*buhl

commission *commissie* ko·mee·see
communications (profession)
 communicatie ko·mew·nee·*kaa·*see
communion (religious) *communie*
 ko·mew·nee
companion *metgezel* met·khuh·zel
company (firm) *zaak* zaak
compass ⓝ *kompas* ⓝ kom·*pas*
complain *klagen* klaa·khuhn
complaint *klacht* klakht
complimentary (free) *gratis khraa·*tis
computer game *computerspel* ⓝ
 kom·pyoo·tuhr·*spel*
concussion *hersenschudding*
 *her·*suhn·skhu·ding
condom *condoom* ⓝ kon·*dohm*
conference (big) *conferentie*
 kon·fey·*ren·*see
conference (small) *bespreking*
 buh·*sprey·*king
confession (religious) *biecht* beekht
confirm (a booking) *bevestigen*
 be·*ves·*ti·khuhn
congratulations *gelukwensen*
 khuh·*luk·*wen·suhn
conjunctivitis *bindvliesontsteking*
 bint·vlees·ont·stey·king
connection (concepts) *verband* ⓝ
 vuhr·*bant*
connection (objects/transport)
 verbinding vuhr·*bin·*ding
conservative *conservatief* kon·ser·va·*teef*
constipation *constipatie* kon·stee·*paa·*see
consulate *consulaat* ⓝ kon·su·*laat*
contact lenses *contactlenzen*
 kon·*takt·*len·zuhn
contact lens solution
 oplossing voor contactlenzen
 *op·*lo·sing vohr kon·*takt·*len·zuhn
contagious *besmettelijk* buh·*sme·*tuh·luhk
contraceptives *anticonceptiemiddelen*
 an·tee·kon·*sep·*see·mi·duh·luhn
convenience store *avondwinkel*
 *aa·*vont·wing·kuhl
convent *klooster* ⓝ *kloh·*stuhr
cook n *kok* kok
cook v *koken* koh·kuhn
cookie *koekje* ⓝ *kook·*yuh
cooking *koken* koh·kuhn
cool (groovy) *leuk* leuk
cool (temperature) *koel* kool
corkscrew *kurkentrekker* kur·kuh·tre·kuhr
corn *maïs* maays/*ma·*yees ⓝ/ⓑ

corner n *hoek* hook
corrupt a *corrupt* ko·*rupt*
corruption *corruptie* ko·*rup*·see
cost n *kost* kost
cost v *kosten* kos·tuhn
cotton n *katoen* ⓝ ka·*toon*
cotton balls *wattenproppen*
 wa·tuh·pro·puhn
cotton buds *wattenstaafjes*
 wa·tuh·*staaf*·yuhs
cough n *hoest* hoost
cough v *hoesten* hoos·tuhn
cough medicine *hoestmiddel* ⓝ
 hoost·mi·duhl
count v *tellen* te·luhn
counter (at bar) *toog* tohk
country *land* ⓝ lant
countryside *platteland* ⓝ pla·tuh·*lant*
court (legal) *gerecht* ⓝ khuh·*rekht*
court (tennis) *plein* ⓝ pleyn
cover charge *bedieningsgeld* ⓝ
 buh·*dee*·nings·khelt
cow *koe* koo
cracker *beschuit* be·skhöyt
crafts *handwerk* ⓝ hant·werk
crash (car) n *aanrijding* aan·rey·ding
crash (plane) n *vliegtuigongeluk* ⓝ
 vleekh·töyk·on·khuh·luk
crazy *gek* khek
cream (food) *room* rohm
cream (lotion) *crème* kreym
credit n *krediet* ⓝ krey·*deet*
credit card *kredietkaart* krey·*deet*·kaart
cross (religious) n *kruis* ⓝ kröys
crowded *stampvol* stamp·vol
cucumber *komkommer* kom·ko·muhr
cup *kop* kop
cupboard *kast* kast
currency exchange *wisselkantoor* ⓝ
 wi·suhl·kan·tohr
current (electricity) *stroom* strohm
current affairs *actualiteiten*
 ak·tew·wa·lee·*tey*·tuhn
custom *gewoonte* khuh·wohn·tuh
customs *douane* doo·*waa*·nuh
cut n *snede* sney·duh
cut v *snijden* sney·duhn
cutlery *bestek* ⓝ buh·*stek*
CV cv ⓝ sey·vey
cycle (ride) v *fietsen* feet·suhn
cycling (casual) *fietsen* feet·suhn
cycling (competitive) *wielersport*
 wee·luhr·sport

cyclist (casual) *fietser* feet·suhr
cyclist (competitive) *wielrenner*
 weel·re·nuhr
cystitis *blaasontsteking* blaas·ont·stey·king

D

dad *pa* paa
daily a&adv *dagelijks* daa·khuh·luhks
dam *dam* dam
damage *schade* skhaa·duh
damage from water *waterschade*
 waa·tuhr·skhaa·duh
dance n *dans* dans
dance v *dansen* dan·suhn
dancing *dansen* dan·suhn
dangerous *gevaarlijk* khuh·*vaar*·luhk
dark (colour/night) *donker* dong·kuhr
date (appointment) n *afspraak* af·spraak
date (day) *dag* dakh
date (fruit) *dadel* daa·duhl
date (go out with) v *uitgaan met*
 öyt·khaan met
date of birth *geboortedatum*
 khuh·*bohr*·tuh·daa·tum
daughter *dochter* dokh·tuhr
dawn *dageraad* daa·khuh·raat
day *dag* dakh
day after tomorrow *overmorgen*
 oh·vuhr·mor·khun
day before yesterday *eergisteren*
 eyr·khis·tuh·ruhn
dead *dood* doht
deaf *doof* dohf
deal (cards) v *delen* dey·leyn
decide *beslissen* be·sli·suhn
deep (water) *diep* deep
deforestation *ontbossing* ont·bo·sing
degrees (temperature) *graden* khraa·duhn
delay n *vertraging* vuhr·traa·khing
delicious *lekker* le·kuhr
deliver *bezorgen* be·zor·khuhn
democracy *democratie* dey·moh·kra·*see*
demonstration (display) *demonstratie*
 dey·mon·straa·see
demonstration (rally) *betoging*
 buh·toh·khing
Denmark *Denemarken* dey·nuh·mar·kuhn
dental floss *tandzijde* tant·zey·duh
dentist *tandarts* tan·darts
deodorant *deodorant* dey·yoh·doh·*rant*
depart *vertrekken* vuhr·*tre*·kuhn

department store
  warenhuis ⑩/*grootwarenhuis* ⑩ Ⓝ/Ⓑ
  waa·ruhn·höys/khroht·waa·ruhn·höys
departure *vertrek* ⑩ vuhr·trek
departure gate *vertrek·hal* vuhr·trek·hal
deposit (money) n *storting* stor·ting
descendant *afstammeling* af·sta·muh·ling
desert n *woestijn* woos·teyn
design n *ontwerp* ⑩ ont·werp
dessert *dessert* ⑩ de·seyr
destination *bestemming* buh·ste·ming
details *details* ⑩ pl dey·tays
diabetes *suikerziekte/diabetes*
  söy·kuhr·zeek·tuh/dee·ya·bey·tis
dial tone *kiestoon* kees·tohn
diamond *diamant* dee·ya·mant
diaper *luier* löy·yuhr
diaphragm (contraceptive) *pessarium* ⑩
  pe·saa·ree·yuhm
diarrhoea *diarree* dee·ya·rey
diary (agenda) *agenda* a·khen·da
diary (personal notes) *dagboek* ⑩
  dakh·book
dice n *dobbelstenen* do·buhl·stey·nuhn
dictionary *woordenboek* ⑩
  wohr·duhn·book
die v *sterven* ster·vuhn
diet n *dieet* ⑩ dee·yeyt
different *verschillend* vuhr·skhi·luhnt
difficult *moeilijk* mooy·luhk
digital a *digitaal* dee·khee·taal
dining car *restauratiewagen*
  res·toh·raa·see·waa·khuhn
dinner *diner* ⑩/*avondmaal* ⑩
  dee·ney/aa·vont·maal
direct a *rechtstreeks* rekh·streyks
direct-dial *rechtstreekse lijn*
  rekh·streyk·suh leyn
direction *richting* rikh·ting
director *directeur/directrice* ⑩/Ⓕ
  dee·rek·teur/dee·rek·tree·suh
dirty *vuil* vöyl
disabled *gehandicapt* khuh·hen·dee·kept/
  khuh·han·dee·kapt Ⓝ/Ⓑ
discount n *korting* kor·ting
discrimination *discriminatie*
  dis·kree·mee·naa·see
disease *ziekte* zeek·tuh
dish n *schotel* skhoh·tuhl
disk (CD-ROM) *schijf* skheyf
diving *duiken* döy·kuhn
diving equipment *duikuitrusting*
  döyk·öyt·rus·ting

divorced *gescheiden* khuh·skhey·duhn
dizzy *duizelig* döy·zuh·likh
do *doen* doon
doctor *dokter* dok·tuhr
dog *hond* hont
dole *werkloosheidsuitkering*
  werk·lohs·heyts·öyt·key·ring
doll *pop* pop
door *deur* deur
double a *dubbel* du·buhl
double bed *tweepersoonsbed* ⑩
  twey·puhr·sohns·bet
double room *tweepersoonskamer*
  twey·puhr·sohns·kaa·muhr
down *naar beneden* naar buh·ney·duhn
downhill *bergaf* berkh·af
downtown *stadscentrum* ⑩ stat·sen·trum
dozen *dozijn* ⑩ do·zeyn
draught beer *getapt bier* ⑩ khuh·tapt beer
dream n *droom* drohm
dress n *jurk/kleed* ⑩/Ⓑ yurk/kleyt
dried *gedroogd* khuh·drohkht
dried fruit *gedroogd fruit* ⑩
  khuk·drohkht fröyt
drink (alcoholic) n *drank/drankje* ⑩
  drangk/drang·kyuh
drink (general) n *drank* drangk
drink v *drinken* dring·kuhn
drive v *rit* rit
drivers licence *rijbewijs* ⑩ rey·buh·weys
drug n *drugs* drukhs
drug addiction *drugsverslaving*
  drukhs·vuhr·slaa·ving
drug dealer *drugdealer* drukh·dee·luhr
drugs (illicit) *drugs* drukhs
drugstore *drogisterij* droh·khis·tuh·rey
drug trafficking *drugshandel*
  drukhs·han·duhl
drug user *(drugs)gebruiker* (drukhs·)
  khuh·bröy·kuhr
drum n *trommel* tro·muhl
drums (kit) *drumstel* ⑩ drum·stel
drunk a *dronken* drong·kuhn
dry a *droog* drohkh
dry (clothes) v *drogen* droh·khuhn
dry (oneself) v *afdrogen* af·droh·khuhn
duck n *eend* eynt
dummy (pacifier) *fopspeen* fop·speyn
Dutch *Nederlands/Hollands*
  ney·duhr·lants/ho·lants
Dutch (language) *Nederlands* ⑩
  ney·duhr·lants
Dutch gable *klokgevel* klok·khey·vuhl

218

Dutch person *Nederlander/Hollander*
ney·duhr·lan·duhr/ho·lan·duhr
Dutch-speaking *Nederlandstalig*
ney·duhr·lants·taa·likh
duty-free shop *taksvrije winkel*
taks·vrey·yuh *wing*·kuhl
DVD *dvd* dey·vey·*dey*
dyke *dijk* deyk

E

each *elke* elk·kuh
ear *oor* ⑩ ohr
early adv *vroeg* vrookh
earn *verdienen* vuhr·*dee*·nuhn
earplugs *oorstoppen* ohr·sto·puhn
earrings *oorringen* oh·ring·uhn
Earth *aarde* aar·duh
earthquake *aardbeving* aart·bey·ving
east n *oosten* ⑩ oh·stuhn
Easter *Pasen* paa·suhn
easy *gemakkelijk* khuh·*ma*·kuh·luhk
eat v *eten* ey·tuhn
education (at home) *opvoeding*
op·duhr·weys
education (at school) *onderwijs* ⑩
on·duhr·weys
egg *ei* ⑩ ey
eggplant *aubergine* oh·ber·*khee*·nuh
election *verkiezing* vuhr·*kee*·zing
electrical store
handel in elektrische apparaten
han·duhl in ey·*lek*·tri·suh a·pa·raa·tuhn
electrician *elektricien* ey·lek·tree·*sye*
electricity *elektriciteit* ey·lek·tree·see·*teyt*
elevator *lift* lift
embarrassed *gegeneerd* khuh·zhuh·*neyrt*
embassy *ambassade* am·ba·*saa*·duh
emergency *noodgeval* ⑩ noot·khuh·val
emotional *emotioneel* ey·moh·syoh·*neyl*
employee *werknemer* werk·*ney*·muhr
employer *werkgever* werk·*khey*·vuhr
empty a *leeg* leykh
end n *einde* ⑩ eyn·duh
endangered species *bedreigde soort*
buh·*dreykh*·duh sohrt
engaged (phone) *bezet* buh·*zet*
engaged (to be married)
verloofd vuhr·*lohft*
engagement (to marry)
verloving vuhr·*loh*·ving
engine *motor* moh·tor
engineer n *ingenieur* in·zhey·*nyeur*

engineering (civil) *burgerlijke bouwkunde*
bur·khur·luh·kuh *baw*·kun·duh
engineering (mechanical) *machine-bouwkunde* ma·*shee*·nuh·baw·kun·duh
England *Engeland* eng·uh·lant
English *Engels* eng·uhls
English (language) *Engels* ⑩ eng·uhls
English-speaking
Engelstalig eng·uhls·*taa*·likh
enjoy (oneself) *(zich) amuseren*
(zikh) a·mew·*sey*·ruhn
enough *genoeg* khuh·*nookh*
enter *binnengaan* bi·nuhn·khaan
entertainment guide *uitgaansgids*
öyt·khaans·khits
entry n *ingang* in·khang
environment *milieu* ⑩ mil·*yeu*
equality *gelijkheid* khuh·*leyk*·heyt
equal opportunity *gelijke kansen* pl
khuh·*ley*·kuh kan·suhn
equipment *uitrusting* öyt·rus·ting
escalator *roltrap* rol·trap
estate agency *makelaarskantoor* ⑩
maa·kuh·laars·kan·tohr
euro *euro/euro's* sg/pl eu·roh/eu·rohs
Europe *Europa* eu·roh·pa
European Union *Europese Unie*
eu·roh·*pey*·suh ew·nee
euthanasia *euthanasie* eu·ta·na·*zee*
evening *avond* aa·vont
every a *elke* el·kuh
everyone *iedereen* ee·duh·*reyn*
everything *alles* a·luhs
exactly *juist* yöyst
example *voorbeeld* ⑩ vohr·beylt
excellent *uitmuntend* öyt·*mun*·tuhnt
excess baggage *overvracht* oh·vuhr·vrakht
exchange (general) v *ruilen* röy·luhn
exchange (money) v *wisselen* wi·suh·luhn
exchange rate *wisselkoers* wi·suhl·koors
excluded *niet inbegrepen*
neet in·buh·khrey·puhn
exhaust (car) *uitlaat* öyt·laat
exhibition *tentoonstelling*
tuhn·*tohn*·ste·ling
exit n *uitgang* öyt·khang
expensive *duur* dewr
experience n *ervaring* er·*vaa*·ring
exploitation *uitbuiting* öyt·*böy*·ting
express mail *expresspost* eks·*pres*·post
extension (visa) *verlenging* vuhr·*leng*·ing
eye *oog* ⑩ ohkh
eye drops *oogdruppels* ohkh·dru·puhls

F

fabric *stof* ⓝ stof
façade *gevel* khey·vuhl
face n *gezicht* ⓝ khuh·zikht
face cloth *washandje* ⓝ was·han·chuh
factory *fabriek* fa·breek
factory worker
  fabrieksarbeider/fabrieksarbeidster
  ⓜ/ⓕ fa·breeks·ar·bey·duhr/
  fa·breeks·ar·beyt·stuhr
fairground *kermis* ker·mis
fall (autumn) *herfst* herfst
fall (down) v *val* val
family *familie* fa·mee·lee
family name *familienaam* fa·mee·lee·naam
famous *bekend* buh·kent
fan (machine) *ventilator* ven·tee·laa·tor
fan belt *ventilatorriem* ven·tee·laa·to·reem
far *ver* ver
fare n *tarief* ⓝ ta·reef
farm n *boerderij* boor·duh·rey
farmer *boer/boerin* ⓜ/ⓕ boor/boo·rin
fashion n *mode* moh·duh
fast a *snel* snel
fat (food) a *vet* vet
fat (objects/people) a *dik* dik
father *vader* vaa·duhr
father-in-law *schoonvader* skhohn·vaa·duhr
faucet *kraantje* ⓝ kraan·chuh
fault (someone's) n *fout* fawt
faulty *stuk* stuk
feed *voeden* voo·duhn
feel (emotions/touch) v *voelen* voo·luhn
feeling (physical) *gevoel* ⓝ khuh·vool
feelings *gevoelens* ⓝ pl khuh·voo·luhns
female a *vrouwelijk* vraw·wuh·luhk
fence n *omheining* om·hey·ning
fencing (sport) *schermen* skher·muhn
ferry n *veerboot/ferry* ⓝ/ⓑ
  veyr·boht/fe·ree
fever *koorts* kohrts
few *enkele* eng·kuh·luh
fiancé/fiancée *verloofde* vuhr·lohf·duh
fiction *fictie* fik·see
field *veld* ⓝ velt
field hospital *veldhospitaal* ⓝ
  velt·hos·pee·taal
fig *vijg* veykh
fight (argument) n *ruzie* rew·zee
fight (physical) n *gevecht* ⓝ khuh·vekht
fill v *vullen* vu·luhn

film speed *filmgevoeligheid*
  film·khuh·voo·likh·heyt
filtered *gefilterd* khuh·fil·tert
find v *vinden* vin·duhn
fine n *boete* boo·tuh
fine a *fijn* feyn
finger *vinger* ving·uhr
finish n *einde* ⓝ eyn·duh
finish v *eindigen* eyn·di·khuhn
fire (general) n *vuur* ⓝ vewr
fire (out of control) n *brand* brant
fire brigade *brandweer* brant·weyr
firewood *brandhout* ⓝ brant·hawt
first a *eerste* eyrs·tuh
first aid *eerste hulp* eyrs·tuh hulp
first-aid kit *EHBO-kist* ey·haa·bey·yoh·kist
first class *eerste klas* eyrs·tuh klas
first name *voornaam* vohr·naam
fish n *vis* vis
fishing *vissen* vi·suhn
fishmonger *vishandelaar* vis·han·duh·laar
fish shop *vishandel* vis·han·duhl
flag n *vlag* vlakh
Flanders *Vlaanderen* vlaan·duh·ruhn
flannel (face cloth) *washandje* ⓝ
  was·han·chuh
flash (camera) *flits* flits
flashlight (torch) *zaklantaarn* zak·lan·taarn
flat (apartment) n *flat/appartement* ⓝ
  ⓝ/ⓑ flet/a·par·tuh·ment
flat a *vlak* vlak
flea *vlo* vloh
flea market *vlooienmarkt* vloh·yuhn·markt
Flemish *Vlaams* vlaams
Flemish (language) *Vlaams* ⓝ vlaams
Flemish Community
  Vlaamse Gemeenschap
  vlaam·suh khuh·meyn·skhap
Flemish person *Vlaming* vlaa·ming
Flemish-speaking
  Vlaamstalig vlaams·taa·likh
flight *vlucht* vlukht
flood n *overstroming* oh·vuhr·stroh·ming
floor n *vloer* vloor
floor (storey) *verdieping* vuhr·dee·ping
florist *bloemist* bloo·mist
flour *bloem* bloom
flower n *bloem* bloom
flu *griep* khreep
fly n *vlieg* vleekh
fly v *vliegen* vlee·khuhn
foggy *mistig* mis·tikh
follow *volgen* vol·khuhn

F

food *voedsel* voot-suhl
food supplies *voedselvoorraad* sg
  voot-suhl-voh-raat
foot (body) *voet* voot
football (soccer) *voetbal* ⓝ voot-bal
footpath *voetpad* ⓝ voot-pat
foreign *buitenlands* böy-tuhn-lants
forest *woud* ⓝ wawt
forever *voor altijd* vohr al-teyt
forget *vergeten* vuhr-khey-tuhn
forgive *vergeven* vuhr-khey-vuhn
fork *vork* vork
fortnight *veertien dagen*
  veyr-teen daa-khuhn
fortune teller *waarzegger/waarzegster*
  ⓜ/ⓕ waar-ze-khuhr/waar-zekh-stuhr
foul (soccer) n *overtreding*
  oh-vuhr-trey-ding
fragile *breekbaar* breyk-baar
France *Frankrijk* frank-reyk
free (available/not bound) a *vrij* vrey
free (gratis) a *gratis* khraa-tis
freeze v *vriezen* vree-zuhn
French *Frans* frans
French (language) *Frans* ⓝ frans
French-speaking *Franstalig* frans-taa-likh
fresh *vers* vers
fridge *ijskast* eys-kast
fried *gebakken* khuh-ba-kuhn
friend *vriend/vriendin* ⓜ/ⓕ
  vreent/vreen-din
Frisian (language) *Fries* ⓝ frees
from *van* van
frost *vorst* vorst
frozen *bevroren* buh-vroh-ruhn
fruit *fruit* ⓝ fröyt
fruit-picking *fruitoogst* fröyt-ohkhst
fry v *bakken* ba-kuhn
frying pan *koekenpan/pan* ⓝ/ⓑ
  koo-kuh-pan/pan
full *vol* vol
full-time *voltijds* vol-teyts
fun a *leuk* leuk
funeral *begrafenis* buh-graa-fuh-nis
funny *grappig* khra-pikh
furniture *meubilair* ⓝ meu-bee-leyr
future n *toekomst* too-komst

G

game (sport) *spel* ⓝ spel
garage *garage* kha-raa-zhuh
garbage *vuilnis* ⓝ vöyl-nis
garbage can *vuilbak* vöyl-bak

garden n *tuin* töyn
gardener *tuinier* töy-neer
gardening *tuinieren* töy-nee-ruhn
garlic *knoflook* knof-lohk
gas (for cooking) *gas* ⓝ khas
gas (petrol) *benzine* ben-zee-nuh
gas cartridge *gasvulling* khas-vu-ling
gauze *gaas* ⓝ khaas
gay (homosexual) *homo* hoh-moh
gears (car, bicycle) *versnellingen* pl
  vuhr-sne-ling-uhn
Germany *Duitsland* döyts-lant
get *bekomen* buh-koh-muhn
get off (bus, train) *uitstappen* öyt-sta-puhn
gift *geschenk* ⓝ khuh-skhengk
gig *optreden* op-trey-duhn
gin *jenever* yuh-ney-vuhr/
  zhuh-ney-vuhr ⓝ/ⓑ
girl *meisje* ⓝ mey-shuh
girlfriend *vriendin* vreen-din
give *geven* khey-vuhn
given name *voornaam* vohr-naam
glandular fever *klierkoorts* kleer-kohrts
glass (drinking) *glas* ⓝ khlas
glasses (spectacles) *bril* sg bril
gloves (clothing/latex) *handschoenen* pl
  hant-skhoo-nuhn
glue n *lijm* leym
go *gaan* khaan
goalkeeper *doelverdediger/keeper*
  dool-vuhr-dey-di-khuhr/kee-puhr
goat *geit* kheyt
god *god* khot
goggles (skiing) *skibril* skee-bril
goggles (swimming) *zwembril* zwem-bril
gold n *goud* ⓝ khawt
golf course *golfterrein* ⓝ kholf-tuh-reyn
good *goed* khoot
goodbye *afscheid* ⓝ af-skheyt
go out *uitgaan* öyt-khaan
go out with (date) *uitgaan met*
  öyt-khaan met
go shopping *gaan winkelen*
  khaan wing-kuh-luhn
government *overheid* oh-vuhr-heyt
grandchild *kleinkind* ⓝ kleyn-kint
grandfather *grootvader*
  khroht-vaa-duhr
grandmother *grootmoeder*
  khroht-moo-duhr
grapes *druiven* dröy-vuhn
grateful *dankbaar* dangk-baar
grave n *graf* ⓝ khraf
great (fantastic) *fantastisch* fan-tas-tis

green *groen* khroon
greengrocer *groenteboer* khroon·tuh·boor
grey *grijs* khreys
grocery shop *kruidenierszaak*
  kröy·duh·neers·zaak
groceries *boodschappen* boht·skha·puhn
group *groep* khroop
grow *groeien* khroo·yuhn
guarantee n *garantie* kha·ran·see
guess v *raden* raa·duhn
guesthouse *pension* ⓝ pen·syon
guide (audio/person) *gids* khits
guidebook *gids* khits
guide dog *geleidehond* khuh·ley·duh·hont
guided tour *rondleiding* ront·ley·ding
guilty *schuldig* skhul·dikh
gum *kauwgom* kaw·khom
gun *geweer* ⓝ khuh·weyr
gym (place) *fitnesscentrum* ⓝ
  fit·nuhs·sen·trum
gymnastics *gymnastiek* kheem·nas·teek
gynaecologist *gynaecoloog*
  khee·ney·koh·lohkh

H

hair *haar* ⓝ haar
hairbrush *haarborstel* haar·bor·stuhl
haircut *kapsel* ⓝ kap·suhl
hairdresser *kapper* ka·puhr
half n *helft* helft
hallucination *hallucinatie*
  ha·lew·see·naa·see
hammer n *hamer* haa·muhr
hammock *hangmat* hang·mat
hand *hand* hant
handbag *handtas* han·tas
handicraft *handwerk* ⓝ hant·werk
handkerchief *zakdoek* zak·dook
handlebars *stuur* ⓝ sg stewr
handmade *handgemaakt* hant·khuh·maakt
handsome *knap* knap
hangover *kater* kaa·tuhr
happy *gelukkig* khuh·lu·kikh
harassment (sexual)
  ongewenste intimiteiten
  on·khuh·wens·tuh in·tee·mee·tey·tuhn
harbour n *haven* haa·vuhn
hard (not soft) *hard* hart
hardware store *doe-het-zelfzaak*
  doo·huht·zelf·zaak
hat *hoed* hoot
have *hebben* he·buhn

have a cold *verkouden zijn*
  vuhr·kaw·duhn zeyn
have fun *plezier hebben* pley·zeer he·buhn
hay fever *hooikoorts* hoy·kohrts
hazelnut *hazelnoot* haa·zuhl·noht
he *hij* hey
head (body) *hoofd* ⓝ hohft
head on beer *schuimkraag*
  skhöym·khraakh
headache *hoofdpijn* hohft·peyn
headlights *koplampen* kop·lam·puhn
health *gezondheid* khuh·zont·heyt
health-food store *reformwinkel*
  rey·form·wing·kuhl
hear *horen* hoh·ruhn
hearing aid *hoorapparaat* ⓝ hohr·a·pa·raat
heart *hart* ⓝ hart
heart attack *hartaanval* hart·aan·val
heart condition *hartkwaal* hart·kwaal
heat n *hitte* hi·tuh
heated (food) *opgewarmd* op·khuh·warmt
heated (place) *verwarmd* vuhr·warmt
heater *verwarmingstoestel* ⓝ
  vuhr·war·mings·too·stel
heating *verwarming* vuhr·war·ming
heavy (weight) *zwaar* zwaar
height *hoogte* hohkh·tuh
height of water *waterstand* waa·tuhr·stant
helmet *helm* helm
help n *hulp* hulp
help v *helpen* hel·puhn
hemp *hennep* he·nuhp
her (possessive) *haar* haar
herb *kruid* ⓝ kröyt
herbalist *kruidkundige* kröyt·kun·di·khuh
here *hier* heer
herring *haring* haa·ring
high (height) *hoog* hohkh
highchair *kinderstoel* kin·duhr·stool
high school *middelbare school*
  mi·duhl·baa·ruh skhohl
highway *snelweg* snel·wekh
hike v *trekken* tre·kuhn
hiking *trekken* tre·kuhn
hiking boots *wandellaarzen*
  wan·duhl·laar·zuhn
hiking route *wandelroute* wan·duhl·roo·tuh
hill *heuvel* heu·vuhl
hire v *huren* hew·ruhn
his *zijn* zeyn
historical *historisch* his·toh·ris
history *geschiedenis* khuh·skhee·duh·nis
hitchhike *liften* lif·tuhn

HIV-positive *seropositief*
  sey·roh·poh·see·*teef*
holiday (day off) n *feestdag* feys·dakh
holiday (vacation) *vakantie* va·*kan*·see
holiday resort *vakantieoord*
  va·*kan*·see·ohrt
holidays *vakantie* va·*kan*·see
Holland *Holland* ho·lant
home *thuis* töys
homeless *dakloos* dak·lohs
homemaker *huisman/huisvrouw* ⑩/①
  höys·man/höys·vraw
homesickness *heimwee* heym·wey
homosexual n *homoseksueel*
  hoh·moh·sek·sew·weyl
honey *honing* hoh·ning
honeymoon (period) *wittebroodsweken*
  wi·tuh·brohts·wey·kuhn
honeymoon (trip) *huwelijksreis*
  hew·wuh·luhks·reys
horse *paard* ⑩ paart
horse racing *paardenwedrennen*
  paar·duhn·wet·re·nuhn
horse riding *paardrijden* ⑩ paart·rey·duhn
hospital *ziekenhuis* ⑩ zee·kuhn·höys
hospitality *gastvrijheid* khast·*vrey*·heyt
hot *warm* warm
(very) hot *heet* heyt
hotel *hotel* ⑩ hoh·*tel*
hot water *warm water* ⑩ warm waa·tuhr
hot water bottle *warmwaterfles*
  warm·*waa*·tuhr·fles
hour *uur* ⑩ ewr
house n *huis* ⑩ höys
housework *huishoudelijk werk* ⑩
  höys·*haw*·duh·luhk werk
how *hoe* hoo
how much/many *hoeveel* hoo·*veyl*
hug v *omhelzen* om·*hel*·zuhn
huge *zeer groot* zeyr khroht
humanities *humaniora* hew·man·*yoh*·ra
human resources *personeelszaken*
  per·soh·*neyls*·zaa·kuhn
human rights *mensenrechten* ⑩ pl
  men·suhn·rekh·tuhn
hundred *honderd* hon·duhrt
hungry *hongerig* hong·uh·rikh
hunting *jacht* yakht
hurt v *pijn doen* peyn doon
husband *echtgenoot* ekht·khuh·noht
hydroponics *watercultuur*
  waa·tuhr·kul·tewr

I

I *ik* ik
ice *ijs* ⑩ eys
ice axe *ijshouweel* ⑩ eys·haw·weyl
ice cream *(room)ijs* ⑩ (rohm·)eys
ice-cream parlour *ijssalon* ⑩ ey·sa·lon
ice hockey *ijshockey* ⑩ eys·ho·kee
icy (road) *glad* khlat
identification *identificatie*
  ee·den·tee·fee·*kaa*·see
identification card (ID) *identiteitsbewijs* ⑩
  ee·den·tee·*teyts*·buh·weys
idiot n *idioot* ee·dee·*yoht*
if *als* als
ill *ziek* zeek
immigration *immigratie* ee·mee·*graa*·see
important *belangrijk* buh·*lang*·ruhk
impossible *onmogelijk* on·*moh*·khul·luhk
in *in* in
in a hurry *gehaast* khuh·*haast*
included *inbegrepen* in·buh·khrey·puhn
income tax *inkomstenbelasting*
  in·kom·stuhn·buh·las·ting
indicator *richtingsaanwijzer*
  rikh·tings·aan·wey·zuhr
indigestion *indigestie* in·dee·*khes*·tee
indoor a *binnen-* bi·nuhn·
indoors adv *binnenshuis* bi·nuhns·*höys*
(brief) industrial action *prikactie* prik·ak·see
industry *industrie* in·dus·*tree*
infection *infectie* in·*fek*·see
inflammation *ontsteking* ont·*stey*·king
influenza *griep* khreep
information *informatie* in·for·*maa*·see
in front of *tegenover* tey·khuhn·*oh*·vuhr
ingredient *ingredient* ⑩ in·khrey·*dyent*
inject *inspuiten* in·spöy·tuhn
injection *inspuiting* in·*spöy*·ting
injured *gekwetst* khuh·*kwetst*
injury *kwetsuur* kwet·*sewr*
inner tube *binnenband* bi·nuhn·bant
innocent *onschuldig* on·*skhul*·dikh
insect repellent *insektwerend middel*
  in·sekt·wey·ruhnt *mi*·duhl
inside adv *binnen* bi·nuhn
instructor *instructeur* in·struk·*teur*
insurance *verzekering* vuhr·*zey*·kuh·ring
interesting *interessant* in·tey·re·*sant*
intermission *pause* paw·zuh
international *internationaal*
  in·tuhr·na·syoh·*naal*
interpreter *tolk* tolk

intersection *kruispunt* ⑩ *krőys*-punt
inundation *overstroming*
  oh-vuhr-*stroh*-ming
invite *uitnodigen* őyt-noh-di-khuhn
iron (for clothes) n *strijkijzer* ⑩
  streyk-ey-zuhr
island *eiland* ⑩ *ey*-lant
it *het* huht
IT *informatica* in-for-*maa*-tee-ka
itch n *jeuk* yeuk
itemised *gedetailleerd* khuh-dey-ta-*yeyrt*
itinerary *reisroute* reys-roo-tuh
IUD *spiraaltje* ⑩ spee-*raal*-chuh

J

jacket (casual) *jas* yas
jacket (dressy) *colbert* ⑪/*vest* ⑩/⑧
  kol-*ber*/vest
jail n *gevangenis* khuh-*vang*-uh-nis
jam n *jam*/*confituur* ⑩/⑧
  zhem/kon-fee-*tewr*
jar *pot*/*bokaal* ⑩/⑧ pot/boh-*kaal*
jaw *kaak* kaak
jealous *jaloers* ya-*loors*
jeans *spijkerbroek*/*jeans* ⑩/⑧
  spey-kuhr-brook/zheens
jellyfish *kwal* kwal
jewellery *juwelen* yew-*wey*-luhn
job *baan*/*werk* ⑩ ⑩/⑧ baan/werk
jogging *joggen* ⑩ *dzho*-guhn
joke n *grap* khrap
journey n *reis* reys
judge n *rechter* rekh-tuhr
juice n *sap* ⑩ sap
jump v *sprong* sprong
jumper (sweater) *trui* trőy
jumper leads *startkabels* start-kaa-buhls

K

key (door etc) *sleutel* sleu-tuhl
keyboard *toetsenbord* ⑩ *toot*-suhn-bort
kick v *schoppen* skho-puhn
kidney *nier* neer
kill v *doden* doh-duhn
kind (nice) *aardig* aar-dikh
kindergarten *kleuterschool* kleu-tuhr-skhohl
king *koning* koh-ning
kiss n *kus* kus
kiss v *kussen* ku-suhn
kitchen *keuken* keu-kuhn
knee *knie* knee

knife n *mes* ⑩ mes
know (someone) *kennen* ke-nuhn
know (something) *weten* wey-tuhn

L

labourer *arbeider*/*arbeidster* ⑪/①
  ar-bey-duhr/ar-beyt-stuhr
lace (fabric) n *kant* kant
lake *meer* ⑩ meyr
lamb (meat) *lamsvlees* ⑩ lams-vleys
land n *land* ⑩ lant
landlady *huisbazin* hőys-baa-zin
landlord *huisbaas* hőys-baas
language *taal* taal
large *groot* khroht
last (final) *laatste* laat-stuh
last (previous) *vorige* voh-ri-khuh
late adv *laat* laat
later *later* laa-tuhr
laugh v *lachen* la-khuhn
laundrette *wasserette* wa-suh-re-tuh
laundry (clothes) *was* was
laundry (place) *wasserij* wa-suh-rey
laundry (room) *wasinrichting*
  was-in-rikh-ting
law (legislation) *wet* wet
law (study/profession) *rechten* ⑩ pl
  rekh-tuhn
lawyer *advocaat* at-voh-*kaat*
laxative *laxeermiddel* ⑩ lak-*seyr*-mi-duhl
lazy *lui* lőy
leader *leider* ley-duhr
leaf n *blad* ⑩ blat
learn *leren* ley-ruhn
leather n *leder* ⑩ ley-duhr
lecturer (at university) *lector* lek-tor
lecturer (general/speaker) *spreker*
  sprey-kuhr
ledge *richel* ri-khul
left (direction) *links* lingks
left luggage *achtergelaten bagage*
  akh-tuhr-khuh-laa-tuhn ba-*khaa*-zhuh
left-luggage office *bagagedepot*
  ba-khaa-zhuh-dey-poh
left-wing *links* lingks
leg (body) *been* ⑩ beyn
legal *wettelijk* we-tuh-luhk
legislation *wetgeving* wet-khey-ving
legume *peulvrucht* peul-vrukht
lemon *citroen* see-*troon*
lentils *linzen* lin-zuhn
lesbian n *lesbische* les-bi-suh

224

less *minder* min·duhr
letter (mail) *brief* breef
lettuce *sla* slaa
liar *leugenaar* leu·khuh·naar
librarian *bibliothecaris* bi·blyoh·tey·*kaa*·ris
library *bibliotheek* bi·blyoh·*teyk*
lice *luizen* löy·zuhn
licence (general) n *vergunning*
   vuhr·*khu*·ning
licence (driving) n *rijbewijs* ⓝ
   rey·buh·weys
license plate number *kentekenplaat*
   ken·tey·kuhn·plaat
licorice *drop* drop
lie (not stand) v *liggen* li·khuhn
lie (not tell the truth) v *liegen* lee·khuhn
life *leven* ley·vuhn
lifeboat *reddingsboot* re·dings·boht
life guard *redder* re·duhr
life jacket *reddingsvest* ⓝ re·dings·vest
light n *licht* ⓝ likht
light (colour/weight) a *licht* likht
light bulb *gloeilamp* khlooy·lamp
lighter (cigarette) *aansteker* aan·stey·kuhr
light meter *lichtmeter* likht·mey·tuhr
like v *houden van* haw·duhn van
lime *limoen* lee·moon
linguist *taalkundige* taal·*kun*·di·khuh
lip balm *lippenbalm* li·puhn·balm
lips *lippen* li·puhn
lipstick *lippenstift* li·puh·stift
liquor store *slijterij/drankenhandel* ⓝ/ⓑ
   sley·tuh·rey/*drang*·kuhn·han·duhl
listen *luisteren* löys·tuh·ruhn
little (quantity) a *weinig* wey·nikh
little (size) a *klein* kleyn
live (life) *leven* ley·vuhn
live (somewhere) *wonen* woh·nuhn
liver *lever* ley·vuhr
lizard *hagedis* haa·khuh·dis
local a *plaatselijk* plaat·suh·luhk
lock n *slot* slot
lock v *sluiten* slöy·tuhn
locked *gesloten* khuh·*sloh*·tuhn
lollies *snoep* snoop
long *lang* lang
look v *kijken* key·kuhn
look after *verzorgen* vuhr·*zor*·khuhn
look for *zoeken* zoo·kuhn
lookout *uitkijk* öyt·keyk
loose *los* los
loose change *kleingeld* ⓝ kleyn·khelt
lose *verliezen* vuhr·*lee*·zuhn

lost *verloren* ver·*loh*·ruhn
lost-property office *gevonden voorwerpen*
   ⓝ pl khuh·*von*·duhn vohr·wer·puhn
(a) lot *veel* veyl
loud *luid* löyt
love n *liefde* leef·duh
love v *houden van* haw·duhn van
lover *minnaar/minares* ⓜ/ⓕ
   mi·naar/mi·naa·*res*
low *laag* laakh
lubricant *smeermiddel* ⓝ smeyr·mi·duhl
lubricant (sex) *glijmiddel* ⓝ khley·mi·duhl
luck *geluk* ⓝ khuh·luk
lucky *gelukkig* khuh·*lu*·kikh
(be) lucky v *boffen* bo·fuhn
luggage *bagage* ba·*khaa*·zhuh
luggage locker *bagagekluis*
   ba·*khaa*·zhuh·klöys
luggage tag *bagage-etiket* ⓝ
   ba·*khaa*·zhuh·ey·tee·*ket*
lump *knobbel* kno·buhl
lunch *lunch/middagmaal* ⓝ
   lunsh/*mi*·dakh·maal
lung *long* long
Luxembourg *Luxemburg* luk·suhm·burkh
luxury *luxueus* luk·sew·*weus*

M

magazine *tijdschrift* ⓝ teyt·skhrift
mail (letters/postal system) n *post* post
mail v *verzenden* vuhr·*zen*·duhn
mailbox *brievenbus* bree·vuh·bus
main a *voornaamste/hoofd-*
   vohr·*naam*·stuh/hohft·
main road *hoofdweg* hohft·wekh
main square *stadsplein* ⓝ stats·pleyn
mansion *herenhuis* ⓝ hey·ruhn·höys
make v *maken* maa·kuhn
man n *man* man
manual worker
   handarbeider/handarbeidster ⓜ/ⓕ
   hant·ar·bey·duhr/hant·ar·beyt·stuhr
many *veel* veyl
map (of building) *plattegrond*
   pla·tuh·*khront*
map (of country/town) *kaart* kaart
marital status *wettelijke stand*
   we·tuh·luh·kuh stant
market n *markt* markt
marriage *huwelijk* ⓝ hew·wuh·luhk
married *gehuwd* khuh·*hewt*
marry *huwen* hew·wuhn

M

mass (Catholic) *mis* mis
mat *mat* mat
match (sports) *wedstrijd* wet·streyt
matches (for lighting) *lucifers* lew·see·fers
mattress *matras* ma·tras
maybe *misschien* mee·*skheen*
mayor *burgemeester* bur·khuh·*mey*·stuhr
me *me* muh
meal *maaltijd* maal·teyt
measles *mazelen* maa·zuh·luhn
meat *vlees* ⓝ vleys
mechanic *mechanicien* mey·ka·nee·*sye*
medicine (medication) *medicijn* ⓝ
  mey·dee·*seyn*
medicine (study/profession)
  medicijnen/geneeskunde ⓝ/®
  mey·dee·*sey*·nuhn/khuh·*neys*·kun·duh
meditation *meditatie* mey·dee·*taa*·see
meet (first time) v *ontmoeten*
  ont·*moo*·tuhn
meet (get together) v *samenkomen*
  saa·muhn·koh·muhn
melon *meloen* muh·*loon*
member *lid* ⓝ lit
memorial *gedenkteken* ⓝ
  khuh·*dengk*·tey·kuhn
memory card *geheugenkaart*
  khuh·*heu*·khuhn·kaart
menstruation *menstruatie*
  men·strew·*waa*·see
menu *menu* ⓝ muh·*new*
message n *bericht* buh·*rikht*
metal n *metaal* ⓝ mey·*taal*
metre *meter* mey·tuhr
metro station *metrostation* ⓝ
  mey·troh·sta·syon
microwave oven
  magnetron/microgolfoven ⓝ/®
  makh·ney·tron/*mee*·kroh·kholf·oh·vuhn
midday *middag* mi·dakh
midnight *middernacht* mi·duhr·*nakht*
migraine *migraine* mee·*khreyn*
military n *leger* ⓝ *ley*·khuhr
military service *legerdienst*
  ley·khuhr·deenst
milk *melk* melk
mill *molen* moh·luhn
million *miljoen* ⓝ mil·*yoon*
mince n *gehakt* ⓝ khuh·*hakt*
mineral water *mineraalwater* ⓝ
  mee·ney·*raal*·waa·tuhr
minute n *minuut* mee·*newt*
mirror n *spiegel* spee·khul

miscarriage *miskraam* mis·kraam
miss *missen* mi·suhn
mistake n *vergissing* vuhr·*khi*·sing
mix v *mengen* meng·uhn
mobile phone *mobiele telefoon* ⓝ/gsm ®
  moh·*bee*·luh tey·ley·*fohn*/khey·es·*em*
moisturiser (cream) *vochtinbrengende*
  crème vokht·in·breng·uhn·duh kreym
monastery *klooster* ⓝ *kloh*·stuhr
money *geld* ⓝ khelt
monk *kloosterling* kloh·stuhr·ling
month *maand* maant
monument *monument* ⓝ mo·new·*ment*
moon *maan* maan
more *meer* meyr
morning *ochtend/morgen* ⓝ/®
  okh·tuhnt/*mor*·khuhn
morning sickness
  zwangerschapsmisselijkheid
  zwang·uhr·skhaps·mi·suh·luhk·heyt
mosque *moskee* mos·*key*
mosquito *mug* mukh
mosquito net *muskietennet* ⓝ
  mus·*kee*·tuhn·net
mother *moeder* moo·duhr
mother-in-law *schoonmoeder*
  skhohn·moo·duhr
motorbike *motorfiets* moh·tor·feets
motorboat *motorboot* moh·tor·boht
motorway *autoweg* aw·toh·wekh
mountain *berg* berkh
mountaineering *bergsport* berkh·sport
mountain path *bergpad* ⓝ berkh·pat
mountain range *bergketen* berkh·key·tuhn
mouse *muis* möys
moustache *snor* snor
mouth *mond* mont
movie *film* film
mud *modder* mo·duhr
mum *mam* mam
mumps *bof* bof
murder n *moord* mohrt
murder v *vermoorden* vuhr·*mohr*·duhn
muscle *spier* speer
museum *museum* ⓝ mew·zey·yuhm
mushroom *paddenstoel* pa·duh·stool
music *muziek* mew·zeek
musician *muzikant* mew·zee·kant
music shop *muziekwinkel*
  mew·zeek·wing·kuhl
mussel *mossel* mo·suhl
mute *doofstom* dohf·stom
my *mijn* meyn

N

nail clippers *nagelknipper* sg
   naa-khuhl-kni-puhr
name n *naam* naam
napkin *servet* ⓝ ser-*vet*
nappy *luier* löy-yuhr
nappy rash *luieruitslag* löy-yuhr-öyt-slakh
narrow *smal* smal
nationality *nationaliteit* na-syoh-na-lee-*teyt*
national park *nationaal park* ⓝ
   na-syoh-*naal* park
nature *natuur* na-*tewr*
naturopathy *natuurgeneeskunde*
   na-*tewr*-khuh-neys-kun-duh
nausea *misselijkheid* mi-suh-luhk-heyt
near prep *bij* bey
nearby *dichtbij* dikht-bey
nearest *dichtsbijzijnde* dikhts-bey-zeyn-duh
necessary *noodzakelijk* noht-*zaa*-kuh-luhk
neck *nek* nek
necklace *halsketting* hals-ke-ting
need v *nodig hebben* noh-dikh he-buhn
needle (sewing/syringe) *naald* naalt
negative a *negatief* ney-kha-teef
negatives (photos) *negatieven*
   ney-kha-*tee*-vuhn
neither adv *evenmin* ey-vuh-*min*
nephew *neef* neyf
(The) Netherlands *Nederland* ney-duhr-lant
network (phone) *netwerk* ⓝ net-werk
never *nooit* noyt
new *nieuw* neew
news *nieuws* neews
newsagency (selling newspapers)
   krantenzaak kran-tuh-zaak
newspaper *krant* krant
newsstand *krantenkiosk* kran-tuh-kee-*yosk*
New Year's Day *nieuwjaarsdag*
   neew-yaars-*dakh*
New Year's Eve *oudejaarsavond*
   aw-duh-yaars-*aa*-vont
New Zealand *Nieuw-Zeeland* neew-zey-lant
next (following) *volgend* vol-*khuhnt*
next to *naast* naast
nice *leuk/fijn* leuk/feyn
nickname *bijnaam* bey-naam
niece *nicht* nikht
night *nacht* nakht
nightclub *nachtclub* nakht-klup
night out *avondje-uit* ⓝ *aa*-vont-chuh-öyt
no *nee* ney
noisy *lawaaierig* la-*waa*-yuh-rikh

none *geen* kheyn
nonsmoking *niet-roken* neet-roh-kuhn
noodles *noedels* noo-duhls
noon *middag* mi-dakh
north n *noorden* ⓝ nohr-duhn
nose *neus* neus
not *niet* neet
notebook *notitieboekje* ⓝ
   noh-tee-see-book-yuh
nothing *niets* neets
no vacancy *vol/volzet* vol/vol-zet ⓝ/ⓑ
now *nu* new
not yet *nog niet* nokh neet
nuclear energy *kernenergie*
   kern-ey-ner-khee
nuclear testing *atoomtesten* pl
   a-*tohm*-tes-tuhn
nuclear waste *atoomafval* ⓝ a-*tohm*-af-val
number n *nummer* ⓝ nu-muhr
numberplate *nummerplaat* nu-muhr-plaat
nun *non* non
nurse n *zuster* zus-tuhr
nut (food) *noot* noht

O

oats *havermout* haa-vuhr-mawt
ocean *oceaan* oh-sey-yaan
occupied *bezet* buh-zet
off (power) *uit* öyt
off (spoilt) *bedorven* buh-dor-vuhn
office *kantoor* ⓝ kan-tohr
office worker *kantoorwerker*
   kan-*tohr*-wer-kuhr
often *vaak* vaak
oil (cooking) *olie* oh-lee
oil (petrol) *benzine* ben-zee-nuh
old *oud* awt
old city *oude stad* aw-duh stat
olive *olijf* oh-leyf
olive oil *olijfolie* oh-leyf-oh-lee
on *op* op
on (power) *aan* aan
once *één keer* eyn keyr
one *één* eyn
one-way ticket *enkele reis* eng-kuh-luh reys
onion *ui* öy
only adv *alleen* a-leyn
on time *op tijd* op teyt
open v *openen* oh-puh-nuhn
opening hours *openingsuren* ⓝ pl
   oh-puh-nings-ew-ruhn

opera house *operagebouw* ⋈
oh·*pey*·ra·khuh·*baw*
operation (medical) *operatie*
oh·pey·*raa*·see
operator (telephone) *telefonist*
tey·ley·foh·*nist*
opinion *opinie* o·*pee*·nee
opposite prep *tegenover*
tey·khuhn·*oh*·vuhr
optometrist *opticien* op·tee·*sye*
or *of* of
orange (colour) *oranje* oh·*ran*·yuh
orange (fruit) *sinaasappel/appelsien*
⋈/⋈ see·*naas*·a·puhl/a·puhl·*seen*
orchestra *orkest* ⋈ or·*kest*
order n *bestelling* buh·*ste*·ling
order v *bestellen* be·*ste*·luhn
ordinary *gewoon* khuh·*wohn*
orgasm *orgasme* ⋈ or·*khas*·muh
original a *origineel* o·ree·zhee·*neyl*
other *andere* an·duh·ruh
our *onze* on·zuh
out of order *stuk* stuk
outside adv *buiten* böy·tuhn
ovarian cyst *gezwel op de eileiders* ⋈
khuh·*zwel* op duh ey·ley·duhrs
ovary *eileider* ey·ley·duhr
overcoat *jas* yas
overdose n *overdosis* oh·vuhr·doh·sis
overnight (during the night) adv
gedurende de nacht
khuh·*dew*·ruhn·duh duh nakht
overnight (lasting one night) adv
één nacht durend eyn nakht dew·ruhnt
overseas *overzees* oh·vuhr·zeys
overseas (abroad) adv *in het buitenland*
in huht *böy*·tuhn·lant
owe *schuldig zijn* skhul·dikh zeyn
owner *eigenaar/eigenares* ⋈/⋈
ey·khuh·naar/ey·khuh·naa·res
oxygen *zuurstof* zewr·stof
oyster *oester* oos·tuhr
ozone layer *ozonlaag* oh·zon·laakh

P

pacifier (dummy) *fopspeen* fop·speyn
package n *pak* ⋈/*pakket* ⋈ pak/pa·*ket*
packet (general) *pak* ⋈/*pakket* ⋈ pak/
pa·*ket*
padlock *hangslot* ⋈ hang·slot
page n *pagina* paa·khee·na
pain n *pijn* peyn

painful *pijnlijk* peyn·luhk
painkiller *pijnstiller* peyn·sti·luhr
painter (artist/tradesperson) *schilder*
skhil·duhr
painting (the art) *schilderkunst*
skhil·duhr·kunst
painting (a work) *schilderij* ⋈ skhil·duh·*rey*
pair (couple) n *paar* ⋈ paar
palace *paleis* ⋈ pa·*leys*
pan *pan* pan
pants (trousers) *broek* brook
pantyhose *panty* pen·tee/*pan*·tee ⋈/⋈
panty liners *inlegkruisjes* ⋈ pl
in·lekh·kröy·shuhs
paper n *papier* ⋈ pa·*peer*
paperwork *papieren* ⋈ pl pa·*pee*·ruhn
pap smear *uitstrijkje* ⋈ öyt·streyk·yuh
paraplegic n *aan beide benen verlamd*
aan bey·duh bey·nuhn vuhr·*lamt*
parcel n *pak* ⋈/*pakket* ⋈ pak/pa·*ket*
parents *ouders* aw·duhrs
park (a car) v *parkeren* par·*key*·ruhn
parliament *parlement* ⋈ par·luh·*ment*
part (component) n *onderdeel* ⋈
on·duhr·deyl
part-time *deeltijds* deyl·teyts
party (entertainment) *feestje* ⋈/*fuif* ⋈/⋈
fey·shuh/föyf
party (politics) *partij* par·*tey*
pass (go by) v *voorbijgaan* vohr·bey·khaan
pass (kick/throw) v *passen* pa·suhn
passenger *passagier* pa·sa·*kheer*
passionfruit *passievrucht* pa·see·vrukht
passport *paspoort* ⋈ pas·pohrt
passport number *paspoortnummer* ⋈
pas·pohrt·nu·muhr
past n *verleden* ⋈ vuhr·ley·duhn
pastry *gebak* ⋈ khuh·*bak*
path *pad* ⋈ pat
pavement *voetpad* ⋈ voot·pat
pay v *betalen* buh·*taa*·luhn
payment *betaling* buh·*taa*·ling
pea *erwt* erwt
peace *vrede* vrey·duh
peach *perzik* per·zik
peak (mountain) *piek* peek
peak hour *piekuur* ⋈ peek·ewr
peanut *pinda* pin·da
pear *peer* peyr
pedal n *pedaal* ⋈ pey·*daal*
pedal boat *waterfiets* waa·tuhr·feets
pedestrian n *voetganger* voot·gang·uhr
pencil *potlood* ⋈ pot·*loht*

penknife *zakmes* ⓝ *zak*·mes
pensioner *gepensioneerde* khuh·pen·syoh·*neyr*·duh
people *mensen* *men*·suhn
pepper (bell) *paprika* pa·*pree*·ka
per (day) *per (dag)* puhr (dakh)
per cent *procent* proh·*sent*
performance *voorstelling* *vohr*·ste·ling
perfume n *parfum* ⓝ par·*föy*
period pain *menstruatiepijn* men·strew·*waa*·see·peyn
permission *toestemming* *too*·ste·ming
permit n *toestemmen* *too*·ste·muhn
person *persoon* puhr·*sohn*
petition n *petitie* pey·*tee*·see
petrol *benzine* ben·*zee*·nuh
petrol station *benzinestation* ⓝ ben·*zee*·nuh·sta·syon
pharmacist *apotheker/apothekeres* ⓜ/ⓕ a·poh·*tey*·kuhr/a·poh·*tey*·kuh·*res*
pharmacy *apotheek* a·poh·*teyk*
phone book *telefoonboek* ⓝ tey·ley·*fohn*·book
phone box *telefooncel* tey·ley·*fohn*·sel
phonecard *telefoonkaart* tey·ley·*fohn*·kaart
photograph v *fotograferen* foh·toh·khra·*fey*·ruhn
photographer *fotograaf* foh·toh·*khraaf*
photography *fotografie* foh·toh·khraa·*fee*
phrasebook *taalgids* *taal*·khits
pickaxe *houweel* ⓝ *haw*·weyl
pickles *ingemaakt zuur* ⓝ *in*·khuh·maakt zewr
pie (big) *taart* taart
pie (small) *pastei* pas·*tey*
piece n *stuk* ⓝ stuk
pig *varken* ⓝ *var*·kuhn
(the) pill *de pil* duh pil
pillow *kussen* ⓝ *ku*·suhn
pillowcase *kussensloop* *ku*·suhn·slohp
pineapple *ananas* *a*·na·nas
pink *roze* *roh*·zuh
pistachio *pistachenoot* pees·ta·shuh·noht
place n *plaats* plaats
place of birth *geboorteplaats* khuh·*bohr*·tuh·plaats
plane *vliegtuig* ⓝ *vleekh*·töykh
plastic a *plastic/plastieken* *ples*·tik/plas·*tee*·kuhn
plate *bord* ⓝ bort
platform (train station) *perron* ⓝ pe·*ron*
play (cards) v *kaartspelen* *kaart*·spey·luhn
play (instrument) v *spelen* *spey*·luhn

play (theatre) n *toneelstuk* ⓝ toh·*neyl*·stuk
pleasant *prettig* *pre*·tikh
plug (bath) n *stop* stop
plug (electricity) n *stekker* *ste*·kuhr
plum *pruim* pröym
plumber *loodgieter* *loht*·khee·tuhr
poached *gepocheerd* khuh·po·*sheyrt*
pocket n *zak* zak
pocketknife *zakmes* ⓝ *zak*·mes
poetry *dichtkunst* *dikht*·kunst
point v *wijzen* *wey*·zuhn
poisonous *giftig* *khif*·tikh
police *politie* poh·*leet*·see
police officer *politieagent* poh·*leet*·see·a·*khent*
police station *politiebureau* ⓝ poh·*leet*·see·bew·*roh*
policy (code of conduct) *gedragslijn* khuh·*drakhs*·leyn
policy (insurance) *polis* poh·*lis*
politician *politicus* poh·*lee*·tee·kus
politics *politiek* poh·*lee*·teek
pollution *vervuiling* vuhr·*vöy*·ling
pond *vijver* *vey*·vuhr
pool (game) *biljart* ⓝ *bil*·yart
pool (swimming) *zwembad* ⓝ *zwem*·bat
poor (wealth) *arm* arm
popular *populair* poh·pew·*leyr*
pork *varkensvlees* ⓝ *var*·kuhns·vleys
port (river/sea) *haven* *haa*·vuhn
positive a *positief* poh·*zee*·teef
possible *mogelijk* *moh*·khuh·luhk
post (mail) n *post* post
post v *op de post doen* op duh post doon
postage *portkosten* *port*·kos·tuhn
postcard *ansichtkaart/postkaart* ⓝ/ⓑ *an*·zikht·kaart/*post*·kaart
poster *poster/affiche* *pos*·tuhr/a·*fee*·shuh
post office *postkantoor* ⓝ *post*·kan·tohr
pot (cooking) *kookpot* *kohk*·pot
potato *aardappel* *aart*·a·puhl
pottery *aardewerk* ⓝ/*keramiek* *aar*·duh·werk/*key*·ra·meek
pound (money) *pond* ⓝ pont
pound (weight) *pond* ⓝ pont
poverty *armoede* ar·moo·duh
powder n *poeder* ⓝ *poo*·duhr
power (electricity) n *elektriciteit* ey·lek·tree·see·*teyt*
power (physical) n *kracht* krakht
power (politics) n *macht* makht
prawn *garnaal* khar·*naal*
prayer *gebed* ⓝ khuh·*bet*

prayer book *gebedenboek*
khuh·*bey*·duhn·book
prefer *verkiezen* vuhr·*kee*·zuhn
pregnancy test kit *zwangerschapstest*
zwang·uhr·skhaps·test
pregnant *zwanger* *zwang*·uhr
premenstrual tension *pms*
(*premenstrueel syndroom*) pey·em·es
(*prey*·men·strew·*weyl* seen·*drohm*)
prepare (for something) *voorbereiden*
vohr·buh·rey·duhn
prepare (food) *klaarmaken* *klaar*·maa·kuhn
prescription *recept* ⓝ/*voorschrift* ⓝ/ⓑ
rey·*sept*/*vohr*·skhrift
present (gift) n *geschenk* ⓝ khuh·*skhengk*
present (time) n *heden* ⓝ *hey*·duhn
president *president* prey·zee·*dent*
pressure (tyre) n *druk* druk
pretty *mooi* moy
price n *prijs* preys
priest *priester* *prees*·tuhr
prime minister *minister-president* ⓝ/*eerste
minister* ⓑ mee·*nis*·tuhr·prey·zee·*dent*/
eyr·stuh mee·*nis*·tuhr
prince *prins* prins
prince consort *prins-gemaal*
prins·khuh·*maal*
prince regent *prins-regent* prins·rey·*khent*
princess *prinses* prin·*ses*
prison *gevangenis* khuh·*vang*·uh·nis
prisoner *gevangene* khuh·*vang*·uh·nuh
private *privé* pree·*vey*
produce v *produceren* proh·dew·*sey*·ruhn
profit n *winst* winst
program n *programma* ⓝ proh·*khra*·ma
projector *projector* proh·*yek*·tor
promise v *beloven* buh·*loh*·vuhn
prostitute n *prostituée* pros·tee·tew·*wey*
prostitution *prostitutie* pros·tee·*tew*·see
protect v *beschermen* buh·*skher*·muhn
protected *beschermd* buh·*skhermt*
protest v *protesteren* proh·tes·*tey*·ruhn
provisions (food) *proviand* proh·*vyant*
pub (bar) *café* ⓝ/*kroeg* ka·*fey*/krookh
public gardens *openbaar park* ⓝ
oh·puhn·baar park
public phone *openbare telefoon*
oh·puhn·bah·ruh tey·ley·*fohn*
public relations *pr* pey·*eyr*
public toilet *openbaar toilet* ⓝ
oh·puhn·baar twa·*let*
pull v *trekken* *tre*·kuhn

pump n *pomp* pomp
pumpkin *pompoen* pom·*poon*
puncture n *lek* ⓝ lek
puppet theatre *marionettentheater* ⓝ
mar·yoh·ne·tuhn·tee·*yaa*·tuhr
pure *puur* pewr
purple *purper* pur·*puhr*
purse *portemonnee* por·tuh·moh·*ney*
push v *duwen* *dew*·wuhn
put *zetten* *ze*·tuhn

Q

quadriplegic n *volledig verlamd*
vo·ley·dikh vuhr·*lamt*
qualifications *kwalificaties*
kwa·lee·fee·*kaa*·sees
quality n *kwaliteit* kwa·lee·*teyt*
quarantine *quarantaine* ka·ran·*tey*·nuh
quarter (15 minutes) n *kwartier* ⓝ
kwar·*teer*
quarter (a fourth) n *kwart* ⓝ kwart
quay *kaai/kade* kaay/*kaa*·duh
queen *koningin* koh·ning·*khin*
Queen Mother *koningin-moeder*
koh·ning·*khin*·moo·duhr
question n *vraag* vraakh
queue n *rij* rey
quick *snel* snel
quiet *stil* stil
quit (job) *ontslag nemen*
ont·*slakh* ney·muhn
quit (something) *ophouden met*
op·haw·duhn met

R

rabbit *konijn* ⓝ koh·*neyn*
race (sport) n *wedstrijd* wet·streyt
racetrack *renbaan* *ren*·baan
racing bike *racefiets* *reys*·feets
racism ⓝ *racisme* ra·*sis*·muh
radiator *radiator* ra·dee·*yaa*·tor
radio n *radio* *raa*·dee·yoh
radish *radijs* ra·*deys*
railway *spoorweg* *spohr*·wekh
railway station (trein)station ⓝ (treyn·)
sta·syon
rain n *regen* *rey*·khuhn
raincoat *regenjas* *rey*·khuhn·yas
raisin *rozijn* roh·*zeyn*
rally (protest) n *betoging* buh·*toh*·khing

rape n *verkrachting* vuhr·*krakh*·ting
rape v *verkrachten* vuhr·*krakh*·tuhn
rare (steak) *kort gebakken* Ⓝ/*saignant* Ⓑ
   kort khuh·*ba*·kuhn/*sey*·*nya*
rare (uncommon) *zeldzaam* zelt·zaam
rash *uitslag* öyt·slakh
raspberry *framboos* fram·*bohs*
rat *rat* rat
raw *rauw* row
razor (electric) *scheerapparaat* Ⓝ
   skheyr·a·pa·raat
razor (manual) *scheermes* Ⓝ *skheyr*·mes
razor blade *scheermesje* Ⓝ *skheyr*·me·shuh
read v *lezen* *ley*·zuhn
reading *lectuur* lek·*tewr*
ready a *klaar* klaar
real estate agent *makelaar* *maa*·kuh·laar
realistic *realistisch* rey·ya·*lis*·tis
rear (location) a *aan de achterkant*
   aan duh *akh*·tuhr·kant
reason n *reden* *rey*·duhn
receipt n *kwitantie* kwee·*tan*·see
recently *onlangs* on·*langs*
recommend *aanbevelen* aan·buh·*vey*·luhn
record (in writing) v *optekenen*
   op·tey·kuh·nuhn
record (music) v *opnemen* op·ney·muhn
recording *opname* op·naa·muh
recyclable *recyclebaar/herbruikbaar*
   ree·*say*·kuhl·baar/her·*bröyk*·baar
recycle *recyclen/herbruiken*
   ree·*say*·kluhn/her·*bröy*·kuhn
red *rood* roht
red wine *rode wijn* roh·duh weyn
referee n *scheidsrechter* skheyts·rekh·tuhr
reference n *referentie* rey·fey·*ren*·see
refrigerator *koelkast* kool·kast
refugee *vluchteling* vlukh·tuh·ling
refund n *terugbetaling*
   tuh·*rukh*·buh·taa·ling
refuse v *weigeren* *wey*·khuh·ruhn
regional *regionaal* rey·khyoh·*naal*
registered mail *aangetekende post*
   aan·khuh·tey·kuhn·duh post
rehydration salts *rehydratie-oplossing*
   rey·hee·*dra*·see·op·lo·sing
relationship *relatie* ruh·*laa*·see
relax *ontspannen* ont·*spa*·nuhn
religion *godsdienst* khots·deenst
religious *godsdienstig* khots·*deens*·tikh
remote a *afgelegen* af·khuh·ley·khuhn
remote control *afstandsbediening*
   af·stants·buh·dee·ning

rent n *huur* hewr
rent v *huren* hew·ruhn
repair v *herstellen* her·*ste*·luhn
republic *republiek* rey·pew·*bleek*
reservation (booking) *reservatie*
   rey·ser·vaa·see
rest v *rusten* rus·tuhn
restaurant *restaurant* Ⓝ res·toh·*rant*
retired *gepensioneerd* khuh·pen·syo·*neyrt*
return v *terugkomen* tuh·*rukh*·koh·muhn
return ticket
   retourtje Ⓝ/*heen- en terugreis* Ⓝ/Ⓑ
   ruh·*toor*·chuh/heyn·en·tuh·*rukh*·reys
review n *recensie* rey·sen·see
rice *rijst* reyst
rich (wealthy) *rijk* reyk
ride v *rijden* rey·duhn
ride (bike, horse) v *rijden* rey·duhn
ridiculous *belachelijk* buh·*la*·khuh·luhk
right (correct) *juist* yöyst
right (direction) *rechts* rekhs
right-wing *rechts* rekhs
ring (phone) v *rinkelen* ring·kuh·luhn
rip-off n *bedrog* Ⓝ be·*drokh*
risk n *risico* Ⓝ *ree*·zee·koh
river *rivier* ree·*veer*
road *weg* wekh
road map *wegenkaart* *wey*·khuhn·kaart
rob *overvallen* oh·vuhr·*va*·luhn
rock n *rots* rots
rock (music) *rockmuziek* rok·mew·zeek
rock climbing *rotsklimmen* Ⓝ *rots*·kli·muhn
rock group *band/groep* Ⓝ/Ⓑ bent/khroop
roll (bread) *broodje* Ⓝ *broh*·chuh
rollerblading *inlineskaten* Ⓝ
   in·layn·*skey*·tuhn
rollerskating *rolschaatsen* Ⓝ
   rol·skhaat·suhn
romantic a *romantisch* roh·*man*·tees
room n *kamer* kaa·muhr
room number *kamernummer* Ⓝ
   kaa·muhr·nu·muhr
rope *touw* Ⓝ taw
round (drinks) *rondje* Ⓝ *ron*·chuh
round a *rond* ront
roundabout *rotonde* roh·*ton*·duh
route n *route* roo·tuh
rowing *roeien* Ⓝ *roo*·yuhn
rubbish *afval* Ⓝ *af*·val
rubella *rodehond* roh·duh·*hont*
rug *kleed* Ⓝ/*mat* Ⓝ/Ⓑ kleyt/mat
ruins *ruïnes* rew·*wee*·nuhs
rule (historic) n *heerschappij* heyr·skha·*pey*

rule (law) n *regel* rey·khuhl
rum *rum* rum
run v *rennen/lopen* Ⓝ/Ⓑ
re·nuhn/loh·puhn
runny nose *loopneus* lohp·neus
rush hour *spitsuur/piekuur* Ⓝ
spits·ewr/peek·ewr

S

sad *droevig* droo·vikh
saddle *zadel* Ⓝ zaa·duhl
safe n *kluis* klöys
safe a *veilig* vey·likh
safe sex *veilig vrijen* Ⓝ vey·likh vrey·yuhn
sailboarding *plankzeilen* Ⓝ/*windsurfen* Ⓝ
plank·zey·luhn/wint·sur·fuhn
saint *heilige* hey·li·khuh
salary *loon* Ⓝ lohn
sale *verkoop* vuhr·kohp
sale (specials) *koopjes* Ⓝ pl kohp·yuhs
sales assistant *verkoper/verkoopster* Ⓜ/Ⓕ
vuhr·koh·puhr/vur·kohp·stuhr
sales tax *verkoopbelasting*
vuhr·kohp·buh·las·ting
salmon *zalm* zalm
salt *zout* Ⓝ zawt
same *dezelfde* Ⓜ&Ⓕ/*hetzelfde* Ⓝ
duh·zelf·duh/huht·zelf·duh
sand *zand* Ⓝ zant
sandals *sandalen* san·daa·luhn
sanitary napkin *maandverband* Ⓝ
maant·vuhr·bant
sardine *sardientje* Ⓝ sar·deen·chuh
saucepan *pan/kookpot* Ⓝ/Ⓑ pan/kohk·pot
sausage *saucijs/worst* Ⓝ/Ⓑ saw·seys/worst
say *zeggen* ze·khuhn
scalp *hoofdhuid* hohft·höyt
scarf *sjaal* shaal
school *school* skhohl
science *wetenschap* wey·tuhn·skhap
scientist *wetenschapper*
wey·tuhn·skha·puhr
scissors *schaar* sg skhaar
score v *scoren* skoh·ruhn
sculpture *beeldhouwwerk* Ⓝ
beylt·haw·werk
sea *zee* zey
seal (animal) n *zeehond* zey·hont
seasick *zeeziek* zey·zeek
seaside n *kust* kust
season *seizoen* Ⓝ sey·zoon
seat (place) *zitje* Ⓝ zi·chuh

seatbelt *veiligheidsriem* vey·likh·heyts·reem
second n *seconde* suh·kon·duh
second a *tweede* twey·duh
second class n *tweede klas* twey·duh klas
secondhand *tweedehands* twey·duh·hants
secondhand shop *tweedehandswinkel*
twey·duh·hants·wing·kuhl
secretary *secretaris/secretaresse* Ⓜ/Ⓕ
sey·krey·taa·ris/sey·krey·taa·re·suh
see *zien* zeen
self-employed *zelfstandig* zelf·stan·dikh
selfish *egoïstisch* ey·khoh·wis·tis
self-service a *zelfbediening*
zelf·buh·dee·ning
sell *verkopen* vuhr·koh·puhn
send *sturen* stew·ruhn
sensible *verstandig* vuhr·stan·dikh
sensitive *gevoelig* khuh·voo·likh
sensual *sensueel* sen·sew·weyl
separate a *afzonderlijk* af·zon·duhr·luhk
serious *ernstig* ern·stikh
service n *dienst* deenst
service charge *bedieningstoeslag*
buh·dee·nings·too·slakh
service station *benzinestation* Ⓝ
ben·zee·nuh·sta·syon
serviette n *servet* Ⓝ ser·vet
several *verscheidene* vuhr·skhey·duh·nuh
sew *naaien* naa·yuhn
sex education *seksuele voorlichting*
sek·sew·wey·luh vohr·likh·ting
sexism *seksisme* Ⓝ sek·sis·muh
shade *schaduw* skhaa·dew
shadow *schaduw* skhaa·dew
shallow *ondiep* on·deep
shape n *vorm* vorm
share (with) v *delen* dey·luhn
shave v *scheren* skhey·ruhn
shaving cream *scheerschuim* Ⓝ
skheyr·skhöym
she *zij* zey
sheep *schaap* Ⓝ skhaap
sheet (bed) *laken* Ⓝ laa·kuhn
shelf *plank* plangk
shingles (illness) *gordelroos* khor·duhl·rohs
ship n *schip* Ⓝ skhip
shirt *hemd* Ⓝ hemt
shoes *schoenen* skhoo·nuhn
shoelace *schoenveters* skhoon·vey·tuhrs
shoe shop *schoenenzaak* skhoo·nuhn·zaak
shoot v *schieten* skhee·tuhn
shop n *winkel* wing·kuhl
shop v *winkelen* wing·kuh·luhn

shopping *winkelen* ⓝ *wing*·kuh·luhn
shopping centre *winkelcentrum* ⓝ *wing*·kuhl·sen·trum
short (height) *klein* kleyn
short (length) *kort* kort
shortage *tekort* ⓝ tuh·*kort*
shorts *short* sg short
shoulder *shouder* skhaw·duhr
shout v *roepen* roo·puhn
show v *tonen* toh·nuhn
shower n *douche* doo·shuh
shrine *schrijn* ⓝ skhreyn
shut a *gesloten* khuh·*sloh*·tuhn
shy *verlegen* vuhr·*ley*·khuhn
sick *ziek* zeek
sick bag *papieren zak* pa·*pee*·ruhn zak
side *kant* kant
sidewalk *voetpad* ⓝ *voot*·pat
sign (general) n *teken* ⓝ *tey*·kuhn
sign (traffic) n *bord* bort
sign v *tekenen* *tey*·kuh·nuhn
signature *handtekening* hant·*tey*·kuh·ning
silk n *zijde* *zey*·duh
silver n *zilver* ⓝ *zil*·vuhr
similar *gelijkaardig* khuh·*leyk*·*aar*·dikh
simple *eenvoudig* eyn·*vaw*·dikh
since (time) *sinds* sins
sing v *zingen* *zing*·uhn
singer *zanger/zangeres* ⓜ/ⓕ *zang*·uhr/zang·uh·*res*
single (person) *vrijgezel* *vrey*·khuh·zel
single room *éénpersoonskamer* eyn·puhr·*sohns*·kaa·muhr
singlet *hemdje* ⓝ *hem*·chuh
sister *zus* zus
sit *zitten* *zi*·tuhn
size (general) *maat* maat
skate v *schaatsen* *skhaat*·suhn
ski v *skiën* *skee*·yuhn
skiing *skisport* *skee*·sport
skim milk *taptemelk* ⓝ/*afgeroomde melk* ⓑ *tap*·tuh·melk/*af*·khuh·rohm·duh melk
skin n *huid* höyt
skirt *rok* rok
skull *schedel* *skhey*·duhl
sky *lucht* lukht
sleep n *slaap* slaap
sleep v *slapen* *slaa*·puhn
sleeping bag *slaapzak* *slaap*·zak
sleeping berth *slaapplaats* *slaap*·plaats
sleeping car *slaapwagen* *slaap*·waa·khuhn
sleeping pills *slaappillen* *slaap*·pi·luhn
sleepy *slaperig* *slaa*·puh·rikh

slice n *plak/snee* ⓝ/ⓑ plak/sney
slide film *diafilm* dee·ya·film
slow *traag* traakh
slowly *traag* traakh
small *klein* kleyn
smaller *kleiner* *kley*·nuhr
smallest *kleinst* kleynst
smell n *geur* kheur
smile v *glimlachen* *khlim*·la·khuhn
smoke v *roken* *roh*·kuhn
snack n *snack* snek/snak ⓝ/ⓑ
snail *slak* slak
snake *slang* slang
snorkelling *snorkelen* ⓝ *snor*·kuh·luhn
snow n *sneeuw* sneyw
snow v *sneeuwen* *sney*·wuhn
snowball *sneeuwbal* sneyw·bal
snowboarding *snowboarden* ⓝ *snohw*·bor·duhn
snowman *sneeuwpop* sneyw·pop
snowscape *sneeuwlandschap* ⓝ *sneyw*·lant·skhap
snowy *sneeuwachtig* sneyw·*akh*·tikh
soap *zeep* zeyp
soccer *voetbal* ⓝ *voot*·bal
socialist n *socialist* soh·sya·list
social welfare *sociale zekerheid* soh·*syaa*·luh zey·kuhr·*heyt*
socks *sokken* *so*·kuhn
soft drink *frisdrank* fris·drangk
soldier *soldaat* sol·*daat*
some *enkele* *eng*·kuh·luh
someone *iemand* *ee*·mant
something *iets* eets
sometimes *soms* soms
son *zoon* zohn
song *lied* ⓝ leet
soon *gauw* khaw
sore a *pijnlijk* *peyn*·luhk
south n *zuiden* ⓝ *zöy*·duhn
souvenir shop *souvenirwinkel* soo·vuh·*neer*·wing·kuhl
soy milk *sojamelk* *soh*·ya·melk
soy sauce *sojasaus* *soh*·ya·saws
space (room) *ruimte* *röym*·tuh
sparkling wine *mousserende wijn* ⓝ/*schuimwijn* ⓑ moo·*sey*·ruhn·duh weyn/*skhöym*·weyn
speak *praten* *praa*·tuhn
special a *special* spey·*syaal*
specialist n *specialist* spey·sya·list
speed (travel) n *snelheid* snel·*heyt*

233

speed limit *maximumsnelheid* mak·see·mum·snel·heyt
speedometer *snelheidsmeter* snel·heyts·mey·tuhr
spider *spin* spin
spinach *spinazie* spee·naa·zee
spoilt (food) *bedorven* buh·dor·vuhn
spoke *spaak* spaak
spoon *lepel* ley·puhl
sportsperson *sportman/sportvrouw* ⓜ/ⓕ sport·man/sport·vraw
sports store *sportwinkel* sport·wing·kuhl
sprain n *verstuiking* vuhr·stöy·king
spring (coil) *veer* veyr
spring (season) *lente* len·tuh
square (town) *plein* ⓝ pleyn
stadium *stadion* ⓝ staa·dee·yon
staff *personeel* ⓝ per·soh·neyl
stairway *trap* trap
stale *oudbakken* awt·ba·kuhn
stamp (postage) n *postzegel* post·zey·khul
star n *ster* ster
(four-)star *(vier)sterren* (veer·)ste·ruhn
start v *starten* star·tuhn
station *station* ⓝ sta·syon
stationer *kantoorboekhandel* kan·tohr·book·han·duhl
statue *standbeeld* ⓝ stant·beylt
stay (at a hotel) v *logeren* loh·zhey·ruhn
stay (in place) v *verblijven* vuhr·bley·vuhn
STD *seksueel overdraagbare aandoening* sek·sew·weyl oh·vuhr·draakh·baa·ruh aan·doo·ning
steak (beef) *biefstuk* beef·stuk
steal *stelen* stey·luhn
steep *steil* steyl
step n *stap* stap
step (stair/threshold) n *trede* trey·duh
stepped gable *trapgevel* trap·khey·vuhl
still water *spa blauw* ⓝ/*plat water* ⓝ ⓑ spa blaw/plat waa·tuhr
stock (food) *bouillon* boo·yon
stockings *kousen* kaw·suhn
stolen *gestolen* khuh·stoh·luhn
stomach *maag* maakh
stomachache *maagpijn* maakh·peyn
stone n *steen* steyn
stop (bus, tram) n *halte* hal·tuh
stop (cease) v *stoppen* sto·puhn
stop (prevent) v *tegenhouden* tey·khuhn·haw·duhn
story *verhaal* ⓝ vuhr·haal
stove *fornuis* ⓝ for·nöys
straight *recht* rekht

strange *raar* raar
stranger n *onbekende* on·buh·ken·duh
strawberry *aardbei* aart·bey
stream n *stroom* strohm
street *straat* straat
strike n *staking* staa·king
string *touw* ⓝ taw
stroke (health) *beroerte* buh·roor·tuh
stroller *wandelwagen* wan·duhl·waa·khuhn
strong *sterk* sterk
stubborn *koppig* ko·pikh
student *student* stew·dent
stupid *dom* dom
style n *stijl* steyl
subtitles *ondertitels* on·duhr·tee·tuhls
suburb *buitenwijk* böy·tuhn·weyk
subway (train) *metro* mey·troh
sugar *suiker* söy·kuhr
suit *pak* ⓝ/*kostuum* ⓝ ⓑ pak/kos·tewm
suitcase *koffer* ko·fuhr
sultana *sultanarozijn* sul·taa·na·roh·zeyn
summer *zomer* zoh·muhr
sun *zon* zon
sunburn *zonnebrand* zo·nuh·brant
sunglasses *zonnebril* sg zo·nuh·bril
sunny *zonnig* zo·nikh
sunrise *zonsopgang* zons·op·khang
sunscreen (lotion) *zonnecrème* zo·nuh·kreym
sunset *zonsondergang* zons·on·duhr·khang
sunstroke *zonneslag* zo·nuh·slakh
superstition *bijgeloof* ⓝ bey·khuh·lohf
supporter (politics) *aanhanger* aan·hang·uhr
surf n *branding* bran·ding
surf v *surfen* sur·fuhn
surface mail (land/sea) *gewone post* khuh·woh·nuh post
surfboard *surfplank* surf·plangk
surfing *surfsport* surf·sport
surname *familienaam* fa·mee·lee·naam
surprise n *verrassing* vuh·ra·sing
sustainable *duurzaam* dewr·zaam
sweater *trui* tröy
sweet a *zoet* zoot
sweets *snoep* sg snoop
swelling *gezwel* ⓝ khuh·zwel
swim v *zwemmen* zwe·muhn
swimming *zwemsport* zwem·sport
swimming pool *zwembad* ⓝ zwem·bat
swimsuit *zwempak* ⓝ zwem·pak

synagogue *synagoog* see·na·*khohkh*
synthetic *synthetisch* sin·*tey*·tis
syringe *spuit* spöyt

T

table *tafel* taa·fuhl
tablecloth *tafellaken* ⓝ taa·fuh·laa·kuhn
table tennis *tafeltennis* ⓝ taa·fuhl·te·nis
tail n *staart* staart
tailor n *kleermaker* kleyr·maa·kuhr
take v *nemen* ney·muhn
take a photo *een foto nemen*
   uhn foh·toh ney·muhn
talk v *praten* praa·tuhn
tall *groot* khroht
tampon *tampon* tam·pon
tanning lotion *zonnebrandolie*
   zo·nuh·brant·oh·lee
tap n *kraantje* ⓝ kraan·chuh
tap (beer) v *(bier) tappen* (beer) ta·puhn
tapestry *tapisserie* ta·pi·suh·ree
tap water *kraantjeswater* ⓝ
   kraan·chuhs·waa·tuhr
tasty *lekker* le·kuhr
tax n *belasting* buh·las·ting
taxi stand *taxistandplaats*
   tak·see·stant·plaats
tea *thee* tey
teacher *leraar/lerares* ⓜ/ⓕ
   ley·raar/ley·raa·res
team *ploeg* plookh
teaspoon *theelepeltje* ⓝ tey·ley·puhl·chuh
technique *techniek* tekh·*neek*
teeth *tanden* tan·duhn
telephone n *telefoon* tey·ley·fohn
telephone v *telefoneren*
   tey·ley·foh·ney·ruhn
telephone centre *telefoonkantoor* ⓝ
   tey·ley·fohn·kan·tohr
television *televisie* tey·ley·vee·see
tell *zeggen* ze·khuhn
temperature (fever) *koorts* kohrts
temperature (weather) *temperatuur*
   tem·pey·ra·*tewr*
temple (body) *slaap* slaap
tennis court *tennisbaan* te·nis·baan
tent peg *(tent)haring* (tent·)haa·ring
terrible *verschrikkelijk* vuhr·skhri·kuh·luhk
terrorism *terrorisme* ⓝ te·roh·ris·muh
thank *bedanken* buh·dang·kuhn
that a *die* ⓜ&ⓕ/*dat* ⓝ dee/dat
theatre *theater* ⓝ tey·yaa·tuhr

theatre (building) *schouwburg* ⓝ
   skhaw·burkh
their *hun* hun
there *daar* daar
they *zij* zey
thick *dik* dik
thief *dief* deef
thin *dun* dun
think *denken* deng·kuhn
third a *derde* der·duh
thirsty *dorstig* dors·tikh
this a *deze* ⓜ&ⓕ/*dit* ⓝ dey·zuh/dit
thread n *draad* draat
throat *keel* keyl
thrush (health) *candida* kan·dee·da
thunderstorm *onweer* on·weyr
ticket *kaartje* ⓝ/*ticket* ⓝ ⓝ/ⓑ
   kaar·chuh/ti·ket
ticket collector *kaartjesknipper*
   kaar·chus·kni·puhr
ticket machine *kaartjesautomaat*
   kaar·chus·aw·toh·maat
ticket office *loket* ⓝ loh·ket
tide *getij* ⓝ khuh·tey
tight *strak* strak
time n *tijd* teyt
time difference *tijdsverschil* ⓝ
   teyts·vuhr·skhil
timetable (general) *tijdschema* ⓝ
   teyt·skhey·ma
timetable (transport) *dienstregeling*
   deenst·rey·khuh·ling
tin (can) *blikje* ⓝ blik·yuh
tin opener *blikopener* blik·oh·puh·nuhr
tiny *miniem* mee·neem
tip (gratuity) n *fooi* foy
tire n *band* bant
tired *moe* moo
to *naar* naar
toast (food) n *geroosterd brood* ⓝ
   khuh·*roh*·stuhrt broht
toaster *broodrooster* broht·roh·stuhr
tobacco *tabak* ta·bak
tobacconist *sigarenhandel*
   see·khaa·ruhn·han·duhl
tobogganing *sleetje rijden* ⓝ
   sley·chuh rey·duhn
today *vandaag* van·daakh
toe *teen* teyn
tofu *tahoe/tofoe* ta·hoo/toh·foo
together *samen* saa·muhn
toilet *toilet* ⓝ twa·let
toilet paper *toiletpapier* ⓝ twa·let·pa·peer

tollway *tolweg* tol·wekh
tomato *tomaat* toh·*maat*
tomorrow *morgen* mor·khuhn
tonight *vanavond* van·*aa*·vont
too (also) *ook* ohk
too (much) *te* tuh
tooth *tand* tant
toothache *kiespijn/tandpijn* Ⓝ/Ⓑ
   kees·peyn/tant·peyn
toothbrush *tandenborstel*
   tan·duhn·bor·stuhl
toothpaste *tandpasta* tant·pas·ta
toothpick *tandenstoker*
   tan·duhn·stoh·kuhr
torch (flashlight) *zaklantaarn* zak·lan·taarn
touch v *aanraken* aan·raa·kuhn
tour (city/outdoors) n *tocht* tokht
tour (short, eg museum) n *rondleiding*
   ront·ley·ding
tourist *toerist* too·*rist*
tourist office *VVV/toerismebureau* Ⓝ
   Ⓝ/Ⓑ vey·vey·*vey*/too·ris·muh·bew·roh
towards *naar ... toe* naar ... too
towel *handdoek* han·dook
tower *toren* toh·ruhn
town *stad* stat
town hall *stadhuis* Ⓑ stat·*höys*
toxic waste *toxisch afval* Ⓝ tok·sis af·val
toy shop *speelgoedwinkel*
   speyl·khoot·wing·kuhl
track (path) *pad* Ⓝ pat
track (sport) *baan* baan
trade (commerce) n *handel* han·duhl
trade (profession) n *vak* Ⓝ vak
tradesperson *stielman* steel·man
traffic n *verkeer* Ⓝ vuhr·*keyr*
traffic jam *verkeersopstopping*
   vuhr·keyrs·op·sto·ping
traffic light *verkeerslicht* Ⓝ vuhr·*keyrs*·likht
trail n *pad* Ⓝ pat
train n *trein* treyn
train station *(trein)station* Ⓝ (treyn·)
   sta·*syon*
tram *tram* trem/tram Ⓝ/Ⓑ
tram stop *tramhalte* tram·hal·tuh
transit lounge *lounge voor doorgaande*
   reizigers laawnzh vohr *dohr*·khaan·duh
   rey·zi·khuhrs
translate *vertalen* vuhr·*taa*·luhn
translator *vertaler* vuhr·*taa*·luhr
travel v *reizen* rey·zuhn
travel agency *reisbureau* Ⓝ reys·bew·roh
travellers cheque *reischeque* reys·shek
travel sickness *reisziekte* reys·zeek·tuh

tree *boom* bohm
trenches (war) *loopgraven* lohp·khraa·vuhn
trip (journey) *reis* reys
trolley *rolwagentje* Ⓝ rol·waa·khun·chuh
trousers *pantalon* sg/*broek* sg Ⓝ/Ⓑ
   pan·ta·*lon*/brook
truck *vrachtwagen* vrakht·waa·khuhn
trust v *vertrouwen* vuhr·*traw*·wuhn
try (attempt) v *proberen* proh·*bey*·ruhn
tube (tyre) *binnenband* bi·nuhn·bant
tuna *tonijn* toh·*neyn*
tune n *deuntje* Ⓝ deun·chuh
turkey *kalkoen* kal·*koon*
turn v *draaien* draa·yuhn
turn (right/left) v *(links/rechts) afslaan*
   (lingks/rekhs) af·slaan
TV *tv* tey·*vey*
tweezers *pincet* Ⓝ pin·*set*
twice *tweemaal* twey·maal
twin beds *lits jumeaux* lee zhew·moh
twins *tweeling* twey·ling
two *twee* twey
type n *soort* sohrt
typical *typisch* tee·pis
tyre *band* bant

U

ugly *lelijk* ley·leyk
ultrasound *echografie* e·khoh·khra·*fee*
umbrella (rain) *paraplu* pa·ra·*plew*
umbrella (sun) *parasol* pa·ra·*sol*
uncle *oom* ohm
uncomfortable *ongemakkelijk*
   on·khuh·*ma*·kuh·luhk
understand *begrijpen* buh·*khrey*·puhn
underwear *ondergoed* Ⓝ on·duhr·khoot
unemployed *werkloos* werk·lohs
unfair *oneerlijk* on·*eyr*·leyk
universe *heelal* Ⓝ hey·*lal*
university *universiteit* ew·nee·ver·see·*teyt*
unleaded petrol *loodvrije benzine*
   loht·*vrey*·yuh ben·*zee*·nuh
unsafe *onveilig* on·*vey*·likh
until *tot* tot
unusual *ongewoon* on·khuh·*wohn*
up *omhoog* om·*hohkh*
uphill *bergop* berkh·*op*
urgent *dringend* dring·uhnt
urinary infection
   infectie van de urinewegen
   in·*fek*·see van duh ew·*ree*·nuh·wey·khun
useful *nuttig* nu·tikh

236

V

vacancy (accommodation) *kamer te huur* kaa·muhr tuh hewr
vacancy (job) *vacature* va·ka·tew·ruh
vacant (available) *vrij* vrey
vacant (empty) *leeg* leykh
vacation *vakantie* va·kan·see
vaccination *inenting* in·en·ting
vagina *vagina* vaa·khee·na
validate *valideren* va·lee·dey·ruhn
valley *valei* va·ley
valuable *waardevol* waar·duh·vol
value (price) n *waarde* waar·duh
van *transportwagen* trans·port·waa·khuhn
VAT *btw* bey·tey·wey
veal *kalfsvlees* ⓝ *kalfs*·vleys
vegan n *veganist* vey·kha·*nist*
vegetable n *groente* khroon·tuh
vegetarian n *vegetariër* vey·khey·*taa*·ree·yuhr
vegetarian a *vegetarisch* vey·khey·*taa*·ris
vein *ader* aa·duhr
venereal disease *seksueel overdraagbare aandoening* sek·sew·*weel* oh·vuhr·*draakh*·baa·ruh aan·doo·ning
venue *plaats* plaats
very *zeer* zeyr
video tape *videofilm* vee·dey·yoo·film
view n *uitzicht* ⓝ öyt·zikht
village *dorp* ⓝ dorp
vine *wijnstok* weyn·stok
vinegar *azijn* a·zeyn
vineyard *wijngaard* weyn·khaart
violin *viool* vee·yohl
virgin *maagd* maakht
virus *virus* vee·rus
visa *visum* ⓝ vee·zum
visit n *bezoek* ⓝ buh·*zook*
visually impaired *visueel gehandicapt* vee·sew·*weel* khuh·*hen*·dee·kept/ khuh·*han*·dee·kapt ⓝ/ⓑ
vitamins *vitaminen* vee·ta·*mee*·nuhn
voice n *stem* stem
volunteer n *vrijwilliger* vrey·*wi*·li·khuhr
volunteer v *vrijwilligen* vrey·*wi*·li·khuhn
vote v *stemmen* ste·muhn

W

wage n *loon* ⓝ lohn
wait v *wachten* wakh·tuhn
waiter *ober/kelner* oh·buhr/kel·nuhr

Waiter! Meneer!/Mevrouw! ⓜ/ⓕ muh·*neyr*/muh·*vraw*
waitress *serveerster/dienster* ser·*veyr*·stuhr/deen·stuhr
waiting room *wachtkamer* wakht·kaa·muhr
wake someone up *wakker maken* wa·kuhr *maa*·kuhn
wake up *wakker worden* wa·kuhr wor·duhn
walk v *lopen/gaan* ⓝ/ⓑ loh·puhn/khaan
walk (go for a walk) v *wandelen* wan·duh·luhn
wall *muur* mewr
wallet *portemonnee* por·tuh·mo·*ney*
want v *willen* wi·luhn
war n *oorlog* ohr·lokh
wardrobe *klerenkast* kley·ruhn·kast
war graves *oorlogsgraven* ohr·lokhs·khraa·vuhn
warm a *warm* warm
warn *waarschuwen* waar·skhew·wuhn
wash (oneself) *(zich) wassen* (zikh) wa·suhn
wash (something) *(iets) wassen* (eets) wa·suhn
wash cloth (flannel) *washandje* ⓝ was·han·chuh
washing machine *wasmachine* was·ma·shee·nuh
wasp *wesp* wesp
watch n *horloge* ⓝ hor·*loh*·zhuh
watch v *kijken* key·kuhn
water n *water* ⓝ waa·tuhr
water bottle *veldfles* velt·fles
(hot) water bottle *warmwaterfles* warm·waa·tuhr·fles
water engineering *hydraulisch engineering* hee·*draw*·lis en·zhi·*nee*·ring
water excursion *watertocht* waa·tuhr·tokht
waterfall *waterval* waa·tuhr·val
waterfront *waterkant* waa·tuhr·kant
water gate *vloeddeur* vloot·deur
water level *waterstand* waa·tuhr·stant
waterlogged *volgelopen met water* vol·khuh·loh·puhn met waa·tuhr
watermelon *watermeloen* waa·tuhr·muh·loon
waterproof (building/structure) *waterdicht* waa·tuhr·*dikht*
water-skiing *waterskiën* ⓝ waa·tuhr·skee·yuhn
watertight *waterdicht* waa·tuhr·*dikht*
wave (beach) n *golf* kholf
way (method) *manier* ma·*neer*

237

way (route) *weg* wekh
we *wij* wey
weak *zwak* zwak
wealthy *rijk* reyk
wear *dragen* draa·khuhn
weather n *weer* ⓝ weyr
wedding *huwelijk* ⓝ hew·wuh·luhk
wedding cake *huwelijkstaart*
  hew·wuh·luhks·taart
wedding present *huwelijkscadeau* ⓝ
  hew·wuh·lukhs·ka·*doh*
week *week* weyk
weigh *wegen* wey·khuhn
weight *gewicht* ⓝ khuh·*wikht*
weights *gewichten* khuh·*wikh*·tuhn
weir *waterkering* waa·tuhr·key·ring
welcome v *verwelkomen*
  vuhr·*wel*·koh·muhn
welfare *welzijn* ⓝ *wel*·zeyn
well adv *goed* khoot
west n *westen* ⓝ *wes*·tuhn
wet a *nat* nat
what *wat* wat
wharf *aanlegplaats* aan·lekh·plaats
wheel *wiel* ⓝ weel
wheelchair *rolstoel* rol·stool
when *wanneer* wa·*neyr*
where *waar* waar
which *welke* *wel*·kuh
white *wit* wit
white wine *witte wijn* wi·tuh weyn
who *wie* wee
wholemeal bread *volkorenbrood* ⓝ
  vol·*koh*·ruhn·broht
why *waarom* waa·*rom*
wide *breed* breyt
wife *echtgenote* ekht·khuh·noh·tuh
win v *winnen* wi·nuhn
wind n *wind* wint
windmill *windmolen* wint·moh·luhn
window *raam* ⓝ raam
windscreen *voorruit* vohr·röyt
wine *wijn* weyn
wings *vleugels* vleu·khuls
winner *winnaar* wi·naar
winter *winter* win·tuhr
wire n *ijzerdraad* ey·zuhr·draat
wish v *wensen* wen·suhn
with *met* met
within (time) *binnen* bi·nuhn
without *zonder* zon·duhr
witness n *getuige* khuh·*töy*·khuh

wok *wadjan/wok* wa·dyan/wok
woman *vrouw* vraw
wonderful *prachtig* prakh·tikh
wood (forest) *bos* ⓝ bos
wood (material) *hout* ⓝ hawt
wool *wol* wol
word *woord* ⓝ wohrt
work n *baan/werk* ⓝ ⓝ/ⓑ baan/werk
work v *werken* wer·kuhn
work experience *werkervaring*
  werk·er·vaa·ring
workout n *conditietraining*
  kon·*deet*·see·trey·ning
work permit *werkvergunning*
  werk·vuhr·khu·ning
workshop (discussion)
  discussiebijeenkomst
  dis·*kew*·see·bey·eyn·komst
workshop (place) *werkplaats* werk·plaats
world *wereld* wey·ruhlt
worried *bezorgd* buh·*zorkht*
worse *slechter* slekh·tuhr
worship v *vereren* vuhr·*ey*·ruhn
wrist *pols* pols
write *schrijven* skhrey·vuhn
writer *schrijver* skhrey·vuhr
wrong *fout* fawt

Y

year *jaar* ⓝ yaar
yellow *geel* kheyl
yes *ja* yaa
yesterday *gisteren* khis·tuh·ruhn
(not) yet *al* al
you inf sg *jij/je* yey/yuh
you pol sg&pl *u* ew
you inf pl *jullie* yew·lee
young *jong* yong
your inf sg *jouw* yaw
your inf pl *jullie* yew·lee
your pol sg&pl *uw* ew
youth hostel *jeugdherberg*
  yeukht·her·berkh

Z

zebra crossing *zebrapad* ⓝ zey·bra·pat
zip/zipper *rits* rits
zodiac *dierenriem* dee·ruhn·reem
zoo *dierentuin* dee·ruhn·töyn
zucchini *courgette* koor·*zhet*

In this dictionary, words are marked as n (noun), a (adjective), v (verb), adv (adverb), prep (preposition), pron (pronoun), sg (singular), pl (plural), inf (informal) and pol (polite) where necessary. Note that we've only indicated Dutch nouns which have neuter gender with ⓝ after the translation – the nouns which have common gender are left unmarked. Where a word has different masculine and feminine forms, both options are given and indicated with ⓜ/ⓕ (for more on gender in Dutch, see the **phrasebuilder**). If it's a plural noun, you'll also see pl. We've used the symbols Ⓝ and Ⓑ for words which are different in the Netherlands and Belgium respectively. For food terms, see the **culinary reader**.

A

aanbevelen aan-buh-vey-luhn recommend
aan boord aan bohrt aboard
aangetekende post aan-khuh-tey-kuhn-duh post registered mail
aankomst aan-komst arrival • arrivals
aansteker aan-stey-kuhr cigarette lighter
aantrekkelijk aan-tre-kuh-luhk attractive
aardig aar-dikh kind (nice)
accommodatie a-koh-moh-daa-see accommodation
accu a-kew battery (car)
achter akh-tuhr behind
acteur/actrice ⓜ/ⓕ ak-teur/ak-tree-suh actor
adapter a-dap-tuhr adaptor
adres ⓝ a-dres address n
advocaat at-voh-kaat lawyer
afgesloten af-khuh-sloh-tuhn blocked (access/road)
afscheid ⓝ af-skheyt goodbye
afspraak af-spraak appointment
afstandsbediening af-stants-buh-dee-ning remote control
agenda a-khen-da diary (agenda)
aktetas ak-tuh-tas briefcase
alle a-luh all
alleen a-leyn alone
allergie a-ler-khee allergy
alles a-luhs everything
ambassade am-ba-saa-duh embassy

ambulance am-bew-lans ambulance
andere an-duh-ruh other
annuleren a-new-ley-ruhn cancel
ansichtkaart an-zikht-kaart postcard
antibiotica ⓝ pl an-tee-bee-yo-tee-ka antibiotics
antiek an-teek antique n
apotheek a-poh-teyk chemist (pharmacy)
apotheker/apothekeres ⓜ/ⓕ a-poh-tey-kuhr/a-poh-tey-kuh-res chemist (pharmacist)
architectuur ar-khee-tek-tewr architecture
arm arm arm (body)
artiest ar-teest artist
asbak as-bak ashtray
aspirine as-pee-ree-nuh aspirin
auto aw-toh car
autoverhuur aw-toh-vuhr-hewr car hire
autoweg aw-toh-wekh motorway
avond aa-vont evening
avondje-uit ⓝ aa-vont-chuh-öyt night out
avondmaal ⓝ aa-vont-maal dinner
avondwinkel aa-vont-wing-kuhl convenience store

B

baan baan job Ⓝ • road Ⓑ
baar geld ⓝ baar khelt cash n
babyvoeding bey-bee-voo-ding baby food
bad ⓝ bat bath n
badkamer bat-kaa-muhr bathroom

bagage ba-*khaa*-zhuh *luggage (baggage)*
bagage band ba-*khaa*-zhuh bant
    baggage claim
bagagedepot ba-*khaa*-zhuh-*dey*-poh
    left-luggage office
bagage-inleverpunt
    ba-*khaa*-zhuh-*in*-ley-vuhr-punt
    baggage claim
bagagekluis ba-*khaa*-zhuh-klöys
    luggage locker
bakken ba-kuhn *bake • fry* v
bakkerij ba-kuh-*rey bakery*
bakkerswinkel
    ba-kuhrs-*wing*-kuhl *bakery*
band bant *tire (tyre)* n
band bent *band (music)*
bank bangk *bank* n
bankbiljet bangk-bil-yet *banknote*
banketbakkerij bang-*ket*-ba-kuh-*rey*
    cake shop
bankrekening bangk-rey-kuh-ning
    bank account
batterij ba-tuh-*rey battery (general)*
bed beyn *bed*
beddegoed
    be-duh-khoot *bed linen*
bedieningsgeld
    buh-*dee*-nings-khelt *cover charge*
bedieningstoeslag
    buh-*dee*-nings-*too*-slakh *service charge*
bedlinnen bet-li-nuhn *linen (sheets)*
beeldhouwwerk
    beylt-how-werk *sculpture*
been beyn *leg (body)*
beha bey-*haa bra*
beide bey-duh *both*
belangrijk buh-*lang*-ruhk *important*
benzine ben-*zee*-nuh *gas (petrol)*
benzinestation ben-*zee*-nuh-*sta*-syon
    petrol station (service station)
berg berkh *mountain*
bericht buh-*rikht message* n
bespreking buh-*sprey*-king
    conference (small)
beste *bes*-tuh *best*
bestek buh-*stek cutlery*
bestemming buh-*ste*-ming *destination*
betaling buh-*taa*-ling *payment*
beter bey-tuhr *better*
bevestigen be-*ves*-ti-khuhn
    confirm (a booking)
bevroren buh-*vroh*-ruhn *frozen*
bezig bey-zikh *busy (person)*

bezorgen be-*zor*-khuhn *deliver*
bibliotheek bi-blyoh-*teyk library*
bier beer *beer*
bij bey *at • near*
binnengaan bi-nuhn-khaan *enter*
bioscoop bee-yos-*kohp cinema*
bitter bi-tuhr *bitter*
blaar blaar *blister* n
blauw blaw *blue*
blik blik *can (tin)* n
blikopener blik-oh-puh-nuhr
    can (tin) opener
bloed bloot *blood*
bloedgroep bloot-khroop *blood group*
bloemist bloo-*mist florist*
boek book *book* n
boekhandel book-han-duhl *book shop*
boodschappen boht-*skha*-puhn *groceries*
boot boht *boat*
bord bort *plate*
borst borst *chest (body)*
borstel bor-stuhl *brush* n
branden bran-duhn *burn* n
brandweer brant-weyr *fire brigade*
brasserie bra-suh-*ree café*
breekbaar breyk-baar *fragile*
brief breef *letter (mail)*
brievenbus bree-vuh-bus *mailbox*
bril sg bril *glasses (spectacles)*
brochure broh-*shew*-ruh *brochure*
broek sg brook *trousers*
broer broor *brother*
brood broht *bread*
broodrooster broht-roh-stuhr *toaster*
brug brukh *bridge (structure)* n
bruin bröyn *brown*
budget bu-*dzhet budget* n
buiten böy-tuhn *outside* adv
buitenlands böy-tuhn-lants *foreign*
burgerlijke bouwkunde bur-khur-luh-kuh
    baw-kun-duh *civil engineering*
bus bus *bus*
bushalte bus-hal-tuh *bus stop*
busstation bus-sta-syon *bus station*

C

café ka-*fey pub (bar)*
camera *kaa*-mey-ra *camera (film/video)*
centrum sen-trum *centre* n
chef-kok shef-*kok chef*
cheque shek *check (banking)* n
chocolade shoh-koh-*laa*-duh *chocolate*

coachen *koh*·chuhn *coach* v
colbert Ⓜ Ⓝ *kol*·ber *dressy jacket*
collega ko·*ley*·kha *colleague*
comfortabel kom·for·*taa*·buhl
  comfortable
commissie ko·*mee*·see *commission*
communicatie ko·mew·nee·*kaa*·see
  communicate • communications
condoom Ⓝ kon·*dohm condom*
conferentie kon·fey·*ren*·see
  conference (big)
constipatie kon·stee·*paa*·see
  constipation
consulaat Ⓝ kon·su·*laat consulate*
contactlenzen kon·*takt*·len·zuhn
  contact lenses
couchette koo·*shet berth (train)* n

D

daar daar *there*
dag dakh *date • day*
dagboek Ⓝ *dakh*·book
  diary (personal notes)
dagelijks *daa*·khuh·luhks *daily* a&adv
dageraad *daa*·khuh·raat *dawn*
dankbaar *dangk*·baar *grateful*
dans dans *dance* n
dansen *dan*·suhn *dance* v • *dancing*
dat dat *that* a&pron
deken *dey*·kuhn *blanket*
delen *dey*·leyn *share (with)* v
dessert Ⓝ de·*seyr dessert*
diafilm *dee*·ya·film *slide film*
diarree *dee*·ya·*rey diarrhoea*
dichtbij dikht·*bey close* a • *nearby*
dichtsbijzijnde *dikhts*·bey·zeyn·duh
  nearest
die dee *that (one)* pron
dienst deenst *service* n
dienster *deen*·stuhr *waitress*
dienstregeling *deenst*·rey·khuh·ling
  timetable (transport)
dierentuin *dee*·ruhn·töyn *zoo*
dik dik *fat (objects/people)* a
diner Ⓝ dee·*ney dinner*
dit dit *this* a&pron
dochter *dokh*·tuhr *daughter*
doden *doh*·duhn *kill* v
dokter *dok*·tuhr *doctor*
donker *dong*·kuhr *dark*
doos dohs *box* n
dorstig *dors*·tikh *thirsty*

douane doo·*waa*·nuh *customs*
douche doo·*shuh shower* n
drank drangk *drink (general)* n
drankenhandel Ⓑ *drang*·kuhn·han·duhl
  bottle shop (liquor store)
drankje Ⓝ *drang*·kyuh *alcoholic drink* n
dringend *dring*·uhnt *urgent*
drinken *dring*·kuhn *drink* v
drogen *droh*·khuhn *dry* v
drogisterij droh·khis·tuh·*rey drugstore*
dronken *drong*·kuhn *drunk* a
droog drohkh *dry* a
drugs drukhs *illicit drugs*
druk druk *busy (place)* a
duur dewr *expensive*

E

echtgenoot *ekht*·khuh·noht *husband*
echtgenote *ekht*·khuh·noh·tuh *wife*
één eyn *one*
een andere uhn *an*·duh·ruh *another*
een foto nemen
  uhn *foh*·toh *ney*·muhn *take a photo*
éénpersoonskamer
  eyn·puhr·sohns·kaa·muhr *single room*
eergisteren *eyr*·khis·tuh·ruhn
  day before yesterday
eerste *eyrs*·tuh *first* a
eerste hulp *eyrs*·tuh hulp *first aid*
eerste klas *eyrs*·tuh klas *first class*
EHBO-kist ey·haa·bey·*yoh*·kist *first-aid kit*
eiland Ⓝ *ey*·lant *island*
elke *elk*·kuh *each • every* a
en en *and*
Engels Ⓝ *eng*·uhls *English (language)*
enkel *eng*·kuhl *ankle*
enkel *eng*·kuhl *only* adv
enkele *eng*·kuh·luh *some*
enkele reis *eng*·kuh·luh reys
  one-way ticket
envelop en·vuh·*lop envelope*
eten *ey*·tuhn *eat*
euro/euro's sg/pl *eu*·roh/*eu*·rohs *euro/
  euros*
exprespost eks·*pres*·post *express mail*

F

familie fa·*mee*·lee *family*
familienaam fa·*mee*·lee·naam
  family name (surname)
fantastisch fan·*tas*·tis *great (fantastic)*

fax faks *fax • fax machine*
feestje ⓝ *fey-shuh party (entertainment)*
ferry *fe-ree ferry*
fiets feets *bicycle*
filmgevoeligheid
  film-khuh-voo-likh-heyt film speed
fitnesscentrum ⓝ
  fit-nuhs-sen-trum gym (place)
fles fles *bottle*
flesopener *fles-oh-puh-nuhr bottle opener*
fooi foy *tip (gratuity)* n
fopspeen fop-speyn *dummy (pacifier)*
foto *foh-toh photo*
fotograaf foh-toh-*khraaf photographer*
fotografie foh-toh-khraa-*fee photography*
fototoestel ⓝ *foh-toh-too-stel*
  camera (photos)
fruit ⓝ *fröyt fruit*
fuif ⓑ *föyf party (entertainment)*

G

gaan khaan *go*
gaan ⓑ khaan *walk* v
gaan winkelen khaan *wing-kuh-luhn*
  go shopping
gangpad ⓝ *khang-pat aisle (on plane)*
garantie kha-*ran-see guarantee* n
garderobe khar-duh-*roh-buh cloakroom*
gas ⓝ khas *gas (for cooking)*
gauw khaw *soon*
geboortedatum
  khuh-*bohr-tuh-daa-tum date of birth*
gebouw ⓝ khuh-*baw building*
gebroken khuh-*broh-khun broken*
geel kheyl *yellow*
gehaast khuh-*haast in a hurry*
gehandicapt khuh-*hen-dee-kept/*
  khuh-*han-dee-kapt* ⓝ/ⓑ *disabled*
gehuwd khuh-*hewt married*
gekwetst khuh-*kwetst injured*
geld ⓝ khelt *money*
geldautomaat ⓑ *khelt-aw-toh-maat ATM*
gelukkig khuh-*lu-kikh happy*
geneeskunde khuh-*neys-kun-duh*
  medicine (study/profession)
genoeg khuh-*nookh enough*
gepensioneerde
  khuh-*pen-syoh-neyr-duh pensioner*
gescheiden khuh-*skhey-duhn divorced*
geschenk ⓝ khuh-*skhengk gift*
gesloten khuh-*sloh-tuhn closed • locked*
gestolen khuh-*stoh-luhn stolen*

geur kheur *smell* n
gevaarlijk khuh-*vaar-luhk dangerous*
gevoel ⓝ khuh-*vool feeling*
gevonden voorwerpen khuh-*von-duhn*
  vohr-wer-puhn *lost-property office*
gewone post khuh-*woh-nuh post*
  surface mail (land/sea)
gewoonte khuh-*wohn-tuh custom*
gezicht ⓝ khuh-*zikht face* n
gids khits *guide (person) • guidebook*
gisteren khis-*tuh-ruhn yesterday*
glas ⓝ khlas *glass (drinking/material)*
goed khoot *good*
goedkoop khoot-*kohp cheap*
goud ⓝ khawt *gold*
gram khram *gram*
grappig khra-*pikh funny*
gratis khraa-*tis complimentary (free)*
griep khreep *flu • influenza*
grijs khreys *grey*
groen khroon *green*
groente khroon-*tuh vegetable* n
groep khroop *band (music)* ⓑ *• group*
groot khroht *big*
grootmoeder khroht-*moo-duhr*
  grandmother
grootst khrohtst *biggest*
grootvader khroht-*vaa-duhr grandfather*
grootwarenhuis ⓝ ⓑ
  khroht-*waa-ruhn-höys department store*
groter khroh-*tuhr bigger*
gsm khey-es-*em mobile (cell) phone* ⓑ

H

haar ⓝ haar *hair* n
haar haar *her (possessive)*
halsketting hals-*ke-ting necklace*
hand hant *hand*
handdoek han-*dook towel*
handgemaakt
  hant-khuh-*maakt handmade*
handschoenen hant-*skhoo-nuhn gloves*
handtas han-*tas handbag*
handwerk ⓝ hant-*werk crafts • handicraft*
hangslot ⓝ *hang-slot padlock*
hard hart *hard (not soft)*
hart ⓝ hart *heart*
hartkwaal hart-*kwaal heart condition*
hebben he-*buhn have*
heen- en terugreis
  heyn-en-tuh-*rukh-reys return ticket*
heet heyt *(very) hot*

helft helft *half* n
helpen *hel*-puhn *help* v
hemd ⓝ hemt *shirt*
hersenschudding
  her-suhn-skhu-ding *concussion*
herstellen her-*ste*-luhn *repair* v
hetzelfde ⓝ huht-*zelf*-duh *same*
hier heer *here*
hij hey *he*
hitte *hi*-tuh *heat* n
hoed hoot *hat*
hoesten *hoos*-tuhn *cough* v
hoestmiddel ⓝ *hoost*-mi-duhl
  cough medicine
homo *hoh*-moh *gay (homosexual)*
homoseksueel hoh-moh-sek-sew-*weyl*
  homosexual n&a
hond hont *dog*
hongerig *hong*-uh-rikh *hungry*
hoofd ⓝ hohft *head (body)*
hoofdpijn hohft-*peyn* *headache*
hooikoorts *hoy*-kohrts *hay fever*
horloge hor-*loh*-zhuh ⓝ *watch* n
houden van *haw*-duhn van *like* v • *love* v
hulp hulp *help* n
huren *hew*-ruhn *hire (rent)* v
hut hut *berth (ship)* n
huur hewr *rent* n
huwelijksreis *hew*-wuh-luhks-reys
  honeymoon (trip)
huwen *hew*-wuhn *marry*
hydraulisch engineering hee-*draw*-lis
  en-zhi-*nee*-ring *water engineering*

I

identificatie ee-den-tee-fee-*kaa*-see
  identification
identiteitsbewijs ⓝ
  ee-den-tee-*teyts*-buh-weys *ID*
iedereen ee-duh-*reyn* *everyone*
ijs ⓝ eys *ice*
(room)ijs ⓝ (rohm-)eys *ice cream*
ijskast *eys*-kast *fridge*
ik ik *I*
inbegrepen in-buh-*khrey*-puhn *included*
incheckbalie in-shek-*ba*-lee
  check-in (desk)
indigestie in-dee-*khes*-tee *indigestion*
inenting in-en-ting *vaccination*
infectie in-*fek*-see *infection*
informatica in-for-*maa*-tee-ka *IT*
informatie in-for-*maa*-see *information*

ingang *in*-khang *entry* n
ingenieur in-zhey-*nyeur* *engineer* n
inlegkruisjes ⓝ pl *in*-lekh-*kröy*-shuhs
  panty liners
(een cheque) innen (uhn shek) *i*-nuhn
  cash (a cheque) v
inschrijvingsbewijs ⓝ
  in-skhrey-vings-buh-*weys* *car registration*
inspuiting *in*-spöy-ting *injection*
instapkaart *in*-stap-kaart *boarding pass*

J

ja yaa *yes*
jaar ⓝ yaar *year*
jas yas *coat* n • *jacket (casual)*
je yuh *you* inf sg
jenever yuh-*ney*-vuhr/zhuh-*ney*-vuhr ⓝ/ⓑ
  gin
jeugdherberg *yeukht*-her-berkh
  youth hostel
jeuk yeuk *itch* n
jij yey *you* inf sg
jongen *yong*-uhn *boy*
journalist zhoor-na-*list* *journalist*
jouw jaw *your* inf sg
juist yöyst *exactly*
jullie *yew*-lee *you* • *your* inf pl
jurk yurk *dress* n
juwelen ⓝ pl yew-*wey*-luhn *jewellery*

K

kaart kaart *map (of country/town)*
kaartje ⓝ *kaar*-chuh *ticket*
kaartjesautomaat *kaar*-chus-aw-toh-*maat*
  ticket machine
kam kam *comb* n
kamer *kaa*-muhr *room* n
kamernummer ⓝ *kaa*-muhr-nu-muhr
  room number
kamer te huur *kaa*-muhr tuh hewr
  vacancy (accommodation)
kantoorboekhandel
  kan-*tohr*-book-han-duhl *stationer*
kapper *ka*-puhr *hairdresser*
kapsel ⓝ *kap*-suhl *haircut*
kassa *ka*-sa *cash register*
kassier/kassierster ⓜ/ⓕ
  ka-*seer*/ka-*seer*-stuhr *cashier*
kasteel ⓝ kas-*teyl* *castle*
katedraal ka-tey-*draal* *cathedral*
katoen ⓝ ka-*toon* *cotton* n
keel keyl *throat*

kelner *kel*-nuhr *waiter*
kerk kerk *church*
kerkhof ⓝ *kerk*-hof *cemetery*
kermis *ker*-mis *fairground*
keuken *keu*-kuhn *kitchen*
kiespijn *kees*-peyn *toothache*
kiestoon *kees*-tohn *dial tone*
kiezen *kee*-zuhn *choose*
kind ⓝ kint *child*
kinderen ⓝ pl *kin*-duh-ruhn *children*
kinderoppasdienst
    kin-duhr-o-pas-deenst
    child-minding service
kinderzitje ⓝ *kin*-duhr-zi-chuh *child seat*
klacht klakht *complaint*
klant klant *client*
klassiek kla-*seek* *classical*
kleding *kley*-ding *clothing*
kledingzaak *kley*-ding-zaak *clothing store*
kleed ⓝ kleyt *dress* n ⑧ • *rug* ⓝ
kleedhokje ⓝ *kleyt*-hok-yuh
    changing room (sport, individual)
kleedkamer *kleyt*-kaa-muhr *changing
    room (sport, communal)*
kleermaker *kleyr*-maa-kuhr *tailor* n
klein kleyn *short (height)* • *small*
kleiner *kley*-nuhr *shorter* • *smaller*
kleingeld ⓝ *kleyn*-khelt
    change (loose coins) n
kleinkind ⓝ *kleyn*-kint *grandchild*
kleinst kleynst *smallest*
kleur kleur *colour* n
kluis klöys *safe* n
knap knap *handsome*
knie knee *knee*
knoop knohp *button* n
koelkast *kool*-kast *refrigerator*
koekenpan *koo*-kuh-pan *frying pan*
koffer *ko*-fuhr *suitcase*
koffie *ko*-fee *coffee*
koffiehuisje *ko*-fee-höy-shuh *café*
koffieshop *ko*-fee-shop
    coffee shop (sells soft drugs)
kok kok *cook* n
koken *koh*-kuhn *cook* v
kom kom *bowl (plate)* n
kookpot *kohk*-pot *saucepan*
kop kop *cup*
kopen *ko*-puhn *buy* v
koplampen *kop*-lam-puhn *headlights*
korting *kor*-ting *discount* n
kost kost *cost* n
kosten *kos*-tuhn *cost* v

koud kawt *cold* a
kousen *kaw*-suhn *stockings*
kraantje ⓝ *kraan*-chuh *faucet (tap)*
krant krant *newspaper*
krantenzaak *kran*-tuh-zaak
    newsagency (selling newspapers)
krediet ⓝ *krey*-deet *credit* n
kredietkaart *krey*-deet-kaart *credit card*
kroeg krookh *pub (bar)*
kruidenierszaak *kröy*-duh-*neers*-zaak
    grocery shop
kunst kunst *art*
kunstgalerie *kunst*-kha-luh-*ree* *art gallery*
kurkentrekker *kur*-kuh-tre-kuhr *corkscrew*
kussen ⓝ *ku*-suhn *pillow*
kussensloop *ku*-suhn-slohp *pillowcase*
kwetsuur kwet-*sewr* *injury*
kwitantie kwee-*tan*-see *receipt* n

L

laat laat *late* adv
laatste *laat*-stuh *last (final)*
laken ⓝ *laa*-kuhn *sheet (bed)*
lang lang *long*
later *laa*-tuhr *later*
lawaaierig la-*waa*-yuh-rikh *noisy*
laxeermiddel ⓝ lak-*seyr*-mi-duhl *laxative*
leder ⓝ *ley*-duhr *leather* n
leeg leykh *vacant (empty)*
lekker *le*-kuhr *delicious* • *tasty*
lelijk *ley*-leyk *ugly*
lens lens *lens*
lente *len*-tuh *spring (season)*
lepel *ley*-puhl *spoon*
leraar/lerares ⓜ/ⓕ *ley*-raar/ley-raa-res
    teacher
lesbische *les*-bi-suh *lesbian* v
licht likht *light (colour/weight)*
licht ⓝ likht *light* n
lichtmeter *likht*-mey-tuhr *light meter*
liefde *leef*-duh *love* n
lift lift *lift (elevator)*
liften *lif*-tuhn *hitchhike*
links lingks *left (direction)*
linnen ⓝ *li*-nuhn *linen (material)*
lits jumeaux lee zhew-*moh* *twin beds*
loket ⓝ loh-*ket* *ticket office*
lopen *loh*-puhn *walk* ⓝ • *run* ⑧
luchthaven *lukht*-haa-vuhn *airport*
luchthavenbelasting
    lukht-haa-vuhn-buh-*las*-ting *airport tax*
luchtpost *lukht*-post *airmail*

luchtvaartmaatschappij
lukht·vaart·maat·skha·pey airline
lucifers *lew·see·fers matches (for lighting)*
luid *löyt loud*
luier *löy·yuhr nappy (diaper)*
luisteren *löys·tuh·ruhn listen*
lunch *lunsh lunch*
luxueus *luk·sew·weus luxurious*

M

maag *maakh stomach*
maagpijn *maakh·peyn stomachache*
maaltijd *maal·teyt meal*
maand *maant month*
maandverband ⓝ *maant·vuhr·bant sanitary napkin*
maat *maat size* n
machinebouwkunde
ma·shee·nuh·baw·kun·duh mechanical engineering
magnetron *makh·ney·tron microwave oven*
makelaarskantoor ⓝ
maa·kuh·laars·kan·tohr estate agency
man *man man* n
mantel *man·tuhl coat* n
markt *markt market* n
matras *ma·tras mattress*
maximumsnelheid
mak·see·mum·snel·heyt speed limit
me *muh me*
medicijn ⓝ *mey·dee·seyn medicine (medication)*
medicijnen *mey·dee·sey·nuhn medicine (study/profession)* ⓝ • *medicines*
meer *meyr more*
meer ⓝ *meyr lake*
meisje ⓝ *mey·shuh girl*
melk *melk milk*
mes ⓝ *mes knife* n
meter *mey·tuhr metre*
metgezel *met·khuh·zel companion*
metrostation ⓝ *mey·troh·sta·syon metro station*
meubilair ⓝ *meu·bee·leyr furniture*
microgolfoven *mee·kroh·kholf·oh·vuhn microwave oven*
middag *mi·dakh afternoon* ⓝ • *midday*
middagmaal ⓝ *mi·dakh·maal lunch*
middernacht *mi·duhr·nakht midnight*
mijn *meyn my*
millimeter *mee·lee·mey·tuhr millimetre*

minder *min·duhr less*
mineraalwater ⓝ *mee·ney·raal·waa·tuhr mineral water*
minuut *mee·newt minute* n
misselijkheid *mi·suh·luhk·heyt nausea*
missen *mi·suhn miss* v
mobiele telefoon *moh·bee·luh tey·ley·fohn mobile/cell phone*
mode *moh·duh fashion* n
modern *moh·dern modern*
moe *moo tired*
moeder *moo·duhr mother*
mond *mont mouth*
mooi *moy beautiful*
morgen *mor·khuhn morning* ⓑ • *tomorrow*
motor *moh·tor engine*
muntstukken *munt·stu·kuhn coins*
museum ⓝ *mew·zey·yuhm museum*
muziek *mew·zeek music*
muziekwinkel *mew·zeek·wing·kuhl music shop*

N

na *naa after*
naald *naalt needle (sewing/syringe)*
naam *naam name* n
naar *naar to*
naast *naast beside*
nacht *nakht night*
nachtclub *nakht·klup nightclub*
nagelknipper sg *naa·khuhl·kni·puhr nail clippers*
namiddag *naa·mi·dakh afternoon*
nee *ney no*
nek *nek neck*
neus *neus nose*
niet-roken *neet·roh·kuhn nonsmoking*
niets *neets nothing*
nieuw *neew new*
nieuws *neews news*
noodgeval ⓝ *noot·khuh·val emergency*
noorden ⓝ *nohr·duhn north* n
notitieboekje ⓝ *noh·tee·see·book·yuh notebook*
nu *new now*
nummer ⓝ *nu·muhr number* n

O

ober *oh·buhr waiter*
ochtend ⓝ *okh·tuhnt morning*
olie *oh·lee oil (cooking)*

omhoog om·*hohkh* up
ondergoed ⓝ on·duhr·*khoot* underwear
ondertitels on·duhr·tee·tuhls subtitles
ongemakkelijk on·khuh·*ma*·kuh·luhk
  uncomfortable
ongeval ⓝ on·khuh·val accident
onmogelijk on·*moh*·khul·luhk impossible
ontbijt ⓝ ont·*beyt* breakfast
ontsmettend ont·*sme*·tuhnt antiseptic a
onze on·zuh our
oog ⓝ ohkh eye
oor ⓝ ohr ear
oorringen oh·ring·uhn earrings
oosten ⓝ *oh*·stuhn east n
op op on
openbare telefoon oh·puhn·bah·ruh
  tey·ley·*fohn* public phone
openbaar toilet ⓝ
  oh·puhn·baar twa·*let* public toilet
openingsuren ⓝ pl
  oh·puh·nings·ew·ruhn opening hours
opgewarmd op·khuh·warmt heated (food)
opnieuw op·*neew* again
op tijd op teyt on time
optreden op·trey·duhn gig
oranje oh·*ran*·yuh orange (colour)
oud awt old
ouders aw·duhrs parents
oude stad aw·duh stat old city
overmorgen oh·vuhr·mor·khun
  day after tomorrow
overvracht oh·vuhr·vrakht excess baggage

P

pak/pakket ⓝ pak/pa·*ket*
  package n • packet • parcel n
paleis ⓝ pa·*leys* palace
pantalon sg ⓝ pan·ta·*lon* trousers
panty pen·tee/pan·tee ⓝ/ⓑ pantyhose
papier ⓝ pa·*peer* paper n
papieren ⓝ pl pa·*pee*·ruhn paperwork
paraplu pa·ra·*plew* umbrella (rain)
parasol pa·ra·*sol* umbrella (sun)
parfum ⓝ par·*föy* perfume n
parkeren par·*key*·ruhn park (a car) v
paskamer pas·kaa·muhr
  changing room (shop)
paspoort ⓝ *pas*·pohrt passport
paspoortnummer ⓝ *pas*·pohrt·nu·muhr
  passport number
passagier pa·sa·*kheer* passenger
patisserie ⓑ pa·tee·suh·*ree* cake shop

pause *paw*·zuh intermission
pension ⓝ pen·*syon*
  boarding house • guesthouse
per (dag) puhr (dakh) per (day)
perron ⓝ pe·*ron* platform (train station)
personeel ⓝ per·soh·*neyl* staff
picknick *pik*·nik picnic n
pijn peyn pain
pijnlijk *peyn*·luhk painful
pijnstiller peyn·sti·luhr painkiller
pil pil pill
pin-automaat ⓝ *pin*·aw·toh·maat
  automated teller machine (ATM)
pincet ⓝ pin·*set* tweezers
plaatselijk *plaat*·suh·luhk local a
plak ⓝ plak slice n
plattegrond pla·tuh·*khront*
  map (of building)
plein ⓝ pleyn court (tennis) • square (town)
pleister *pley*·stuhr Band-Aid
politie poh·*leet*·see police
politieagent poh·*leet*·see·a·khent
  police officer
politiebureau ⓝ poh·*leet*·see·bew·roh
  police station
portemonnee por·tuh·mo·*ney*
  purse • wallet
post post mail (letters/postal system) n
postkaart *post*·kaart postcard
postkantoor ⓝ *post*·kan·tohr post office
postzegel *post*·zey·khul stamp (postage) n
potlood ⓝ *pot*·loht pencil
praten *praa*·tuhn speak
prijs preys price n
privé pree·*vey* private
proberen proh·*bey*·ruhn try (attempt) v
programma ⓝ proh·*khra*·ma program n
proper ⓑ *proh*·puhr clean a
prostituée pros·tee·tew·*wey* prostitute n
purper *pur*·puhr purple

R

raam ⓝ raam window
radio *raa*·dee·yoh radio
recept ⓝ rey·*sept* prescription
rechten ⓝ pl *rekh*·tuhn
  law (study/profession)
rechts rekhs right (direction)
rechtstreeks rekh·*streyks* direct a
rechtstreekse lijn rekh·*streyk*·suh leyn
  direct-dial
reddingsvest ⓝ *re*·dings·vest life jacket

regen *rey*·khuhn *rain* n
regenjas *rey*·khuhn·yas *raincoat*
reisbureau ⓝ *reys*·bew·roh *travel agency*
reischeque *reys*·shek *travellers cheque*
reisroute *reys*·roo·tuh *itinerary*
reisziekte *reys*·zeek·tuh *travel sickness*
rekening *rey*·kuh·ning
   account • bill • check n
rekenmachine *rey*·kuhn·ma·shee·nuh
   calculator
remmen *re*·muhn *brakes*
reservatie rey·ser·*vaa*·see
   reservation (booking)
reserveren rey·ser·*vey*·ruhn
   book (make a booking) v
restaurant ⓝ res·toh·*rant* *restaurant*
restauratiewagen
   res·toh·*raa*·see·waa·khuhn *dining car*
retourtje ⓝ ruh·*toor*·chuh
   return ticket
richting *rikh*·ting *direction*
rijbewijs ⓝ *rey*·buh·weys *drivers licence*
rit rit *drive* n
rits rits *zip/zipper*
rivier ree·*veer* *river*
rockmuziek *rok*·mew·zeek *rock (music)*
rok rok *skirt*
roken *roh*·kuhn *smoke* v
rolstoel *rol*·stool *wheelchair*
roltrap *rol*·trap *escalator*
rolwagentje ⓝ *rol*·waa·khun·chuh *trolley*
romantisch roh·*man*·tees *romantic* a
rondleiding *ront*·ley·ding *guided tour*
rood roht *red*
roze *roh*·zuh *pink*
rug rukh *back (body)*
rugzak *rukh*·zak *backpack (rucksack)*
ruilen *röy*·luhn *exchange (general)* v
ruïnes rew·*wee*·nuhs *ruins*

S

saai *saay* *boring*
samen *saa*·muhn *together*
schaar sg *skhaar* *scissors*
schade *skhaa*·duh *damage*
schaduw *skhaa*·dew *shade*
scheerapparaat ⓝ *skheyr*·a·pa·raat
   razor (electric)
scheermes ⓝ *skheyr*·mes *razor (manual)*
scheermesje ⓝ *skheyr*·me·shuh
   razor blade
scheerschuim ⓝ *skheyr*·skhöym
   shaving cream

scheren *skhey*·ruhn *shave* v
schijf *skheyf* *disk*
schoenen *skhoo*·nuhn *shoes*
schoenenzaak *skhoo*·nuhn·zaak *shoe shop*
schoon *skhohn* *beautiful* ⓑ • *clean* a ⓝ
schoonheidssalon *skhohn*·heyt·sa·lon
   beauty salon
schoonmaak *skhohn*·maak *cleaning*
schoonmaken *skhohn*·maa·kuhn *clean* v
schoonmoeder *skhohn*·moo·duhr
   mother-in-law
schoonvader *skhohn*·vaa·duhr
   father-in-law
schotel *skhoh*·tuhl *dish*
schouwburg *skhaw*·burkh
   theatre (building)
schrijven *skhrey*·vuhn *write*
seizoen ⓝ sey·*zoon* *season* n
seks seks *sex*
serveerster ser·*veyr*·stuhr *waitress*
servet ⓝ ser·*vet* *napkin*
short sg short *shorts*
shouder *skhaw*·duhr *shoulder*
sigaar see·*khaar* *cigar*
sigaret see·kha·*ret* *cigarette*
sim-kaart *sim*·kaart *SIM card*
sjaal *shaal* *scarf*
skisport *skee*·sport *skiing*
slaapkamer *slaap*·kaa·muhr *bedroom*
slaapwagen *slaap*·waa·khuhn
   sleeping car
slaapzak *slaap*·zak *sleeping bag*
slagerij slaa·khuh·*rey* *butcher's shop*
slapen *slaa*·puhn *sleep* v
slecht *slekht* *bad*
slechter *slekh*·tuhr *worse*
sleutel *sleu*·tuhl *key (door etc)*
slijterij ⓝ *sley*·tuh·rey
   bottle shop (liquor store)
slot *slot* *lock* n
sluiten *slöy*·tuhn *close* v
smeermiddel ⓝ *smeyr*·mi·duhl *lubricant*
snee ⓑ *sney* *slice* n
sneeuw *sneyw* *snow* n
snel *snel* *fast* a
snelweg *snel*·wekh *highway*
snijden *sney*·duhn *cut* v
sokken *so*·kuhn *socks*
souvenirwinkel soo·vuh·*neer*·wing·kuhl
   souvenir shop
spiegel *spee*·khul *mirror* n
sportwinkel *sport*·wing·kuhl *sports store*
stad *stat* *city • town*

T

stadhuis ⑩ stat·*höys* town hall
stadsbus stats·bus city bus
stadscentrum ⑩ stat·sen·trum
  city centre (downtown)
stadsplein ⑩ stats·pleyn main square
staking staa·king strike n
station ⑩ sta·syon station
stekker ste·kuhr plug (electricity) n
stil stil quiet
stoel stool chair n
stoeltjeslift stool·chuhs·lift
  chairlift (skiing)
stop stop plug (bath) n
storting stor·ting deposit (money) n
straat straat street
strand strant beach
strijkijzer ⑩ streyk·ey·zuhr
  iron (for clothes) n
stroom strohm current (electricity)
student stew·dent student
stuk stuk broken down • faulty • out of order
suiker söy·kuhr sugar
suikerziekte söy·kuhr·zeek·tuh diabetes

T

taal taal language
taalgids taal·khits phrasebook
taksvrije winkel taks·vrey·yuh wing·kuhl
  duty-free shop
tandarts tan·darts dentist
tandenborstel tan·duhn·bor·stuhl
  toothbrush
tandpasta tant·pas·ta toothpaste
tandpijn tant·peyn toothache
tandzijde tant·zey·duh dental floss
tarief ⑩ ta·reef fare n
tas tas bag
taxistandplaats tak·see·stant·plaats
  taxi stand
te tuh too (much)
telefoneren tey·ley·foh·*ney*·ruhn
  telephone v
telefoon tey·ley·*fohn* telephone n
telefoonboek ⑩ tey·ley·*fohn*·book
  phone book
telefooncel tey·ley·*fohn*·sel phone box
telefoongesprek ⑩
  tey·ley·*fohn*·khuh·sprek phone call v
telefoonkaart tey·ley·*fohn*·kaart
  phonecard
televisie tey·ley·*vee*·see television
temperatuur tem·pey·ra·*tewr*
  temperature (weather)

tennisbaan te·nis·baan tennis court
tentoonstelling tuhn·*tohn*·ste·ling
  exhibition
terugbetaling tuh·*rukh*·buh·taa·ling
  refund n
terugkomen tuh·*rukh*·koh·muhn return v
theater ⑩ tey·*yaa*·tuhr theatre
theelepeltje ⑩ tey·ley·puhl·chuh teaspoon
thuis töys home
ticket ⑩ ti·*ket*/ti·kuht ⑤/⑧ ticket
tijdschema ⑩ teyt·skhey·ma
  timetable (general)
tijdsverschil ⑩ teyts·vuhr·skhil
  time difference
tocht tokht hike • tour • trek n
toegangsprijs too·khangs·preys
  admission (price)
toer toor tour (short, eg museum) n
toerismebureau ⑩
  too·ris·muh·bew·roh tourist office
toerist too·rist tourist n
toilet ⑩ twa·*let* toilet
toiletpapier ⑩ twa·*let*·pa·peer
  toilet paper
tolk tolk interpreter
tolweg tol·wekh tollway
toneelstuk ⑩ toh·*neyl*·stuk
  play (theatre) n
tonen toh·nuhn show v
tot tot until
touringcar too·ring·kar coach (bus) n
traag traakh slowly
trap trap stairway
trein treyn train n
treinstation ⑩ treyn·sta·syon
  train station
trekken tre·kuhn hike v • hiking • pull v
trui tröy jumper (sweater)
tuin töyn garden n
tv tey·*vey* TV
twee twey two
tweede klas twey·duh klas second class n
tweepersoonsbed ⑩
  twey·puhr·sohns·bet double bed
tweepersoonskamer ⑩
  twey·puhr·sohns·kaa·muhr
  double room

U

u ew you pol sg&pl
uw ew your pol sg&pl
uitgaan öyt·khaan go out

uitgaansgids öyt·khaans·khits
entertainment guide
uitgang öyt·khang *exit* n
uitstappen öyt·sta·puhn *get off (bus etc)*
uitzicht ⓝ öyt·zikht *view* n
universiteit ew·nee·ver·see·teyt *university*
uur ⓝ ewr *hour*
uw ew *your* pol sg&pl

V

vacature va·ka·tew·ruh *vacancy (job)*
vader vaa·duhr *father*
vakantie va·kan·see *holidays • vacation*
valideren va·lee·dey·ruhn *validate*
van van *from*
vanavond van·aa·vont *tonight*
vandaag van·daakh *today*
veerboot veyr·boht *ferry* n
veertien dagen veyr·teen daa·khuhn
fortnight
vegetariër vey·khey·taa·ree·yuhr
vegetarian n
vegetarisch vey·khey·taa·ris *vegetarian* a
veiligheidsriem vey·likh·heyts·reem
seatbelt
veilig vrijen ⓝ vey·likh vrey·yuhn
safe sex
ventilator ven·tee·laa·tor *fan (machine)*
ver ver *far*
verandering vuhr·an·duh·ring
change (general) n
verband ⓝ vuhr·bant *bandage*
verdieping vuhr·dee·ping *floor (storey)*
verjaardag vuhr·yaar·dakh *birthday*
verloofd vuhr·lohft
engaged (to be married)
verloofde vuhr·lohf·duh *fiancé/fiancée*
verloren ver·loh·ruhn *lost*
verloving vuhr·loh·ving
engagement (to marry)
vers vers *fresh*
verschillend vuhr·skhi·luhnt *different*
verschrikkelijk vuhr·skhri·kuh·luhk *awful*
versnellingen vuhr·sne·ling·uhn *gears*
verstopt vuhr·stopt *blocked (drain/nose)*
verstuiking vuhr·stöy·king *sprain* n
vertalen vuhr·taa·luhn *translate*
vertraging vuhr·traa·khing *delay* n
vertrek ⓝ vuhr·trek *departure*
vertrekken vuhr·tre·kuhn *depart*
vervelend ⑧ vuhr·vey·luhnt *boring*
verwarmd vuhr·warmt *heated (place)*

verwarmingstoestel ⓝ
vuhr·war·mings·too·stel *heater*
verzekering vuhr·zey·kuh·ring *insurance*
vest ⑧ vest *jacket (dressy)*
vest ⓝ vest *jacket (casual)*
vestiaire ves·tyer *cloakroom*
vet vet *fat (food)*
videofilm vee·dey·yoo·film *video tape*
vinger ving·uhr *finger*
vishandel vis·han·duhl *fish shop*
vissen ⓝ vi·suhn *fishing* n
visum ⓝ vee·zum *visa*
vlees ⓝ vleys *meat*
vliegen vlee·khuhn *fly* v
vliegtuig ⓝ vleekh·töykh
aeroplane (airplane)
vlooienmarkt vloh·yuhn·markt *flea market*
vlucht vlukht *flight*
voedsel voot·suhl *food*
voedselvoorraad voot·suhl·voh·raat
food supplies
voelen voo·luhn *feel (emotions/touch)* v
voet voot *foot (body)*
voetbal ⓝ voot·bal *football (soccer)*
voetpad ⓝ voot·pat *footpath*
vol vol *full*
volgend vol·khuhnt *next (following)*
volzet vol·zet *no vacancy*
voor vohr *before*
voornaam vohr·naam *first name*
voorschrift ⓝ ⑧ vohr·skhrift *prescription*
vorige voh·ri·khuh *last (previous)*
vork vork *fork*
vriend vreent *boyfriend • friend*
vriendin vreen·din *friend • girlfriend*
vrij vrey *free (available)* a • *vacant*
vrijgezel vrey·khuh·zel *single (person)*
vrijwilligen vrey·wi·li·khuhn *volunteer* v
vrijwilliger vrey·wi·li·khuhr *volunteer* n
vroeg vrookh *early* adv
vrouw vraw *woman*
vrouwelijk vraw·wuh·luhk *female* a
vuil vöyl *dirty*
vuilbak vöyl·bak *garbage can*
VVV ⓝ vey·vey·vey *tourist office*

W

waar waar *where*
waardevol waar·duh·vol *valuable*
waarom waa·rom *why*
wachten wakh·tuhn *wait* v

wachtkamer *wakht·kaa·muhr waiting room*
wagen *waa·khuhn car*
wakker maken *wa·kuhr maa·kuhn wake someone up*
wakker worden *wa·kuhr wor·duhn wake up*
wandelen *wan·duh·luhn walk (go for a walk)* v
wandelwagen *wan·duhl·waa·khuhn stroller*
wanneer *wa·neyr when*
warenhuis Ⓐ Ⓝ *waa·ruhn·höys department store*
warm *warm hot • warm* a
warmwaterfles *warm·waa·tuhr·fles hot water bottle*
was *was laundry (clothes)*
wasmachine *was·ma·shee·nuh washing machine*
(iets) wassen *(eets) wa·suhn wash (something)* v
wasserette *wa·suh·re·tuh laundrette*
water Ⓝ *waa·tuhr water* n
wattenproppen *wa·tuh·pro·puhn cotton balls*
wedstrijd *wet·streyt match (sport)*
week *weyk week*
weekend Ⓝ *wey·kent weekend*
weg *wekh road • route*
wekker *we·kuhr alarm clock*
welke *wel·kuh which*
werk *werk job* Ⓑ *• task*
westen Ⓝ *wes·tuhn west* n
wetenschap *wey·tuhn·skhap science*
wetenschapper *wey·tuhn·skha·puhr scientist*
wie *wee who*
wijn *weyn wine*
wijzen *wey·zuhn point* v
winkel *wing·kuhl shop* n
winkelcentrum Ⓝ *wing·kuhl·sen·trum shopping centre*
winkelen *wing·kuh·luhn shop* v
(geld) wisselen *(khelt) wi·suh·luhn change (money)* v
wisselgeld Ⓝ *wi·suhl·khelt change (money given back)* n
wisselkantoor Ⓝ *wi·suhl·kan·tohr currency exchange*
wisselkoers *wi·suhl·koors exchange rate*
wit *wit white*

wittebroodsweken pl *wi·tuh·brohts·wey·kuhn honeymoon (period)*
wol *wol wool* n
woordenboek Ⓝ *wohr·duhn·book dictionary*
woud Ⓝ *wawt forest*

Z

zaak *zaak company (firm)*
zakdoek *zak·dook handkerchief*
zaken pl *zaa·kuhn business* n
zakenreis *zaa·kuhn·reys business trip*
zaklantaarn *zak·lan·taarn flashlight (torch)*
zakmes Ⓝ *zak·mes penknife*
zee *zey sea*
zeep *zeyp soap*
zeldzaam *zelt·zaam rare (uncommon)*
zelfbediening *zelf·buh·dee·ning self-service* a
ziek *zeek ill • sick*
ziekenhuis Ⓝ *zee·kuhn·höys hospital*
zijde *zey·duh silk* n
zijn *zeyn his (possessive)*
zijn *zeyn to be* v
zilver *zil·vuhr silver* n
zitje Ⓝ *zi·chuh seat (place)* n
zoet *zoot sweet* a
zomer *zoh·muhr summer*
zon *zon sun*
zonder *zon·duhr without*
zonnebrand *zo·nuh·brant sunburn*
zonnebrandolie *zo·nuh·brant·oh·lee tanning lotion*
zonnebril sg *zo·nuh·bril sunglasses*
zonnecrème *zo·nuh·kreym sunscreen (lotion)*
zonsondergang *zons·on·duhr·khang sunset*
zonsopgang *zons·op·khang sunrise*
zoon *zohn son*
zout Ⓝ *zawt salt* n
zuiden Ⓝ *zöy·duhn south* n
zus *zus sister*
zuster *zus·tuhr nurse* n
zwaar *zwaar heavy (weight)*
zwanger *zwang·uhr pregnant*
zwart *zwart black*
zwart-wit (film) *zwart·wit (film) B&W (film)*
zwembad Ⓝ *zwem·bat swimming pool*
zwemmen *zwe·muhn swim* v

D

E

F

255

KEY PATTERNS

When's (the next bus)?	Hoe laat gaat (de volgende bus)?	hoo laat khaat (duh *vol*·khun·duh bus)
Where's (the station)?	Waar is (het station)?	waar is (huht sta·*syon*)
Where can I (buy a ticket)?	Waar kan ik (een kaartje kopen)?	waar kan ik (uhn *kaar*·chuh *koh*·puhn)
How much is (a room)?	Hoeveel kost (een kamer)?	hoo·*veyl* kost (uhn *kaa*·muhr)
I'm looking for (a hotel).	Ik ben op zoek naar (een hotel).	ik ben op zook naar (uhn hoh·*tel*)
Do you have (a map)?	Heeft u (een kaart)?	heyft ew (uhn kaart)
Is there (a toilet)?	Is er (een toilet)?	is uhr (uhn *twa*·let)
I'd like (the menu).	Ik wil graag (een menu).	ik wil khraakh (uhn me·*new*)
I'd like (to hire a car).	Ik wil graag (een auto huren).	ik wil khraakh (uhn *aw*·toh *hew*·ruhn)
Can I (enter)?	Kan ik (binnengaan)?	kan ik (*bi*·nuhn·khaan)
Could you please (help me)?	Kunt u alstublieft (helpen)?	kunt ew al·stew·*bleeft* (*hel*·puhn)
Do I have to (get a visa)?	Moet ik (een visum hebben)?	moot ik (uhn *vee*·zum *he*·buhn)